FOCUS

0.1 Family

Grammar: Present Simple and Present Continuous
Vocabulary: Family

SHOW WHAT YOU KNOW

1 In pairs, list all the family members you can think of in sixty seconds. Then use them to describe yourselves.

I'm a son, I'm a nephew, I'm a ...

2 Tell your partner about three members of your family.

Mark is my uncle. He's my mum's brother. He lives ...

3 CD·1.2 MP3·2 Look at Vicky's family photos and guess how each person is related to Vicky. Then listen and check.

I think 1 is Vicky's mum.

Chats | Friends | Vicky | Photos | Info

My family

Vicky
View | Download | 08.32

View | Download | 08.35

View | Download | 08.37

View | Download | 08.40

View | Download | 08.42

Comment

+ Add photos

4 CD·1.2 MP3·2 Complete the sentences about Vicky's family with the correct form of the verbs in brackets. Then listen again and check.

1 Her mum _____ (write) for a magazine.
2 Her dad _____ (work) in a bank.
3 Her sisters _____ (argue) all the time.
4 Her brother and family _____ (live) in Paris.
5 Her grandpa often _____ (go) to Spain.

5 Use the phrases in the box to describe what Vicky's family are doing in the photos.

> have a cup of tea   laugh
> play football   play golf   sit in the park

1 *Her mum is having a cup of tea.*

6 Read REMEMBER THIS. Then complete the cartoon caption with the correct form of the verbs in brackets.

REMEMBER THIS

- You use the **Present Simple** to talk about facts, habits and routines.
- You use the **Present Continuous** to talk about actions in progress.

My dad ¹_____ (work) in a bank, but today he ²_____ (play) football.

Grammar Focus page 108

7 Write true sentences from the prompts. Use the Present Simple or Present Continuous and an affirmative or negative form.

1 I / live / near the school
  I don't live near the school.
2 we / have / a family pet
3 I / read / a good book at the moment
4 my parents / speak / English
5 I / wear / my favourite shoes today
6 my best friend / like / shopping
7 I / play / the guitar
8 it / rain

8 In pairs, take turns to ask and answer questions using the prompts in Exercise 7.

A: *Do you live near the school?*
B: *No, I don't.*

0.2 How we met

Grammar: Past Simple affirmative
Vocabulary: Music

SHOW WHAT YOU KNOW

1 **CD·1.3** **MP3·3** Listen and tick the six music styles you hear.

folk ☐ heavy metal ☐ hip-hop ☐ house ☐ jazz ☐
pop ☐ punk ☐ reggae ☐ rock ☐ R & B ☐

2 **List all the bands you can think of in sixty seconds. What music style are they? Then compare your 'Top 5' with a partner.**

3 **Read the text and answer the questions. Do you know how any of your favourite bands first met?**

1 Which bands appeared on *The X Factor*?
2 Which band members grew up in the same neighbourhood?
3 Which band members met at school?
4 Which band got together at university?
5 Which band did a record company create?

HOW THEY MET

CD·1.4 **MP3·4**

Do you know how your favourite bands first got together?

Coldplay

Many of the most famous bands were friends at school or college. International superstars U2 met in secondary school. When he was fourteen, Larry, the drummer, planned to start a band, so he put an ad on the school notice board. The other members of U2 answered it and they are still together forty years later!

British band Coldplay met in their first week at university. Singer Chris Martin studied Latin and Greek and got a first class degree. The same year, Coldplay had a number one hit.

The Arctic Monkeys grew up together. Their families were neighbours and two of them went to the same primary school. When they were fifteen, they all received guitars for Christmas. They played music together in Alex Turner's garage and did their first gig when they were sixteen years old.

Some bands started in a different way. When record companies wanted new bands, they created them. The Spice Girls began in this way.

Several boy and girl bands became famous after appearing on a TV reality show; successful British bands JLS and One Direction both appeared on *The X Factor*.

4 **Find the Past Simple form of these verbs in the text. Then answer the questions.**

be – _____ , _____   do – _____   have – _____
become – _____   get – _____   meet – _____
begin – _____   grow up – _____ put – _____

1 Are the verbs regular or irregular?
2 How many Past Simple forms are there for *be*?
3 How many Past Simple forms are there for all other verbs?

5 **Complete the table with more examples of regular verbs from the text.**

Spelling	Examples
add -*ed*	work**ed**, …
add -*d*	liv**ed**, …
delete -*y* + add -*ied*	tr**ied**, …
double the consonant + add -*ed*	stop**ped**, …

6 **CD·1.5** **MP3·5** **Listen and repeat. Which verbs have an extra syllable in the Past Simple form?**

asked   needed   started
talked   wanted   lived

7 **Read REMEMBER THIS. Then complete the cartoon caption with the correct form of the verbs in brackets.**

REMEMBER THIS

- You use the **Past Simple** to talk about finished actions in the past. You often say when they happened.
- There is only one past form for every verb (except *be*).

We ¹_____ (meet) at primary school.
We ²_____ (be) seven years old.

Grammar Focus page 109

8 **Complete the sentences with the Past Simple form of the verbs in brackets.**

1 I _____ (meet) my best friend *three years ago*.
2 I _____ (buy) some music *a few days ago*.
3 My dad _____ (cook) *last Sunday*.
4 I _____ (go) to a great party *last Saturday*.
5 I _____ (wear) my favourite jeans *yesterday*.
6 I _____ (see) a good film *two weeks ago*.
7 I _____ (be) very tired *last night*.
8 I _____ (wake up) *before 6 a.m.*

9 **Change the time expressions *in italics* in Exercise 8 to make the sentences true for you.**

I met my best friend five years ago.

5

0.3 Mr Bean

Grammar: Past Simple negative and questions
Vocabulary: Verbs

SHOW WHAT YOU KNOW

1 In pairs, try to note down a verb for each letter of the alphabet. How many can you think of in sixty seconds?

ask   be   can   do

2 Complete the table with the Past Simple form of the verbs in Exercise 1. Do you have more regular or irregular verbs?

Regular verbs	Irregular verbs
ask – asked	be – was/were
	can – could
	do – did

3 **CD·1.6 MP3·6** What do you know about Mr Bean? Choose what you think is true. Then listen and check.

1 The film 'Mr Bean on Holiday' *was / wasn't* very successful.
2 Mr Bean *started / didn't start* as a TV series.
3 The person who plays Mr Bean *studied / didn't study* acting.
4 Mr Bean *was / wasn't* the original name for the character.

Rowan Atkinson as Mr Bean

4 **CD·1.6 MP3·6** Put the words in the correct order to form the interview questions. Then listen again and check.

1 see/for the first time/did/Mr Bean/you/when?
   When did you see Mr Bean for the first time?
2 it/like/you/did/why?
3 Mr Bean/begin/did/how?
4 the idea for Mr Bean/come from/did/where?
5 Mr Bean/similar to/Rowan Atkinson/was?
6 study/acting/he/did?

5 Read REMEMBER THIS. Then complete the cartoon captions.

> **REMEMBER THIS**
>
> • For all verbs (except *be*) you form **Past Simple** negatives with *did not* (*didn't*) + infinitive.
> • You form **Past Simple** questions with *did + subject + infinitive*.

> ¹_____ you enjoy primary school?

> No, we ²_____ . But we liked the school uniform.

Grammar Focus page 109

6 Rewrite the sentences in the negative. Then tick the sentences that are true for you.

1 Mr Bean was on TV when I was younger. ☐
   Mr Bean wasn't on TV when I was younger. ☐
2 My friend told me a good joke this morning. ☐
   _____ ☐
3 I saw a really funny advert online yesterday. ☐
   _____ ☐
4 My parents gave me a funny DVD for Christmas. ☐
   _____ ☐
5 My grandad liked silent Charlie Chaplin films. ☐
   _____ ☐
6 I watched cartoons when I was younger. ☐
   _____ ☐

7 Put the verbs in brackets in the correct Past Simple form to make the sentences true for you.

1 I *watched/didn't watch* (watch) a funny film last week.
2 I _____ (be) very busy yesterday.
3 I _____ (have) eggs for breakfast this morning.
4 I _____ (play) tennis last weekend.
5 My mother and father _____ (meet) at university.
6 I _____ (go) to primary school near here.
7 My grandparents _____ (get) married in a church.
8 My best friend and I _____ (grow up) together.

8 In pairs, ask and answer questions about the sentences in Exercise 7.

A: *Did you watch a funny film last week?*
B: *Yes, I did./No, I didn't.*

0.4 Experiences

Grammar: Present Perfect
Vocabulary: Leisure activities

SHOW WHAT YOU KNOW

1 In pairs, complete the table with all the different leisure activities you can think of in sixty seconds.

do	go	play
yoga	horse-riding	the guitar

2 Mark the leisure activities you do often ✓✓✓, sometimes ✓ and never ✗. Then compare with a partner.

3 Complete the questionnaire. Put ✓ for yes and ✗ for no.

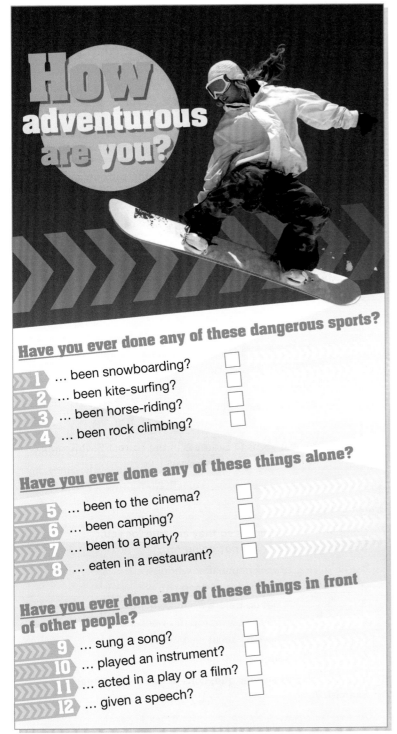

How adventurous are you?

Have you ever done any of these dangerous sports?

1 ... been snowboarding? ☐
2 ... been kite-surfing? ☐
3 ... been horse-riding? ☐
4 ... been rock climbing? ☐

Have you ever done any of these things alone?

5 ... been to the cinema? ☐
6 ... been camping? ☐
7 ... been to a party? ☐
8 ... eaten in a restaurant? ☐

Have you ever done any of these things in front of other people?

9 ... sung a song? ☐
10 ... played an instrument? ☐
11 ... acted in a play or a film? ☐
12 ... given a speech? ☐

4 In pairs, ask and answer the questions in the questionnaire. Who is more adventurous?

A: Have you ever been snowboarding?
B: No, I haven't.

5 Read REMEMBER THIS. Then complete the cartoon caption with the correct question.

REMEMBER THIS

You use the **Present Perfect** to talk about finished actions in time up to now. You never say when they happened.

Note: *been* is the past participle of *go* when you mean 'go and come back'.

horse-riding (you/ever/go)?

No, I haven't. Help!

Grammar Focus page 109

6 Complete the sentences so they are true for you. Then compare with a partner.

1 The most famous city I've ever been to is …
2 The fastest car I've ever been in is …
3 The most beautiful place I've ever been to is …
4 The tallest building I've ever been in is …
5 The most expensive shop I've ever been in is …
6 The best party I've ever been to is …

7 How well do you know your partner? Write sentences that you think are true from the prompts. Use the Present Perfect.

1 go to a rock concert
   My partner hasn't been to a rock concert.
2 write a poem
3 see a James Bond film
4 go to London
5 win a prize
6 meet a famous person
7 stay up all night
8 lose a phone

8 In pairs, ask and answer questions to check your ideas in Exercise 7.

A: Have you ever been to a rock concert?
B: Yes, I have.
A: Oh, I was wrong.

0.5 Adventure

Grammar: *be going to*
Vocabulary: Collocations

SHOW WHAT YOU KNOW

1 In pairs, make as many verb + noun collocations as you can in sixty seconds.

do go have make	+	~~camping~~ some cooking a fire a great time a haircut on holiday some homework a mistake a party a promise swimming the washing-up

go camping

2 In pairs, ask and answer questions about the last time your partner did the activities in Exercise 1.

A: *When was the last time you went camping?*

B: *Two years ago.*

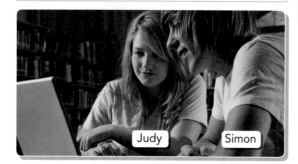
Judy   Simon

3 [CD·1.7] [MP3·7] Judy and Simon are discussing a holiday they are going on. Listen and mark what they have decided to do. Write *J* (Judy) or *S* (Simon).

The Forest Adventure Camp

ACTIVITIES	JOBS
☐ rock climbing	☐ put up tents
☐ swimming	☐ collect firewood
☐ yoga	☐ make a fire
☐ forest walks	☐ do the cooking
☐ sailing	☐ do the washing-up
☐ guitar and singing	☐ organise games

4 Put the words in the correct order to form questions. Then answer them.

1 is / Simon / rock climbing / to / going / try?
2 Judy / to / is / in the afternoon / going / what / do?
3 is / do / which jobs / going / Judy / to?
4 Simon / is / the washing-up / to / going / do?
5 sing / Simon and Judy / to / going / are?

8

5 What do they think is going to happen? Complete the cartoon captions with the correct form of *be going to* and the verbs in the box.

crash   fall   get lost   rain

A — She _____.
No, she isn't. She's got ropes. Don't worry!

B — Oh dear! I think it _____!

C — It's dark. We _____.
No, we're not. I've got a map.

D — Oh no! Simon _____.

6 Read REMEMBER THIS. Then complete the cartoon captions with one word in each gap.

REMEMBER THIS

You use *be going to* for:
- future intentions (when you have already decided to do something and you tell people about it).
- predictions based on what you can see or what you know.

1 _____ you going to take your waterproof?
No, I'm 2 _____. It's going 3 _____ be a lovely, sunny day.

Grammar Focus page 110

7 Complete the sentences so they are true for you. Use *I'm going to* or *I'm not going to*.

1 *I'm going to* walk home after school.
2 _____ stay in this evening.
3 _____ get up before 7 a.m. tomorrow.
4 _____ buy a new laptop this weekend.
5 _____ have a haircut next week.
6 _____ be rich and famous one day!

8 In pairs, ask and answer questions about the sentences in Exercise 7.

A: *Are you going to walk home after school?*

B: *Yes, I am.*

Grammar: *will* for predictions
Vocabulary: Travel

SHOW WHAT YOU KNOW

1 Work in pairs. How many nouns and verbs to do with transport can you think of in sixty seconds? Add them to the diagrams.

ferry   sail   helicopter

land   water   air

car   ride   fly

2 Has your partner ever travelled in the ways listed in Exercise 1? Ask and answer in pairs.

A: Have you ever ridden a motorbike?
B: Yes, I have.

3 How will people travel in 2050? Discuss in pairs. Put ✓ for *it will happen* and ✗ for *it won't happen*.

1 High-speed trains will replace air travel. ☐

2 People will have holidays in space. ☐

3 Planes won't have pilots. ☐

4 Cars will fly. ☐

5 There will be an elevator into space. ☐

6 Planes will be transparent. ☐

4 CD·1.8 MP3·8 Listen to an expert discussing the predictions in Exercise 3 and compare his opinions with yours.

5 CD·1.8 MP3·8 Listen again. Which two things won't happen in the expert's opinion? Why?

6 Read REMEMBER THIS. Then add *will* in the correct place in the sentence to complete the cartoon caption.

REMEMBER THIS

• You use *will* for future predictions – things you think or guess about the future.
• Use *I don't think ... + will ...*
  NOT ~~I think ... + won't~~

One day you travel to the moon.

Grammar Focus page 110

7 Complete the predictions about 2050 with *will* or *won't*. Then tick the predictions you agree with for your country.

1 There _____ (not be) any petrol cars. ☐
2 People _____ (work) till they are seventy. ☐
3 Pollution _____ (be) worse. ☐
4 There _____ (be) more extreme weather. ☐
5 Food _____ (not be) cheaper. ☐
6 Everybody _____ (speak) English. ☐
7 Robots _____ (not replace) teachers in school. ☐
8 There _____ (be) a female president. ☐

8 Make predictions about your partner. Use *I think/I don't think you will ...*

1 be famous
   I don't think you will be famous.
2 travel round the world
3 live and work in a foreign country
4 have five or more children
5 learn how to fly a plane
6 study English at university
7 win a sports prize one day
8 write a best-selling book

9 In pairs, read your predictions in Exercise 8. Does your partner agree?

A: I don't think you will be famous.
B: I don't agree with you. I think I will be famous.

0.7 Sport

Grammar: *must, have to* and *should*
Vocabulary: Sport

SHOW WHAT YOU KNOW

1 In pairs, list all the sports you can think of in sixty seconds.

2 Put the sports from Exercise 1 in the correct group. Some sports can go in more than one group.

1 team sports: _football,_ _____
2 indoor sports: _____
3 sports that collocate with *play*: _football,_ _____
4 expensive sports: _____
5 sports you have tried: _football,_ _____
6 sports you don't like: _____

3 Complete a sports teacher's sentences with *must* or *mustn't*. Which sport do you think he/she is teaching?

1 You _____ respect the other team.
2 You _____ accept the referee's decisions.
3 You _____ argue with the referee.
4 You _____ keep your eye on the ball.
5 You _____ criticise your own team mates.
6 You _____ get angry when you lose.

4 `CD·1.9` `MP3·9` Listen to a gymnast and a triathlete talking about their diets. Answer the questions. Write G (gymnast) or T (triathlete).

1 Who has to train seven hours a day? ☐
2 Who mustn't eat more than 1,500 calories a day? ☐
3 Who has to eat six times a day? ☐
4 Who mustn't eat after 5 p.m.? ☐
5 Who has to eat a lot of carbohydrates (e.g. pasta)? ☐
6 Who has to have protein (e.g. fish) for lunch? ☐

5 `CD·1.9` `MP3·9` Based on the interview in Exercise 4, complete the advice for a triathlete with *should* or *shouldn't* .

Before a race, a triathlete:
1 _____ drink lots of water.
2 _____ eat things like rice and pasta.
3 _____ eat lots of red meat.
4 _____ rest and sleep at least eight hours.
5 _____ drink coffee.

6 Read REMEMBER THIS. Then complete the cartoon captions with *should* or *have to*.

REMEMBER THIS

- You use **must** and **have to** to say, 'This is necessary.'
- You use **mustn't** to say, 'Don't do this.'
- You use **should** (or **shouldn't**) to say, 'This is (or isn't) a good idea.'

Remember, you ¹_____ drink three litres of water a day.

I do. That's why I ²_____ go to the bathroom every five minutes!

Grammar Focus page 111

7 Rewrite the sentences using *should, shouldn't, mustn't* or *have to*.

1 It is necessary for sumo wrestlers to be very heavy.
Sumo wrestlers _____ .
2 If you're a woman, don't enter the *dohyo* (or sumo ring).
Women _____ .
3 It's a good idea for a sumo wrestler to eat around 20,000 calories a day.
Sumo wrestlers _____ .
4 When you watch a sumo training session, don't speak.
When you watch a sumo training session, you _____ .
5 It is necessary for sumo wrestlers to throw salt into the ring at the beginning of a match.
Sumo wrestlers _____ .
6 It isn't a good idea for sumo wrestlers to show their feelings.
Sumo wrestlers _____ .

8 Write three sentences about your favourite sport. Use *should/shouldn't, must/mustn't* and *have to*. Then compare with a partner.

Before you run, you should stretch.

0.8 Food

Grammar: Countable and uncountable nouns •
Articles
Vocabulary: Food

SHOW WHAT YOU KNOW

1 In pairs, complete the table with all the different food you can see in photos A–D. You have sixty seconds.

Protein	Carbohydrates	Fruit and vegetables	Other
meat	rice	banana	chocolate

2 In pairs, look at the photos and discuss the questions.

1 Which school lunch do you think is the healthiest?
2 Which school lunch is most similar to yours?
3 Which school lunch would you most like to eat?

3 CD·1.10 MP3·10 Listen to four students describing the school lunches. Match photos A–D with countries 1–4.

1 Brazil ☐   2 France ☐   3 England ☐   4 Australia ☐

4 Look at the photos again. Find examples of three countable nouns and three uncountable nouns. Use your dictionary if necessary.

- Countable nouns: _a banana_ , _____ , _____ , _____
- Uncountable nouns: _rice_ , _____ , _____ , _____

5 In pairs, ask and answer questions about food items in the photos. Use *Is/Are there any …?*

A: Is there any rice in photo D?
B: Yes, there is.
A: Are there any sandwiches in photo D?
B: No, there aren't.

6 CD·1.11 MP3·11 Complete the text with *a/an*, *the* or Ø (no article). Then listen and check.

My school day starts early. For breakfast I usually have [1] _Ø_ bread, [2] _____ hot chocolate and [3] _____ banana. I love [4] _____ fruit, so I always put [5] _____ apple and [6] _____ orange in my school bag for later. We have [7] _____ dog and I have to take [8] _____ dog out before I go to school. There's [9] _____ school bus. I know I should walk to school, but [10] _____ bus stops right outside my house and I'm lazy! I have lunch at school. [11] _____ lunches are healthy and because [12] _____ pasta is my favourite food, I usually have that. I get home around five o'clock. Luckily, my mum's [13] _____ great cook, so we always eat well at home.

7 Read REMEMBER THIS. Then complete the cartoon caption with *a/an*, *the* or Ø (no article).

REMEMBER THIS

- You use *a* or *an* with singular countable nouns. Use *a/an* to talk about a thing or a person for the first time.
- You use *the* to talk about that thing or that person again. You also use *the* when there is only one of something.
- Don't use *a/an* or *the* to talk about things in general.

What have you got for lunch today?

I've got some sandwiches and [1] _____ apple. [2] _____ sandwiches look OK, but I don't want [3] _____ apple. I can't stand [4] _____ fruit!

Grammar Focus page 111

8 Complete the sentences with *a/an*, *the* or Ø (no article).

1 _____ fast food is bad for you.
2 _____ Italian food is the best in _____ world!
3 _____ men cook better than _____ women.
4 I can't live without _____ chocolate.
5 It's wrong to eat _____ animals.

9 In pairs, discuss the sentences in Exercise 8. Which ones do you agree with?

I agree with number 1.

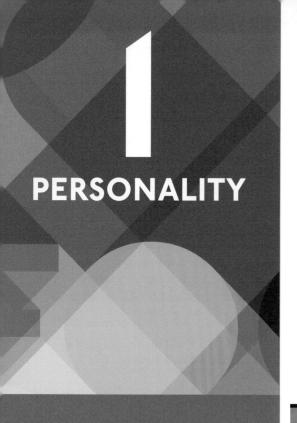

1
PERSONALITY

Wanting to be someone else is a waste of the person you are.

KURT COBAIN (1967–1994), AN AMERICAN MUSICIAN

UNIT LANGUAGE AND SKILLS

Vocabulary:
- *Show what you know* – personality adjectives
- adjective antonyms
- negative prefixes: *un-*, *in-*, *ir-*, *dis-*
- adjective + preposition
- word families

Grammar:
- present tenses – question forms
- subject and object questions
- *wh-* questions ending with prepositions
- verb + *-ing* or verb + *to*-infinitive

Listening:
- an interview and a conversation about voluntary work

Reading:
- a text on teenage stereotypes

Speaking:
- showing interest

Writing:
- a personal email/letter

FOCUS EXTRA

- Grammar Focus page 112
- WORD STORE booklet pages 2–3
- Workbook pages 8–19 or MyEnglishLab

1.1 Vocabulary

Personality adjectives · Adjective + preposition
I can describe people and talk about personal qualities.

SHOW WHAT YOU KNOW

1 Match adjectives 1–5 with their opposites a–e.

1	clever	*d*	**a**	boring
2	funny		**b**	negative
3	interesting		**c**	serious
4	kind		**d**	stupid
5	positive		**e**	unkind

2 In pairs, look at the photos and choose an adjective from Exercise 1 to describe each person.

3 CD·1.12 MP3·12 Listen to Rani and check your answers to Exercise 2.

---

4 CD·1.13 MP3·13 What do Sara, David and Rani want to be? Listen and complete the interview with the jobs they want to do.

TEENAGE DREAMS AND AMBITIONS

THEY'RE YOUNG, AMBITIOUS AND OPTIMISTIC. WE MEET THREE TEENAGERS AND ASK THEM ABOUT THEIR DREAMS AND AMBITIONS.

Interviewer: So Sara, what do you want to be?

Sara: I want to be a ¹_____ .

Interviewer: Are your parents <u>involved in</u> journalism?

Sara: No, not at all. In fact, journalists are pretty unpopular in my house. My father's <u>interested in</u> the news, but he isn't very <u>keen on</u> journalists. He thinks most of them are **arrogant**, dishonest and irresponsible.

Interviewer: David, why do you want to be a ²_____ ?

David: I'm really <u>disappointed with</u> our government. Young people have a lot to say, but politicians don't listen to them. They just think teenagers are lazy and **miserable**.

Interviewer: Why do you think you could be a politician?

David: I'm <u>passionate about</u> my country. I also have the right character: I'm not at all shy! In fact, I'm very **outgoing** and I'm <u>good at</u> public speaking. I'm only sixteen now, so I'm very inexperienced, but I'm <u>serious about</u> politics.

Interviewer: Rani, why do you want to be a ³_____ ?

Rani: Well, most surgeons in the UK are men and I think that's unfair and wrong in the twenty-first century. I think my generation is <u>responsible for</u> getting more women into important jobs.

Interviewer: What special qualities do you think you need to be a surgeon?

Rani: I think I need to be **caring**, **sensible** and very **hard-working**.

5 Replace the adjectives in brackets with the adjectives in red in the interview.

1 Surgeons are (not selfish). They are kind and helpful.
Surgeons are caring. They are kind and helpful.

2 Teenagers are (not cheerful). They are always in a bad mood.

3 Business people are (not lazy). They put a lot of effort into their work.

4 Journalists are (not modest). They think they are better than other people.

5 Politicians are (not shy). They are confident and sociable.

6 Farmers are (not crazy). They don't make silly decisions.

6 In pairs, discuss the questions.

1 Do you know anybody like Rani, Sara or David?

2 Which teenager is the most like/unlike you?

3 What are your dreams and ambitions?

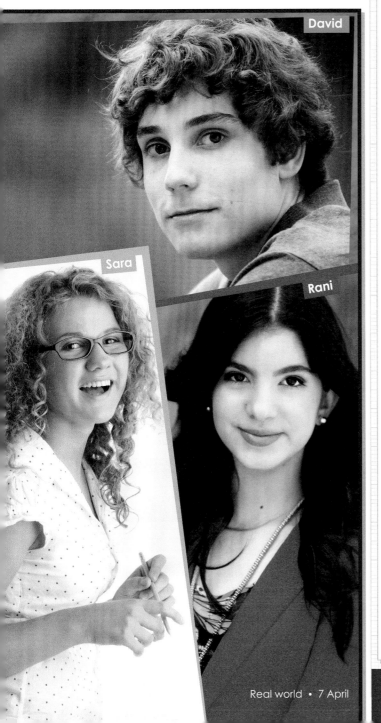

David

Sara

Rani

Real world • 7 April

Go to WORD STORE 1 page 3.

WORD STORE 1A ⟩⟩⟩

7 CD•1.14 MP3•14 Complete WORD STORE 1A with adjectives from Exercise 5. Then listen, check and repeat.

WORD STORE 1B ⟩⟩⟩

8 CD•1.15 MP3•15 Complete WORD STORE 1B. Write the opposites of the adjectives. You can find them in the interview. Then listen, check and repeat.

9 Complete the sentences with adjectives from WORD STORE 1B.

1 Phil is an _____ skier. He goes to the mountains every year.

2 Ted's an _____ guy. He never tells lies.

3 I never ask Sarah to look after my pet. She is so _____ .

4 Mr Morgan is very _____ . He treats all his students equally.

5 Everybody likes Emma. She's really _____ .

6 I'm worried about going in a car with Cara because she's an _____ driver. She only passed her test recently.

7 Paul's only sixteen, but he seems to be much older. He's so sensible and _____ .

10 Can you change the names in Exercise 9 to describe people you know? Tell your partner.

WORD STORE 1C ⟩⟩⟩

11 CD•1.16 MP3•16 Look at the underlined words in the interview. Complete WORD STORE 1C with the correct preposition after the adjectives. Then listen, check and repeat.

12 Complete the questions with the correct prepositions.

1 What sort of things are you interested _____ ?

2 What after-school activities are you involved _____ ?

3 What bands and singers are you keen _____ ?

4 What sports or games are you good _____ ?

5 What sort of things are you serious _____ ?

6 What jobs at home are you responsible _____ ?

7 Which marks in your last exams were you disappointed _____ ?

8 What are you most passionate _____ ?

13 In pairs, ask and answer the questions in Exercise 12.

1.2 Grammar

Present tenses – question forms

I can ask questions using present tense forms.

1 In pairs, discuss who your role models are. Think about business people, sports stars, entertainers, and people you know.

2 `CD·1.17` `MP3·17` Match questions 1–8 with answers a–h. Then listen and check.

1 Who **inspires** you?
2 What **does** he **do**?
3 Why do you admire him?
4 **Does** he **give** any money to charity?
5 Which charities **does** he **give** money to?
6 Have you ever met him?
7 What is he doing now?
8 Are you similar to him in any way?

a No, never.
b Different African charities, I think.
c He's developing the first ever spaceport.
d Richard Branson.
e Yes, in some ways, I am.
f He owns Virgin Atlantic.
g Yes, he's very generous.
h Because he's so energetic and successful.

Richard Branson

3 Read the GRAMMAR FOCUS. Then complete the examples. Look at the questions in blue in Exercise 2.

GRAMMAR FOCUS

Present tenses – question forms

• To make questions, you put an auxiliary verb (*do, be, have*) before the subject of the main verb.

Present Simple: *Why* [1]_____ *you admire him?*

Present Continuous: *What* [2]_____ *he doing now?*

Present Perfect: [3]_____ *you ever met him?*

• When you ask about the subject, you don't use the Present Simple auxiliary *do/does*.

Who inspires you? NOT ~~Who does inspire you?~~

• Notice the position of the preposition in *wh-* questions:

Which charities does he give money to?

4 `CD·1.18` `MP3·18` Complete the questions for the interview about Aung San Suu Kyi. Then listen and check.

1 'Who _____?' 'The person who inspires me is Aung San Suu Kyi.'
2 'Who _____?' 'She's the Burmese Nobel Peace laureate.'
3 'Why _____?' 'I admire her because she's 100 percent loyal to the people of her country.'
4 'What _____?' 'She believes in non-violent action.'
5 'Have _____?' 'No, I haven't seen her, but I've listened to her speaking.'
6 'What _____?' 'She's working for peace, democracy and human rights.'

Aung San Suu Kyi

5 Complete the questions about the subject (a) and about the object (b) of each sentence.

1 a Viv enjoys   b swimming.
   a Who *enjoys swimming* ?
   b What *does Viv enjoy* ?
2 a Neil has tried   b Japanese food.
   a Who _____ ? b What _____ ?
3 a Rosie can speak b three languages.
   a Who _____ ? b How many languages _____ ?
4 a Dave has visited   b London.
   a Who _____ ? b Which capital city _____ ?
5 a Tom is thinking about b food.
   a Who _____ ? b What _____ ?

6 Complete the sentences to make them true for you.

1 I'm reading _____ at the moment.
2 I spend most money on _____ .
3 It takes me _____ minutes to get to school.
4 I go shopping for clothes _____ a year.
5 I usually have lunch with _____ .
6 _____ inspires me.

7 In pairs, ask and answer questions about the information in Exercise 6. Use different question words.

A: *What are you reading at the moment?*
B: *A book about Steve Jobs.*

Grammar Focus page 112

14

1.3 Listening

Gap-fill
I can identify specific detail in a monologue.

1 In pairs, look at some of the places where people do voluntary work. Discuss why you would or wouldn't like to volunteer in each place.

> in a developing country   in a hospital   in a library
> in a nursery   in a prison
> in a soup kitchen for homeless people
> in an old person's home   on a farm

2 `CD·1.19` `MP3·19` **Listen to two volunteers, Karen and Martin. Where do they do their voluntary work?**

Martin   Karen

3 Read questions 1–8 in Exercise 4. Match the underlined words and phrases with these words and phrases from the interview.

> confident 7   elderly ☐   impresses people ☐
> in a team ☐   more likely to do something ☐
> pigs and chickens ☐   Saturday and Sunday ☐
> two or three ☐

4 `CD·1.19` `MP3·19` **Listen again and answer the questions. Write K (Karen) or M (Martin).**

Who:

1 helps <u>old</u> people in the local area? ☐
2 works with <u>farm animals</u>? ☐
3 volunteers <u>a few</u> hours a week? ☐
4 does volunteering work every <u>weekend</u>? ☐
5 thinks that volunteers are <u>more active</u> than other people? ☐
6 enjoys working <u>with other people</u>? ☐
7 thinks that voluntary work makes you more <u>sure of yourself</u>? ☐
8 thinks that doing voluntary work <u>makes a good impression</u>? ☐

5 Imagine you could volunteer anywhere in the world. Which country would you choose? Why? Discuss in pairs.

6 `CD·1.20` `MP3·20` **Listen to Becky talking about international volunteering. Answer the questions.**

1 Who do you think Becky is talking to?
2 Did Becky enjoy her volunteering work?
3 What does she think are the benefits of volunteering?

EXAM FOCUS Gap-fill

7 `CD·1.20` `MP3·20` **Listen again and complete the sentences with a word or short phrase.**

1 Becky did volunteering work in ¹_____ last year.
2 She was there for ²_____ .
3 Becky's job was to care for ³_____ .
4 Becky says that life can be very different in other countries and gives ⁴_____ as an example.
5 She thinks that volunteers need to:
   • be fit and ⁵_____ .
   • have good ⁶_____ skills.
   • be responsible.
6 Becky recommends a volunteering agency which is called ⁷_____ .
7 Their phone number is ⁸_____ .

8 Are you a good candidate for international volunteer work? Why?/Why not? Discuss in pairs.

PRONUNCIATION FOCUS

9 `CD·1.21` `MP3·21` **Listen and put the adjectives the correct group depending on the stress.**

> ~~ambitious~~   disappointed   interested
> optimistic   outgoing   passionate
> responsible   unpopular

A ■▪▪   B ▪■▪   C ▪■▪   D ▪▪■▪
_____   *ambitious*   _____   _____

_____   _____   _____   _____

10 `CD·1.22` `MP3·22` **Listen, check and repeat.**

WORD STORE 1D 〉〉〉〉〉

11 `CD·1.23` `MP3·23` **Complete WORD STORE 1D. Write the adjectives to make pairs of opposites. Then listen, check and repeat.**

1.4 Reading

Gapped text

I can understand the structure of a text.

Andrew, 17　　　Mel, 18　　　Ryan, 16

1 In pairs, look at the phrases in the box and decide whether they are things parents say about teenagers or things teenagers say about themselves.

> able to get up early   bad-tempered
> generous   hard-working
> interested in the world   lazy
> loyal to their friends
> obsessed with their phones
> passionate about music   selfish
> uncommunicative   unhelpful

Parents say teenagers are ...

Teenagers say they are ...

2 Read the survey report and comments. Compare your ideas in Exercise 1 with the information you read.

3 Read the comments again. Choose from sentences A–F the one which fits each gap (1–5). There is one extra sentence.

A Teenagers are definitely not lazy.

B We don't have time to tidy our rooms.

C Why are people so negative about teenagers?

D I don't think I'm selfish.

E I hate stereotypes.

F The most important thing in my life is not my phone.

4 Read the comments again and write the names.

Who thinks that:

1 teenagers work really hard?

_____ , _____

2 teenagers have lots of positive personal qualities? _____

3 teenagers are interested in other people and cultures? _____

4 teenagers are all different people?

_____

5 friends are very important for teenagers?

_____

What are teenagers

CD·1.24 **MP3·24**

A recent survey shows that there are reasons why teenagers behave badly. The study suggests that teenagers need to sleep more and that is why sixty-five percent of parents say their teenagers are bad-tempered, uncommunicative and lazy.
5 The report also shows that most teenagers are obsessed with their phones. They spend more time chatting online or playing computer games than doing homework. Most parents also say that their teenage children are selfish and unhelpful. Only a few of them help with housework at home.

10 **Your comments**

Sarah

1 _____ Most of us are adorable, cheerful, very hard-working, interesting, brave, generous, loyal, helpful and very good cooks. Oh, and very modest!

15
5.54 p.m. 3 May

Janet

2 _____ It's my friends. We love each other. We don't argue or fight. We go to the park after school and we sit under a tree, eat ice cream and talk about
20 guys. We like cooking and camping, not just texting and computer games. I don't have time to read much, but I play the guitar and sing. I'm not a bad-tempered monster – I (usually) apologise when I'm wrong and I like spending time with my
25 grandparents.
7.18 p.m. 3 May

Sarah, 16   Janet, 17

really like?

Andrew

³_____ I get up at 6.30 a.m. every school day and I work hard all day. I never make plans to meet friends in the evening – that's when I do my homework. I

30 think I need about nine and a half hours sleep a night, but I usually get only seven hours. So I'm sometimes a bit grumpy like my parents! 😃

10.13 a.m. 4 May

Ryan

⁴_____ Not all teenagers are the same. Some

35 of us are lazy, some of us aren't. Some of us like chatting online or playing computer games, but some of us prefer to play football or go for a run. OK, some of the things people say about teenagers are true. For example, music is really, really important to us, but we like different kinds

40 of music. We are INDIVIDUALS!

3.22 p.m. 5 May

Mel

⁵_____ I care about other people. I'm interested in the world. I want to travel and learn about other cultures. Then I want to get a job in a

45 developing country. Most of my friends are like me! Where did you find your information? It's wrong!

6.20 p.m. 5 May

---

5 Match 1–5 with a–e to make questions. Then answer the questions.

1 Who likes spending ☐
2 Who wants to get ☐
3 Who doesn't have ☐
4 Who does ☐
5 Who thinks some teenagers play ☐

a his homework in the evening?
b football?
c time with her grandparents?
d a job in a developing country?
e time to read much?

6 Find the opposites of these adjectives in Sarah's comment. Use a dictionary if necessary.

1 arrogant ≠ *modest*
2 cowardly ≠ _____
3 disloyal ≠ _____
4 dull ≠ _____
5 grumpy ≠ _____
6 mean ≠ _____

7 Complete the sentences with adjectives from Exercise 6.

1 Teenagers are _____ . They think they know everything.
2 Teenagers are _____ . They never get enough sleep and are always in a bad mood.
3 Teenagers are _____ to their friends. They are always there for their friends.
4 Teenagers are _____ . They never give money to charity and always buy cheap presents.
5 Teenagers are _____ . They have lots of things to talk about.
6 Teenagers are _____ . They avoid dangerous situations and don't take risks.

8 In pairs, discuss the sentences in Exercise 7. Which ones do you agree/disagree with? Why?

WORD STORE 1E ❯❯❯❯

9 CD·1.25 MP3·25 Complete WORD STORE 1E. Add adjectives to the table. Mark the stress. Then listen, check and repeat.

17

1.5 Grammar

Verb + -ing form or verb + to-infinitive

I can use different verb patterns.

1 In pairs, match the words in the box with the clothes (a–f) in the pictures. Which of the clothes do you own?

> hoodie ☐   jacket ☐   suit ☐
> sweatpants ☐   tie ☐   uniform ☐

2 Tick the sentence that best describes your opinion about clothes.

   1 I want to look good at all times. ☐
   2 I enjoy wearing comfortable things. ☐
   3 I'm not interested in clothes. ☐

3 Read the GRAMMAR FOCUS. Then complete the examples using the verb patterns in blue in Exercise 2.

GRAMMAR FOCUS

Verb + -ing form or verb + to-infinitive

• After some verbs and verb phrases you usually use the -ing form of a verb.

   Examples: *avoid, can't stand, consider, don't mind, enjoy, hate, like, love, miss, prefer, spend time*

   I enjoy [1]_____ *comfortable things.*

• After some verbs and verb phrases you usually use the to-infinitive.

   Examples: *agree, can't afford, choose, decide, hope, manage, need, pretend, refuse, want, would like, would prefer*

   I want [2]_____ *good at all times.*

4 Complete the questionnaire with the correct form of the verbs in brackets.

5 Do the questionnaire. Then compare your answers with a partner.

6 Complete the sentences with *to wear* or *wearing*. Then tick the sentences that are true for you.

   1 I can't stand _____ formal clothes like suits. ☐
   2 I don't mind _____ sweatpants at home. ☐
   3 I refuse _____ skinny jeans. They're too uncomfortable. ☐
   4 I hate _____ heavy winter coats. ☐
   5 I can't afford _____ designer clothes. They're too expensive. ☐
   6 I avoid _____ anything yellow or pink. ☐

7 Complete the sentences with information about you. Write five true sentences and one false one.

   1 I love …   4 I spend a lot of time …
   2 I need …   5 I sometimes pretend …
   3 I've decided …   6 I hope …

8 In pairs, take turns to read your sentences from Exercise 7. Guess which of your partner's sentences is false.

Grammar Focus page 112

18

WHAT IS YOUR ATTITUDE TO CLOTHES?

1 (SPEND)

A I spend a lot of money on clothes.
B I can't afford [1] *to spend* much money on clothes.
C I prefer [2]_____ my money on going out.

2 (GO)

A I enjoy [3]_____ shopping for clothes.
B I don't mind [4]_____ shopping for clothes.
C I refuse [5]_____ shopping for clothes.

3 (BUY)

A I love [6]_____ new clothes every season.
B I only buy clothes when I need them.
C I avoid [7]_____ new clothes for as long as possible.

4 (WEAR)

A I refuse [8]_____ sweatpants.
B I love [9]_____ sweatpants at home for comfort.
C I wear sweatpants all the time.

5 (GET)

A I hope [10]_____ a job where I can wear all my favourite clothes.
B I want [11]_____ a job where I can wear practical, comfortable clothes.
C I'd like [12]_____ a job where I can wear a uniform or a suit.

6 (THINK)

A In the morning, I spend a lot of time [13]_____ about my clothes.
B In the morning, I don't spend much time [14]_____ about my clothes.
C I wear the same clothes every day.

WHAT DOES IT MEAN?

Mainly As   I LOVE THEM

You enjoy [15]_____ (think) about clothes (perhaps a bit too much). The way you look is important for your personal identity.

Mainly Bs   I NEED THEM

You don't mind [16]_____ (think) about clothes, but they are not your priority. You prefer casual clothes because you need [17]_____ (be) comfortable.

Mainly Cs   I HATE THEM

You hate [18]_____ (think) about clothes! You choose [19]_____ (spend) your time and money on other things. But don't forget: clothes can be fun.

1.6 Speaking

Showing interest

I can show interest in what somebody is saying and say whether we are similar.

1 In pairs, look at the activities in the box and discuss the questions.

  1 How much free time do you spend on each activity?

  2 What other things do you do in your free time?

  3 How similar or different are you to your partner?

> being online   doing sport   eating and drinking
> listening to music   shopping   socialising
> travelling   watching TV

2 CD·1.26 MP3·26 Listen to two conversations and answer the questions.

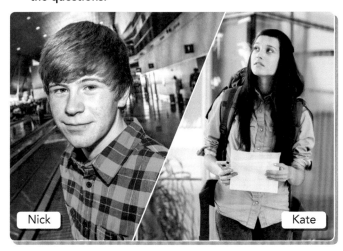

Nick   Kate

  1 What do Ed and Nick have in common?

  2 What do Rachel and Kate have in common?

3 CD·1.26 MP3·26 Listen again and complete the **SPEAKING FOCUS** with responses a–e.

  a Do you? Right …   **d** Really? I love it.

  b ~~Really? That's cool!~~   **e** Me too.

  c Is she?

SPEAKING FOCUS

Statement	Saying you are similar
A: I love travelling and meeting new people.	**B:** ¹_____
A: I don't really like rock or heavy metal.	**B:** Me neither.

Statement	Showing interest
A: I've got loads of friends and they want to meet you.	**B:** ²*Really? That's cool!*
A: I've just got one sister. She's a model.	**B:** ³_____
A: She's training to be a pilot.	**B:** Wow, that's interesting!

Statement	Saying you are different
A: I'm not very keen on tea.	**B:** ⁴_____
A: I don't like travelling.	**B:** Don't you? Oh, I do.
A: I play the violin.	**B:** ⁵_____

4 CD·1.27 MP3·27 **Cross out the incorrect options. Then listen, check and repeat.**

  1 A: I've got thousands of songs on my iPod.

    B: *Have you? / Cool! / Is it?*

  2 A: I love Spanish and Italian food.

    B: *Really? / Are you? / Do you?*

  3 A: My parents have got an apartment in Paris.

    B: *Wow, that's interesting! / Have they? / Are they?*

  4 A: There are forty students in my class.

    B: *Is it? / Are there? / Really?*

  5 A: I can play the guitar.

    B: *Cool! / Are you? / Can you?*

  6 A: I'm passionate about politics.

    B: *Really? / Do you? / Are you?*

5 CD·1.28 MP3·28 **Listen to six conversations and decide if the two speakers are similar or different. Write *S* or *D*.**

  1 ___   3 ___   5 ___

  2 ___   4 ___   6 ___

6 Complete the table.

Statement	Say you are similar	Say you are different
a I'm worried about the world.	Me too.	Are you? ¹*I'm not.*
b I'm not worried about the world.	²_____	Aren't you? I am.
c I love reading poetry.	³_____	⁴_____ ? I don't.
d I don't like reading poetry.	Me neither.	Don't you? ⁵_____ .
e I've got lots of cousins.	⁶_____	⁷_____ ? I haven't.
f I haven't got any cousins.	Me neither.	Haven't you? ⁸_____ .

7 Complete the sentences to make them true for you.

  1 I'm really into …

  2 I haven't got …

  3 I really like …

  4 I'm very interested in …

  5 I'm not very keen on …

  6 I'm not very good at …

8 In pairs, follow the instructions.

Student A: Choose one of your sentences from Exercise 7. Say it to Student B.

Student B: Say if you are similar or different. Use the SPEAKING FOCUS to help you.

1.7 Writing

A personal email/letter

I can write to someone and tell them about myself.

To: Jo

Subject: C U soon!

Hi Jo,

I hope you're well. I'm really excited about coming to stay with you. I'm writing to tell you a bit more about myself.

As you know, I'm sixteen and I live in Venice. My brother and I go to the same school. I'm not crazy about studying, but it's OK – my favourite subject is Art. What about you? What's your favourite subject?

In my free time, I'm keen on sports and I'm pretty good at volleyball. I'm also passionate about music, especially American bands. At the moment I'm listening to Black Eyed Peas all the time.

At weekends, my friends and I love going to the cinema. What do you enjoy doing at weekends? Are you involved in any groups or clubs?

I can't wait to see you next month! I'm sure we'll have fun.

OK, time to finish. Write soon! ☺

Bye 4 now,

Carlo

---

1 In pairs, choose five qualities to describe the ideal exchange student.

- confident and independent
- friendly and outgoing
- generous
- good-looking
- good at sport
- honest
- interested in computers
- into the same music as me
- keen on the same hobbies as me
- sensible

2 Read the email from an exchange student and tick the topics in the box that he writes about.

family ☐	food ☐	hobbies ☐
music ☐	school ☐	sport ☐

3 Write a sentence about each topic in Exercise 2 that is NOT mentioned to add to the email.

4 Put the sentences summarising the email in the correct order (1–5).

a basic information about yourself ☐
b a greeting and information about why you are writing ☐
c say you are looking forward to seeing him/her ☐
d finish with a friendly goodbye ☐
e information about your likes/dislikes/hobbies, etc ☐

5 Which of these phrases are used in the opening of the email and which are used in the closing part? Write *O* or *C*.

1 Time to finish.
2 I hope you're well.
3 Write soon.
4 I can't wait to see you.
5 Bye for now.
6 Give my love/Say hello to …
7 I'm writing to …
8 It was good to hear from you.

6 Complete the WRITING FOCUS with the words in purple in email.

WRITING FOCUS

A personal email/letter

- Start the email/letter with a friendly greeting.
  Dear Nick/[1] ___Hi___ Jo.
- Don't use full forms. Use contractions.
  you're (not ~~you are~~)/[2] _____ (not ~~I am~~).
- Use useful phrases to give information about yourself.
  I'm interested in …/I'm good at …/I'm [3] _____ .
- Ask questions to show you want a reply.
  What do you enjoy doing at weekends?/What [4] _____ ?
- Finish the email/letter with a friendly goodbye.
  All the best/[5] _____

7 Does the person in the email sound like your ideal exchange student? What details would you change? Discuss in pairs.

8 Which of these people do you think would be a good (G) or not so good (NG) exchange student for you? Compare your answers with a partner.

1 I'm quite cheerful, but sometimes I get in a bad mood.

2 I don't like sports very much and I'm quite unfit.

3 I love school and studying and my favourite subjects are Science and Maths.

4 I'm obsessed with pop music.

5 I watch a lot of DVDs, especially horror films.

6 I'm crazy about shopping! I spend lots of money on clothes.

7 I love animals and I'm a volunteer at an animal centre.

Writing task

You recently received an email from Jenny, an English teenager you are going to stay with in England. Read part of her email and write your reply to Jenny.

> It's great to hear that you're going to come and stay with me and my family for two weeks. Please tell me something about yourself. What music and films do you like? What do you do in your free time?

A Write your email in about 100 words. Include these points.

- Thank Jenny for her email.
- Say how you feel about staying in England.
- Tell her about the sort of music and films you like.
- Write about some of the things you do in your free time.
- Ask about Jenny's interests.
- Say goodbye.

Useful language

- Thanks for …
- It was good to hear from you.
- I'm writing to tell you about/apologise for/thank you for …
- How are you?/How are you doing?
- I must be going now.
- Looking forward to hearing from/meeting you.
- See you soon.

B Use the ideas in the WRITING FOCUS and the model to help you.

C Check.

✓ Have you answered all the questions in the task?
✓ Have you organised your email into paragraphs?
✓ Have you used information and phrases from the model, WRITING FOCUS and Useful language box?
✓ Have you checked your spelling and punctuation?

VOCABULARY AND GRAMMAR

1 Complete the sentences with adjectives. The first letter of each adjective is given.

1 Shona never smiles and is always depressed. She's a really **m**_____ person.
2 Tim always thinks he's right. He's so **a**_____.
3 I'm **d**_____ with my exam results. I didn't do well.
4 My parents always give me and my brother the same things. They're very **f**_____.
5 Has Marion always been so **l**_____? She always stays in bed until midday!
6 Everyone knows Katie's name and everyone likes her. She's so **p**_____.

2 Complete the sentences with the correct form of the words in capitals.

1 Tom has some health problems. He's quite _____. **HEALTHY**
2 He saved a boy from the river and won a prize for _____. **BRAVE**
3 Neil eats chips and hamburgers every day and never exercises. He's really _____. **FIT**
4 She sends money to her family. I admire her _____. **GENEROUS**
5 Jo told everyone my secrets. She's so _____. **LOYAL**
6 _____ is not one of Zafira's qualities – she tells everybody that she's the best student in the class. **MODEST**

3 Complete the sentences with the correct form of the verbs in brackets.

1 _____ (you/ever/swim) in a river before?
2 Who _____ (enjoy) eating Italian food? I know a good restaurant.
3 _____ (Eve/usually/go) to bed very late?
4 What music _____ (your friends/like) listening to?
5 What _____ (you/read) at the moment? Is it a novel?
6 Who _____ (take) my book? It's not on the desk!

4 Use the prompts to write sentences.

1 I / not mind / wear / my sister's old clothes / if they suit me

_____

2 they / miss / live / in the city

_____

3 you / ever / refuse / help / your friends?

_____

4 police officers / not always / need / wear a uniform

_____

5 I / always / like / dance

_____

6 you / spend / a long time / studying / when you get home from school?

_____

LANGUAGE IN USE

5 Choose the correct answer, A, B or C.

1 Johann _____ art at all. He has never been to an art gallery or an exhibition.
   A isn't involved in   C isn't responsible for
   B isn't keen on
2 _____ with the project at the moment?
   A Who helps Mary   C Who is helping Mary
   B Who has helped Mary
3 A: I don't like shopping for clothes.
   B: _____
   A Me too.   B Me neither.   C Not me.
4 Sally is a vegetarian and she _____ to wear clothes made of leather.
   A avoids   B refuses   C doesn't mind
5 A: My older sister is a fashion designer.
   B: _____
   A Is she?   B Have you?   C Are there?

6 Read the text and choose the correct answer, A, B or C.

WOULD YOU LIKE TO LOOK MORE STYLISH?

Most teenagers want to ¹_____ good, but most of us can't afford ²_____ the latest fashions or designer clothes. But there is another way.

Have you ever ³_____ buying clothes from a charity shop? You can find unique, stylish items at a much lower price than in high-street shops. Tasmin Childs, sixteen, is a big fan of charity shops. 'I enjoy ⁴_____ through all the rails of clothes. I always find something interesting and I prefer ⁵_____ unusual items that no one else has.' Tasmin doesn't mind that someone else has worn the clothes before her. 'I wash the clothes, of course. I'm passionate ⁶_____ recycling. If you're worried about the planet and climate change, reuse old clothes and visit your local charity shop.'

1 A look   B see   C watch
2 A buy   B to buy   C buying
3 A preferred B wanted   C considered
4 A search   B to search   C searching
5 A putting   B wearing   C clothing
6 A about   B with   C to

READING

7 Read the article. Are the statements true (T) or false (F)?

1 You have to pay to join some of the websites. ☐
2 There will be information about other websites in the future. ☐
3 On the *What's your hobby?* website you can learn about new and interesting sports and hobbies. ☐
4 People who have lots of personal problems can get help on the *Serious teenage* talk website. ☐
5 The *Exchange!* website is only for teenagers who want to visit other countries. ☐
6 Teenagers who want to learn a language can find information about schools near them where they can do this. ☐
7 The *Learn a language* website is looking for good teachers. ☐

International Students' Magazine

Would you like to talk to people of your age in another country? Here are just a few of the free websites we can recommend. There's something for everyone here! Go online and make some friends. We'll give you more websites in the next month.

What's your hobby?

This is a website where you can meet people who have the same hobbies and interests as you. You type in the name of something you enjoy, for example, a sport, and then you can find other people in different countries who like the same thing. You can share information about things you do and give advice to each other. Who knows – one day perhaps you'll meet and do your hobby together!

Serious teenage talk

Perhaps you like talking about more important things like politics or education. On this site you can join in group discussions about things that are important to everyone. It's good to hear the opinions of people from different countries. We can learn a lot. So if you care about things like homeless people and human rights, come online and talk about them.

Exchange!

You probably think this site is about exchange visits where students go to other countries for a short time. It is, but that's not all you can do on this site. You can also exchange things with teenagers all round the world. You can exchange music or recipes, books and so on. In this way you can learn a lot about different cultures. And you can meet people and arrange visits too.

Learn a language

Do you want to learn another language? This website can find online language classes for nearly every major language in the world! And you can study in an international group with excellent teachers. So if you'd like to learn Mandarin Chinese or Russian or even Norwegian, go on the website and they will help you.

SPEAKING

8 Work in pairs. You want to spend Saturday afternoon together. Look at the photos and talk about the different things you could do.

WRITING

9 Write one sentence referring to each of the five points in the email from George, your English friend.

> I'm sure you're having a fantastic time in the US. Tell me about your host family and your American friend. Do you have the same interests and hobbies? What's he like?

10 Write your email to George in about 100 words. Use your sentences from Exercise 9, but add some more details.

2 INVENTION

Necessity is the mother of invention.

A PROVERB

2.1 Vocabulary

Technology • Compound nouns • Collocations • Phrasal verbs

I can talk about technology.

SHOW WHAT YOU KNOW

1 In pairs, look at the twentieth-century inventions in the box. Decide which three are the most useful to society.

> washing machine (1907)   refrigerator (1913)   radar (1922)
> television (1925)   antibiotics (1928)   jet engine (1930)
> nuclear power (1942)   communications satellite (1945)
> credit card (1958)   mobile phone (1973)

2 Decide which inventions from Exercise 1 you could/couldn't live without. Then compare your choices with a partner.

3 CD•1.29 MP3•29 In pairs, match the dates in the box with the digital 'firsts' below (1–8). Then listen and check.

> 1971   1984   1990   1991
> 1995   2001   2005   2006

Digital firsts

1 You Tube
the first video on YouTube:
_____

2 the first email:
_____

5 http://www
the first website:
_____

6 Archie Query Form
Search for:
Archie
the first search engine:
_____

4 CD•1.29 MP3•29 Listen again. Are the statements true (T) or false (F)?

1 Lots of people still watch the first YouTube video called *Me at the zoo*. ☐

2 Ray Tomlinson used the @ symbol to separate the username from the name of the Internet server in an email address. ☐

3 You can only <u>download music</u> from the iTunes store. ☐

4 Using a mouse to <u>click on an icon</u> and <u>open a document</u> was a very new idea in 1984. ☐

5 You could <u>visit a website</u> before August 1991. ☐

6 Thanks to Archie, you could <u>go online</u> to find information. ☐

7 Classmates is the most popular social networking site in the world. ☐

8 A tweet is a text message to everybody who <u>follows you on Twitter</u>. ☐

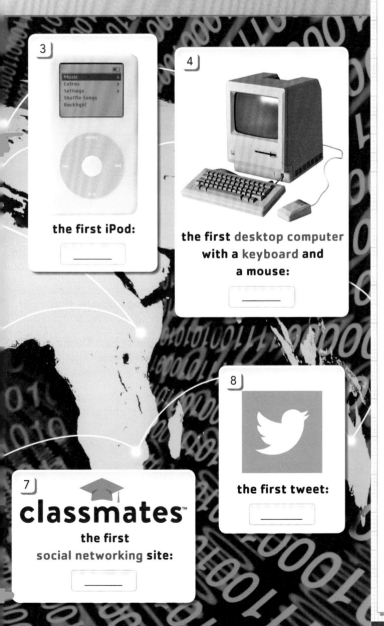

3 the first iPod: _____

4 the first desktop computer with a keyboard and a mouse: _____

8 the first tweet: _____

7 **classmates**™ the first social networking site: _____

Go to **WORD STORE 2** page 5.

WORD STORE 2A ⟩⟩⟩⟩

5 CD•1.30 MP3•30 Complete WORD STORE 2A with the compound nouns in red in Exercises 3 and 4. Then listen, check and repeat.

6 In pairs, complete the questions with compound nouns from WORD STORE 2A. Then ask and answer the questions.

1 How many _____ messages do you send in a day?

2 Do you always use the same _____ name and password online?

3 Have you got a _____ computer or a laptop?

4 Which is the most popular search _____ in your country?

5 How often do you update your profile on a _____ networking site?

6 Have you got a reliable Internet _____ and fast broadband speeds?

WORD STORE 2B ⟩⟩⟩⟩

7 CD•1.31 MP3•31 Complete WORD STORE 2B with the verbs from the underlined phrases in Exercise 4. Then listen, check and repeat.

8 Choose the correct options. Then complete the sentences to make them true for you.

1 The first thing I do when I *visit / go* online is …

2 The last document I *opened / followed* was …

3 The icon I *click on / push* most often is …

4 The person I'd like to *watch / follow* on Twitter is …

5 The website I *visit / go in* most is …

6 The last music I *downloaded / followed* was …

WORD STORE 2C ⟩⟩⟩⟩

9 CD•1.32 MP3•32 Listen to a conversation between a grandma and her grandson. Tick the actions she does.

1 <u>switch on</u> the computer ☐   4 <u>scroll down</u> the page ☐

2 <u>log on</u> to Facebook ☐   5 <u>scroll up</u> the page ☐

3 <u>click on</u> the Skype icon ☐   6 <u>hang up</u> ☐

10 CD•1.33 MP3•33 Complete WORD STORE 2C. Match the underlined phrasal verbs in Exercise 9 with the definitions. Then listen, check and repeat.

11 In pairs, take turns to explain to your partner how to do one of these tasks. Use the words and phrases in WORD STORE 2C to help you.

• attach a photo to an email

• download an album from iTunes

• find a friend on Facebook

2.2 Grammar

Past Continuous and Past Simple

I can use the Past Continuous and the Past Simple to describe past events.

1 In pairs, read what people say about e-books and printed books. Note down some other advantages and disadvantages.

1 When I go on holiday, I don't have to pack heavy books.

2 I like the feel of a real book in my hands.

3 I work with computer screens all day – I don't want to read books on a screen too.

4 Books are so expensive. E-books are cheaper.

2 Read about e-ink. Who was Joe Jacobson and why did he have a 'Eureka!' moment?

Eureka!

In 1997 Joe Jacobson was working as a researcher for the Massachusetts Institute of Technology (MIT). One summer, he went on holiday to the coast. He was lying on a beach when he finished his book. Unfortunately, he didn't have another one with him. At that moment, he imagined an electronic book that he could download any time he wanted and read in direct sunlight. It was a 'Eureka!' moment. His vision became e-ink technology and helped develop the e-readers that we have today.

3 Read the GRAMMAR FOCUS. Then complete the examples using the past forms in blue in the text in Exercise 2.

GRAMMAR FOCUS

Past Continuous and Past Simple

* You use the **Past Continuous** to talk about actions in progress in the past.

  In 1997 Joe Jacobson ¹_____ as a researcher for MIT.

* You often use the **Past Continuous** with the **Past Simple** – in narrative situations, to talk about an action (Past Simple) which interrupted another action in progress in the past (Past Continuous).

  He ²_____ on a beach when he ³_____ his book.

Past Continuous: was/were + -ing

+	He was working ...
–	You weren't working ...
?	Were they working ...?
	Yes, they were./No, they weren't.

4 Complete the opening paragraphs of two famous stories with the Past Simple or Past Continuous form of the verbs in brackets.

LEVEL 3

Pearson English **Readers**

David Copperfield
Charles Dickens

It was a terrible stormy night six months after my father's death. My mother ¹was sitting (sit) alone by the fire, waiting for her baby to arrive. She ²_____ (feel) sad and ill. Suddenly, she ³_____ (hear) a noise outside. 'There's someone at the door, Peggotty,' my mother ⁴_____ (call) . 'Who is it?' Peggotty was her servant and her only real friend. 'I'll go and see,' Peggotty ⁵_____ (reply). She ⁶_____ (go) and ⁷_____ (open) the door.

As the carriage moved quickly along the rough dry road, Jonathan Harker ⁸_____ (look out) at the changing view. Behind him was a land of small green hills and colourful fields of fruit trees. Now he ⁹_____ (drive) into the Transylvanian mountains through a thick forest. It ¹⁰_____ (get) dark and the other people in the carriage ¹¹_____ (be) quiet and afraid. A woman opposite him ¹²_____ (reach) towards him and ¹³_____ (put) something in his hand. It ¹⁴_____ (be) a small, silver cross. 'Wear it around your neck,' she said. 'You'll be safe.'

LEVEL 3

Pearson English **Readers**

Dracula
Bram Stoker

5 Which story would you like to continue reading? Discuss your reasons in pairs.

6 Complete the sentences with the Past Simple or Past Continuous form of the verbs in brackets. Then tick the sentences that are true for you.

1 My parents _____ (study) when they _____ (met). ☐
2 My computer _____ (crash) when I _____ (do) my homework last night. ☐
3 I _____ (watch) TV when my mum _____ (get) home yesterday. ☐
4 It _____ (rain) when I _____ (wake up) this morning. ☐
5 I _____ (burn) myself when I _____ (make) breakfast. ☐
6 A friend _____ (text) me when I _____ (walk) to school. ☐

7 In pairs, write questions for the sentences in Exercise 6. Then ask and answer the questions.

A: Were your parents studying when they met?
B: No, they weren't.

Grammar Focus page 113

Multiple choice

I can identify specific detail in conversations.

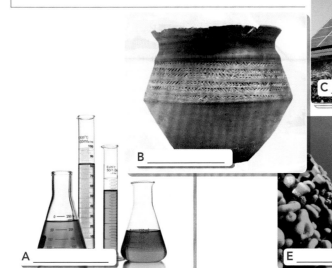

C _____

D _____

B _____

A _____

E _____

F _____

1 CD·1.34 MP3·34 **In pairs, label the photos with the words in the box. Then listen, check and repeat.**

> chemistry   physics   marine biology
> archaeology   geology   ecology

EXAM FOCUS Multiple choice

2 CD·1.35 MP3·35 **Listen and choose the correct answer.**

1 What does the girl want to study in the future?

photo A   photo B   photo C

2 The girl and the boy have both seen one of the documentaries. What was it about?

photo D   photo E   photo F

3 Complete the descriptions with the words in the box.

> an archaeologist   a chemist   an ecologist
> a geologist   a marine biologist   a physicist

1 _____ finds ways to make chemicals useful to society.

2 _____ studies ways of protecting the environment.

3 _____ studies rocks and the history of the earth.

4 _____ asks 'big' questions about the laws of nature.

5 _____ studies people who lived thousands of years ago.

6 _____ studies, observes and protects marine life.

4 CD·1.36 MP3·36 **Listen to five speakers. Choose from the list A–F what each speaker wants. Use the letters only once. There is one extra letter.**

Speaker 1: ☐   Speaker 3: ☐   Speaker 5: ☐
Speaker 2: ☐   Speaker 4: ☐

The speaker wants to:

A find answers to important questions.

B discover new things that help people.

C explore oceans and preserve the ocean environment.

D study our prehistoric ancestors.

E study the evolution of our planet.

F find solutions to nature's problems.

5 CD·1.36 MP3·36 **Complete the questions about the speakers with the words in the box. Then listen and answer the questions.**

> cures   discoveries   evidence
> experiments   hours   research

1 Who wants to collect _____ about global warming?

2 Who wants to make new _____ and find new _____ ?

3 Who loves doing _____ and analysing data?

4 Who spent _____ in the Egyptian Room in the Louvre?

5 Who is doing _____ into climate change?

PRONUNCIATION FOCUS

6 CD·1.37 MP3·37 **Complete the table. Then listen, check and repeat. Mark the stress.**

Subject	Job
1 archae<u>o</u>logy	archaeol<u>o</u>gist
2 biology	_____
3 _____	chemist
4 ecology	_____
5 geology	_____
6 mathematics	mathematician
7 _____	physicist
8 science	_____

WORD STORE 2D ⟩⟩⟩⟩

7 CD·1.38 MP3·38 **Complete WORD STORE 2D. Add nouns or verbs to the table. Mark the stress. Then listen, check and repeat.**

2.4 Reading

Multiple choice

I can find specific details in a story about space travel.

1 In pairs, look at photos A–E on page 29 and match them with headings 1–5. Then discuss what you know about Apollo 13.

1 NASA engineers at mission control in Houston ☐
2 The capsule splashed down in the sea ☐
3 The launch of Apollo 13 ☐
4 Earth seen from the moon ☐
5 Astronauts who were on board the spacecraft ☐

2 Read the text on page 29 and answer the questions.

1 Where was Apollo 13 flying to?
2 Why didn't it get there?
3 Who helped the astronauts solve the problem?
4 How many days in total did the astronauts spend in space?

EXAM FOCUS Multiple choice

3 Read the text again. For questions 1–6, choose the correct answer, A, B, C or D.

1 Reg Turnill found out there was a problem with Apollo 13 when he was
   A sitting at his desk.
   B getting ready for bed.
   C entering mission control.
   D talking to Jim Lovell.

2 The workers at mission control were
   A planning to walk on the moon.
   B not expecting any problems.
   C working hard when the explosion took place.
   D concerned about the spacecraft.

3 The spacecraft lost most of its fuel
   A through the hatch.
   B because of the explosion.
   C several hours after the explosion.
   D very slowly.

4 NASA engineers
   A did not expect the astronauts to return.
   B were not interested in help from outside.
   C immediately formed a big team to fix the problem.
   D continued working as usual.

5 The main problem on board was
   A very little oxygen and water.
   B very little light.
   C a lot of gas.
   D a lot of oxygen and water.

6 Where do you think this text is from?
   A a scientific report
   B a science fiction story
   C a magazine article
   D a newspaper report on 17 April 1970

4 Match the words in blue in the text with the definitions.

1 small door – ____hatch____
2 thought of/produced – _____
3 understand – _____
4 working – _____
5 not be worried any more – _____
6 getting less and less – _____
7 shout happily – _____
8 doing/taking part in – _____

5 [CD·1·40] [MP3·40] Complete the text with the correct form of words from Exercise 4. Then listen and check.

One small step for man

In 1962, US President JF Kennedy promised to put a man on the moon before 1970. It was seven more years before NASA ¹ _figured_ out how to do it. In July 1969, when time was ² _____ out, three astronauts ³ _____ out the historic mission on board Apollo 11. American astronaut Neil Armstrong opened the ⁴ _____ and became the first man to walk on the moon. In Houston, engineers who were on ⁵ _____ at mission control ⁶ _____ a sigh of relief when they saw Armstrong step onto the moon. All over the world, people were watching on TV and they ⁷ _____ as they heard Armstrong say his famous words: 'That's one small step for man, one giant leap for mankind.' Armstrong ⁸ _____ up with his famous words after landing on the moon.

6 In pairs, discuss these opinions about space exploration. Which do you agree with?

- Space exploration is very expensive – we should solve problems on earth first such as poverty and starvation.
- The earth's population is growing – we will need to live on another planet one day.
- We need space exploration to answer the big questions: are we alone? are there other forms of life out there?

WORD STORE 2E ▶▶▶▶▶

7 [CD·1·41] [MP3·41] Complete WORD STORE 2E. Match verbs and nouns to make collocations. Then listen, check and repeat.

'HOUSTON, WE HAVE A PROBLEM'

CD·1.39 MP3·39

It was 13 April 1970, two days after the launch of Apollo 13. BBC journalist, Reg Turnill was reporting on the mission from the space centre in Houston. He describes the moment he realised there was a problem with Apollo 13:

'I looked into mission control just before going to bed. I was going through the door when I heard Jim Lovell say, "Houston, we have a problem".'

Instead of going to bed, the journalist went back to his desk and stayed there for the next three days.

Apollo 13's commander, Jim Lovell, together with his colleagues Fred Haise and Jack Swigert, were carrying out NASA's third mission to the moon. Lovell and Haise were planning to walk on the moon. But this never happened.

Nearly two days into the flight, things were going so smoothly that Joe Kerwin, on duty at mission control, told the crew, 'The spacecraft is in real good shape (…). We're bored to tears down here.'

Several hours later, the crew heard a loud explosion. On board the spacecraft, warning lights were flashing. One of the fuel tanks was empty and one of them was close to zero. Thirteen minutes after the explosion, Jim Lovell looked out of the hatch. Gas was escaping into space.

NASA reacted quickly. They called in all the most experienced astronauts, including Neil Armstrong and Buzz Aldrin. They worked day and night with the NASA engineers and the crew of Apollo 13 to find a solution.

Both mission control and the astronauts remained very calm, but by breakfast time, the media were going crazy. Millions of people were following the events on television. The newspapers reported that the astronauts only had a ten-percent chance of getting home safely.

Meanwhile, on board, the astronauts did not discuss the possibility of not returning home. They were trying to figure out what was happening and how to fix it. Supplies of oxygen and water were running out, but with the help of the engineers at mission control, they came up with a plan.

The spacecraft orbited the moon, using its gravity to return to earth. As the spacecraft left outer space and re-entered into the earth's atmosphere, nobody knew whether the astronauts would live or die.

Under parachutes, the spacecraft appeared through the clouds and exhausted workers at mission control were finally able to breathe a sigh of relief, raise their hands and cheer.

The capsule successfully returned to earth on Friday 17 April 1970. It splashed down in the Pacific Ocean, near Tonga, where a rescue boat was waiting to recover the three astronauts.

2.5 Grammar

used to

I can talk about past states and repeated actions.

1 In pairs, look at the photos and say in what ways these things are different today.

> fashion   friends   music   travel
> school   technology   relationships

People don't buy records now – they download music from the Internet.

2 **CD·1.42** **MP3·42** Listen to Chris talking with his granddad. Are the statements about Chris's granddad true (T) or false (F)?

1 He used to phone people from the phone in the sitting room. ☐
2 He used to send text messages. ☐
3 He didn't use to live near his friends. ☐
4 His mum didn't use to like the loud music in his bedroom. ☐
5 His parents bought him a camera for his sixteenth birthday. ☐
6 He used to have five or six good friends. ☐

3 Read the GRAMMAR FOCUS. Then complete the examples using the past forms in blue in Exercise 2.

GRAMMAR FOCUS

used to

• You use **used to + infinitive** to talk about past states that are no longer true.
  He ¹_____ have five or six good friends.

• You use **used to + infinitive** to talk about regular past actions that don't happen any more.
  He ²_____ phone people from the phone in the sitting room.

• You don't use **used to + infinitive** to talk about a past action that happened once only, you use the **Past Simple**.
  His parents ³_____ him a camera for his sixteenth birthday. (NOT ~~used to buy~~)

used to + infinitive

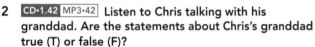

+	*I used to work ...*
–	*He didn't use to work ...*
?	*Did you use to work ...?*
	Yes, we did./No, we didn't.

4 Complete the sentences with the correct form of the verbs in brackets. Use *used to* or the Present Simple.

1 People used to read (read) maps, but now they _____use_____ (use) GPS systems.
2 People _____ (not use) their cars much, but now they _____ (drive) everywhere.
3 People _____ (update) their online profiles now, but they _____ (write) letters.
4 Children _____ (play) inside now, but in the past they _____ (play) outside.
5 Teachers _____ (suggest) books, but now they _____ (give out) website addresses.
6 Families _____ (watch) TV together, but now they _____ (watch) it individually.
7 Students _____ (use) Google now, but they _____ (look up) things in encyclopedias.
8 Parents _____ (not worry) so much, but now they _____ (give) children less freedom.

5 Where possible, replace the Past Simple in the sentences with *used to*.

When I was at primary school:
1 my parents took me to school every day.
2 I didn't go online much.
3 I went on a school trip to the Science Museum.
4 I didn't like school dinners.
5 my parents bought me my first mobile phone.
6 I wanted to be an astronaut.

6 In pairs, write questions for the sentences in Exercise 5. Then ask and answer the questions.

A: *Did your parents use to take you to school?*
B: *Yes, they did.*

Grammar Focus page 113

30

Telling a story

I can tell a story and be a good listener.

1 In pairs, look at the holiday photo of Ed below and answer the questions.

   1 Where was Ed?

   2 What was he doing?

   3 What do you think his problem was?

2 **CD·1.43** **MP3·43** Read and listen to the story. Check your ideas from Exercise 1.

Lisa: Hi, Ed. How was your holiday in Australia?

Ed: It was really good, thanks – except for the day I nearly died. ⌉1

Lisa: What happened?

Ed: I was doing some climbing. <u>At first</u>, the sun <u>was shining</u> and I was enjoying myself. ⌉2

But <u>all of a sudden</u>, the weather changed. It became really foggy and I couldn't see the path. ⌉3

Lisa: Oh dear, <u>that sounds frightening</u>!

Ed: I was pretty worried. I continued for a while, but finally, I realised I was lost.

Lisa: What did you do?

Ed: Fortunately, I had my phone with me, so I called my father – 9,000 miles away in England! He called the Australian police and told them where I was. Then they called me. <u>Unfortunately</u>, my battery went dead after five seconds. It was dark and cold. I sat under a rock, put on my torch and waited. ⌉4

Lisa: Oh no, <u>what a nightmare</u>!

Ed: <u>Eventually</u>, they found me. I was so relieved. I used to go climbing on my own all the time, but <u>I'll never do it again</u>. ⌉5

3 There are often five stages in a story. Match stages 1–5 in Ed's story with labels a–e.

  a background ☐   **d** problem ☐

  b final comment ☐   **e** main events ☐

  c introduction ☐

4 Complete the SPEAKING FOCUS with the underlined phrases in the story in Exercise 2.

SPEAKING FOCUS

Telling a story

Use the right tenses.

• Past Continuous for the 'background':

The sun ¹<u>was shining</u> and I was enjoying myself.

• Past Simple for the 'problem' and the 'main events':

The weather changed. I couldn't see the path.

Use linkers.

• Beginning: To start with,/At ² _____

• Middle: Suddenly/All of a ³ _____ / Luckily/Fortunately/⁴ _____

• End: In the end/Finally/⁵ _____

Say how you felt.

I was excited/frightened/relieved/surprised/shocked/worried, etc.

Make a final comment.

It was the best/worst day of my life!

I'll never forget the look on his face!

I'll never ⁶ _____ .

Listening to a story

Give a neutral response.

Really?/Oh dear!/Oh no!

Give a strong response.

That sounds amazing/funny/⁷ _____ .

What a great story/a ⁸ _____ !

Respond with questions.

What happened?

What did you do?

5 You are going to tell a story and your partner is going to listen and respond. In pairs, follow the instructions.

• Choose a topic from the box or use your own idea.

> a dangerous situation   a nice surprise
> some good or bad luck   a mistake
> something that happened on holiday

• Think about what you are going to say and make notes under the headings for the five stages of a story from Exercise 3.

6 In pairs, follow the instructions to practise telling your stories. Then act out your conversation.

Student A: Use your notes in Exercise 5 to tell the story.

Student B: React and respond to what Student A says. Use the SPEAKING FOCUS to help you.

An informal email/letter

I can write to someone and recount a past event.

To: Adam

Subject: You must see this!

Hi Adam,

I've just come back from a visit to the Copernicus Science Centre – it's really cool! You MUST go! You'll love it. I liked the Planetarium best. If you go, make sure you visit the Robot Room. It's great fun! Write and tell me what you think!

Speak soon.

Love,
Alice

_⤢×

To: Alice

Subject: Re: You must see this!

Hi Alice,

Just a quick message to say a big THANK YOU for suggesting the Copernicus Science Centre. It was fantastic. ¹ First we went to the gallery and did some interactive experiments. ²_____ we went to see the Robotic Theatre. That was amazing – the actors are robots! It was brilliant and we stayed there for ages, but ³_____ it finished and we went to the canteen for lunch.
⁴_____ we went to the Planetarium. We stayed there for at least two hours. ⁵_____ we watched a film about the history of space – I learnt so much. ⁶_____ we watched another film about black holes – that was scary. ⁷_____ we were tired, so we relaxed in the Discovery Park. That was my favourite thing. ⁸_____ we left at six o'clock. We were tired, but happy.

Best wishes,
Adam

---

1 In pairs, list the top three tourist attractions in your area. Compare your answers with other students.

2 Read the emails and answer the questions.

  1 Why does Alice write to Adam?

  2 What did Adam like best in Copernicus Science Centre?

3 Read Adam's email again and choose the correct answer, A, B or C.

  1 A First   **B** Then   **C** Afterwards

  2 A In the end **B** First   **C** Then

  3 A after that **B** eventually **C** first

  4 A First   **B** Afterwards **C** Finally

  5 A Finally   **B** In the end **C** First

  6 A Then   **B** First   **C** Eventually

  7 A Finally   **B** After that **C** First

  8 A Finally   **B** Later   **C** Then

4 Match the sentence halves to describe some of the things Adam did.

  1 He went   ☐   **a** some robots.

  2 He watched ☐   **b** in the Discovery Park.

  3 He saw   ☐   **c** at six o'clock.

  4 He relaxed   ☐   **d** some films.

  5 He left   ☐   **e** some experiments.

  6 He did   ☐   **f** for lunch.

5 Put the events from Exercise 4 in the correct order and add linkers to describe Adam's day.

  First Adam did some experiments. Then …

6 Complete the WRITING FOCUS with the words in purple in the emails.

WRITING FOCUS

An informal email/letter

- Start the email with a short phrase. You don't have to write complete sentences.

  Just a quick ¹_____ to say …

- Use imperatives to make suggestions or give advice.

  If you go, ²_____ sure you visit the Robot Room.

- Use dashes (–) to add comments or more information.

  We watched another film about black holes – ³_____ .

- Use linkers.

  Beginning: First

  Middle: Then/Later/After that/Afterwards

  End: Finally/In the end/Eventually

7 Choose the correct options.

1 We had a great time at the Science Exhibition. *Finally / First* we saw some robots and then we looked at some new mobile phones.

2 We had lunch. *After that / In the end* we went round the shop and bought some cards.

3 We were in the queue to go into the museum for ages but *eventually / afterwards* we bought our tickets.

4 First we went to the supermarket to get some food. *Eventually / Then* we went to the sports shop to look at football boots. *Finally / Then* we went to a jewellery shop to buy Anne a birthday present.

Writing task

You recently received an email from your friend, Sophie. Read part of her email and write your reply to Sophie.

> Have you been to an interesting museum or gallery recently – or maybe an exhibition? I'm looking for somewhere to take my cousin. She's staying with us for a week. Tell me where you went and what it was like. Thanks!

A Write your email in about 100 words. Include these points.

- Thank Sophie for her email.
- Tell her where you've been recently.
- Say if you enjoyed it.
- Describe what you did there.
- Say what you liked best and why.
- Wish Sophie and her cousin a good time.

Useful language

- It's great to hear from you!
- Last week I went/saw/visited …
- It was fantastic!
- I had a great time.
- I really enjoyed … because I love doing experiments.
- If she is interested in history/modern art/science, take her to …
- I think she'll love …
- My favourite part was …
- The best thing was …
- I liked … best.
- You can see …
- I hope you have a wonderful time.
- I'm sure you will enjoy it.

B Use the ideas in the WRITING FOCUS and the model to help you.

C Check.

✓ Have you answered all parts of the task?

✓ Have you used phrases from the model, WRITING FOCUS and Useful language box?

✓ Have you used linkers?

✓ Have you used the correct past tenses?

VOCABULARY AND GRAMMAR

1 Complete the sentences with the correct form of the verbs in the box. There are two extra verbs.

click crash do fix get go open visit

1 Can you help me? I don't know how to _____ a problem with my computer.
2 The instructions say I must _____ on an icon, but I can't see it.
3 I _____ online every day to read the news and answer emails.
4 I usually _____ home very late, so I'm often tired.
5 He _____ a website about cars once a week to check the prices.
6 _____ the text document and complete it.

2 Complete the sentences with the correct form of the words in capitals.

1 The _____ of advanced computers has taken very little time. **DEVELOP**
2 To contact Tom, I often use our favourite social _____ site. **NETWORK**
3 This information is from 2012. Why don't they _____ their website? **DATE**
4 After years of work, the scientist made an important _____ . **DISCOVER**
5 Use your _____ and you will write something creative. **IMAGINE**
6 He works as a _____ in a laboratory. **SCIENCE**

3 Use the the prompts to write sentences.

1 the first moon landing / be / in 1969
_____

2 ten years ago / my brother / still / study / at university
_____

3 Mabel / find / some keys / on the pavement yesterday
_____

4 I / have / my first driving lesson last week
_____

5 I / talk / on my mobile phone / when / my mum / ask / me a question
_____

6 what / you / do / this time last year?
_____

4 Choose the correct options.

1 Did he use to *live / living* here before moving to Oxford?
2 She didn't *use to go / go* shopping yesterday.
3 I *don't like / didn't use to like* spicy food. Now I love it.
4 We *did / used to do* a lot of exercise last weekend.
5 Did you *used / use* to ride a bike to school?
6 Did she *buy / use to buy* a laptop last year?

LANGUAGE IN USE

5 Choose the answer, A, B or C, that is closest in meaning to the underlined words.

1 I'm afraid <u>there isn't any</u> ink, so I can't print anything.
  A we have hung up   C we have run out of
  B we have scrolled up
2 When my brother got his first job, he <u>was a student</u>.
  A studied   B was studying   C used to study
3 Can you help me <u>come up with</u> a solution to my problems?
  A fix   B follow   C find
4 A: When I was a child, I was in a serious car accident and I spent a month in hospital.
  B: <u>What a nightmare!</u>
  A What a great story!   C Really? That's cool!
  B That sounds frightening!
5 I had an accident in the mountains, but <u>luckily</u>, I managed to phone for help.
  A eventually   B fortunately   C suddenly
6 I <u>didn't use to send</u> my homework to my teacher by email five years ago.
  A didn't send   C wasn't sending
  B haven't sent

6 Choose the correct answer, A, B or C, to complete both sentences.

1 Where shall I ____ this picture?
  Please don't ____ up. I have something more to tell you.
  A put   B hang   C give
2 Can you show me how to log ____ to this computer, please?
  I don't like flying ____ board small planes.
  A on   B off   C with
3 I can't ____ this bag any further. It's too heavy!
  I don't like studying chemistry from a book. I'd like to ____ out experiments in our school lab.
  A do   B take   C carry
4 They want to ____ world events, so they buy a newspaper every day.
  Do you ____ your favourite pop stars on Twitter?
  A follow   B watch   C meet
5 I can't figure ____ how to do this exercise.
  Please turn off the light before you go ____ of the room.
  A around   B off   C out
6 Tara uses her mobile phone to ____ online.
  I've got so much homework, I think I'm going to ____ crazy!
  A get   B go   C find

LISTENING

7 `CD·1.44` `MP3·44` **Listen to six recordings. Choose the correct picture, A, B or C, to answer the questions.**

1 When does the Science exam start?

2 What did Eva give her gran for her birthday?

3 What was the weather like when the boy's class went to the beach?

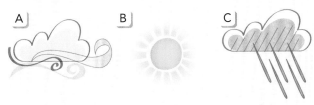

4 What does the man think is good for science lessons?

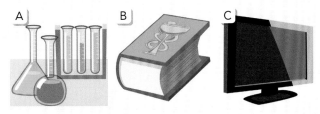

5 How do the boy and girl plan to travel to the exhibition?

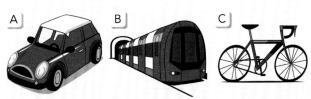

6 What is the boy going to send his brother?

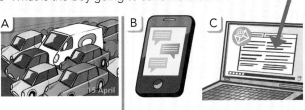

SPEAKING

8 **In pairs, complete the sentences with one word in each gap. Then ask and answer the questions.**

1 _____ you play computer games in your free time?
2 _____ you do anything interesting last weekend?
3 _____ you going to use a social networking site later today?
4 _____ do you enjoy doing at the weekends?

9 **In pairs, write down five words to describe the photo.**

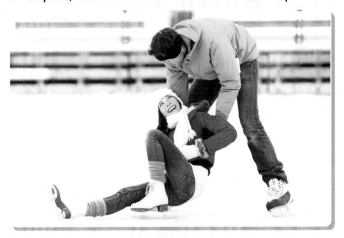

10 **In pairs, talk about what you can see in the photo.**

1 Where are the two people?
2 What are they wearing?
3 How are they feeling?
4 What has just happened?

11 **When was the last time you did any sport? What happened?**

WRITING

12 **Read the writing task and make some notes to plan your story. Then, in pairs, discuss your ideas. Use these questions to help you.**

- When did it happen?
- Why did you go for a walk?
- What was the weather like?
- What did you discover?

Your teacher has asked you to write a story. Read the title and write your story, including the points below.

Story title
An interesting discovery

Include:
1 a walk in the forest
2 a strange light

13 **Write your story in about 100 words.**

3
THE ARTS

Every child is an artist. The problem is how to remain an artist when he grows up.

PABLO PICASSO (1881–1973), A SPANISH PAINTER

UNIT LANGUAGE AND SKILLS

Vocabulary:
- *Show what you know* – art and media
- types of books and writers
- 'a part of a whole'; films, music, art
- adjectives with positive or negative meanings

Grammar:
- Present Perfect with *just, already, (not) yet* and Past Simple
- comparative and superlative adjectives
- *too* and *enough*

Listening:
- a radio programme about a street artist

Reading:
- film descriptions and reviews

Speaking:
- describing a photo

Writing:
- an informal email/letter

FOCUS EXTRA

- Grammar Focus page 114
- WORD STORE booklet pages 6–7
- Workbook pages 32–43 or MyEnglishLab

3.1 Vocabulary

Types of books and writers · Films · Music
I can talk about books, films and music.

SHOW WHAT YOU KNOW

1 In pairs, put the words in the box under the appropriate heading.

> art gallery ballet band best-seller costume
> documentary hit picture stage TV presenter writer

art	books	film/theatre	media	music
art gallery				

2 Think of three more words to add to each group.

---

3 How do you like to study? In pairs, discuss the ideas in the box and your own ideas.

> alone   anywhere   at night   in silence
> in the evening   in my room   in the morning
> with my music or the TV on   with other people

How writers write

Ludwig van Beethoven

Ernest Hemingway

The Beatles

J. K. Rowling

4 Read the text to find out how some famous writers used to write. Who do you think had the most unusual writing habits?

5 Complete the facts about other famous writers with the words in red in the text.

  1 Mary Shelley was a famous English _____ . She wrote *Frankenstein*.
  2 Eugène Ionesco was a Romanian-French _____ . His plays were part of the *Theatre of the Absurd*.
  3 Giuseppe Verdi was an Italian _____ . He wrote famous operas like *Aida*.
  4 Federico García Lorca was a Spanish _____ . His poems were about Andalusia.
  5 Pedro Almodóvar is a Spanish film director and _____ . He won an Oscar for his screenplay *Talk to Her* in 2002.
  6 Bob Woodward was a _____ for *The Washington Post*. After Woodward's famous report on the Watergate scandal in 1972, President Nixon had to resign.

Writers have very clear preferences about where and how they write. For instance, some writers like to have people around them and background noise, but others prefer isolation.

Novelist and journalist Ernest Hemingway used to write standing up. D.H. Lawrence wrote under a tree. Jane Austen, author of romantic fiction, wrote on a small table in her family living room. Children's author and poet Roald Dahl sat in a very old armchair in a shed and French novelist Marcel Proust wrote in bed. Graham Greene, author, playwright and literary critic, used to write only in the morning. After 500 words, he stopped, even in the middle of a sentence.

Nicholson's Café in Edinburgh became famous because J.K. Rowling sat there and wrote some chapters of her first best-selling fantasy novel, Harry Potter and the Philosopher's Stone. She used to sit at the same table, drinking coffee and writing in a notebook with her baby asleep in her pushchair.

Most novelists write alone, but scriptwriters and songwriters often write together. A team of seven writers wrote scripts each week for the popular American sitcom Friends. Lennon and McCartney wrote 180 songs together for the Beatles.

Perhaps the strangest of all was classical composer Beethoven. He was completely deaf when he wrote the famous Ninth Symphony, so he took the legs off his piano and felt the vibrations of the music through the floor.

Go to **WORD STORE 3** page 7.

WORD STORE 3A ⟩⟩⟩⟩⟩

6 CD·2.1 MP3·45 Complete WORD STORE 3A with the words in red in the text. Then listen, check and repeat.

WORD STORE 3B ⟩⟩⟩⟩⟩

7 CD·2.2 MP3·46 Complete WORD STORE 3B. Use these definitions to help you. What is the mystery word in the crossword? Then listen, check and repeat.

  1 a book about a person's life by that person
  2 a story about imaginary future events (often in space)
  3 a book with instructions on how to prepare food
  4 a book with tourist and travel information
  5 a story about detectives and police work
  6 a famous book from the past that has a lot of influence
  7 a book with facts on many different subjects
  8 a frightening story about dead people
  9 traditional children's stories that include magic

8 In pairs, decide if the types of books in WORD STORE 3B are fiction or non-fiction. Then tell your partner which types of books you like or don't like reading.

WORD STORE 3C ⟩⟩⟩⟩⟩

9 CD·2.3 MP3·47 Complete WORD STORE 3C. Cross out the incorrect options. Then listen, check and repeat.

10 Complete the facts with words from WORD STORE 3C.

  1 In total, there were 236 _____ of the _____ *Friends*.
  2 The British National Anthem has three _____ , but most people only know the first one.
  3 'To be or not to be?' comes from Shakespeare's _____ , *Hamlet*: _____ III, _____ 1.
  4 Leo Tolstoy's classic novel *War and Peace* has 365 _____ .
  5 The famous shower _____ in Hitchcock's thriller *Psycho* is only forty-five seconds long.
  6 *Echoes* is a _____ on Pink Floyd's _____ *Meddle*. It is over twenty-three minutes long.

11 In pairs, tell each other about your favourite:
  • track on an album
  • scene in a film
  • episode of a sitcom.

3.2 Grammar

Present Perfect with *just, already, (not) yet* and Past Simple

I can use the Present Perfect and the Past Simple to talk about past actions.

1 What music do you like? Write down your favourite musicians. Then, in pairs, compare your preferences.

- favourite band: _____
- favourite female singer: _____
- favourite male singer: _____

2 Read about the Brit School in London. What do Leona Lewis, Adele and Jessie J all have in common?

A school for stars

The Brit School opened in 1991. Over the years, it has produced many successful graduates. Leona Lewis, Adele and Jessie J are three former students – they have sold millions of albums between them. In 2006, Leona Lewis won *The X Factor* and she has already sold more than ten million albums worldwide. Adele has had number one hits in the British and American charts, including the title track to the James Bond movie *Skyfall*. Singer and songwriter Jessie J has already won numerous music awards and she's written songs for other international artists such as Miley Cyrus.

Another term has just ended at the Brit School. Have they produced new stars? Probably! We haven't heard of them yet, but we will!

3 Read the GRAMMAR FOCUS. Complete the examples with the verbs in blue in the text. Then underline five more Present Perfect verbs in the text.

GRAMMAR FOCUS

Present Perfect Simple and Past Simple

- You use the **Present Perfect Simple** for finished actions in time up to now. You never say when they happened.

  Time expressions: *ever, never, since then, just, already* (usually affirmative), *(not) yet* (usually negative or questions)

  just = has happened very recently

  Another term ¹_____ *just* _____ *at the Brit School.*

  (not) yet = hasn't happened but probably will happen

  We ²_____ *of them yet.*

  already = has happened earlier than expected

  She ³_____ *already* _____ *numerous music awards.*

- You use the **Past Simple** to talk about finished actions in the past. You usually say when they happened.

  In 2006, Leona Lewis ⁴_____ *The X Factor.*

4 Choose the correct time expressions and write them in the correct place in the sentences.

1 I lent my iPod to my sister, but she hasn't given it back ∧yet. (yet / just)
2 I've updated my Facebook profile with some new photos. (just / yet)
3 I want to learn the guitar, but I haven't found a teacher. (already / yet)
4 My favourite band released a new album today and I've downloaded it. (already / yet)
5 I've finished a really good book. (already / just)
6 I can watch TV tonight because I've done my homework. (yet / already)

5 Complete the text with the correct Present Perfect or Past Simple form of the verbs in brackets.

Adele Laurie Blue Adkins ¹_____ (grow up) in London with her mum and ²_____ (begin) singing when she was four. She ³_____ (graduate) from the Brit School in 2006. Adele ⁴_____ (already/earn) millions of pounds, but according to her friends, she ⁵_____ (not change). She's still the same girl they ⁶_____ (know) before she was famous. She ⁷_____ (write) her first two albums about two relationships that ended badly. But now she is in a happy relationship – will she continue to write good songs? Adele says, 'I don't know what's going to happen if my music career goes wrong. I ⁸_____ (not have) a proper job yet!'

6 Write one sentence with *already* and one with *yet* for each item on the list.

6 cultural things to do before you are 18

- ☆ see a live band
- ✱ visit a big art gallery
- ✷ listen to a Beethoven symphony
- ☆ act in a play
- ☆ read a classic novel
- ✱ write a poem or a short story

I've already seen a live band. ✓
I haven't seen a live band yet. ✗

7 In pairs, write questions about the sentences in Exercise 6. Then ask and answer the questions. If your partner answers *yes*, ask three more questions.

A: Have you seen a live band yet?
B: Yes, I have.
A: Who did you see? Where did you see them? What were they like?

Grammar Focus page 114

Multiple choice

I can identify specific detail in a radio programme about a street artist.

1 In pairs, discuss the questions using the words and phrases in the table.

1 What kind of art do you like/not like?
2 When was the last time you saw some art?
3 Where did you go and what did you see?

Type of artist	painter photographer sculptor
Type of art	black-and-white photographs classic oil paintings landscapes modern abstract paintings portraits sculpture street art
Where to see it	at a museum in an art gallery in public places pasted on walls and buildings

2 Look at three works of art by French street artist JR. Which words or phrases from Exercise 1 can you use to describe them?

A

Brazil – the *favelas* (slums)

B

Paris – the city centre

C

Africa – 'Women are heroes'

3 **CD·2.4** **MP3·48** Listen to a radio programme and check your ideas in Exercise 2. Number the photos in the order in which you hear about them.

---

4 **CD·2.4** **MP3·48** Listen again and choose the correct answer, A, B or C.

1 Katy West is
  A a guest artist of the week.
  B an artist in her studio.
  C the editor of a photography magazine.

2 Because most of his work is illegal, JR
  A doesn't want people to know his name.
  B doesn't want people to see his face.
  C uses his full name.

3 JR prefers to have exhibitions in
  A the Pompidou Centre in Paris.
  B public places.
  C art galleries and museums.

4 For his first project, he pasted portraits of
  A poor people in rich parts of Paris.
  B rich people in dangerous parts of Paris.
  C rich people in poor suburbs.

5 In Africa and Brazil he took photographs of women because
  A they have beautiful eyes.
  B the rest of the world wants to hear their story.
  C they don't usually have a chance to tell their story.

6 Which statement describes JR and his work?
  A He is interested in people and their identity.
  B He wants to have exhibitions everywhere.
  C He only likes taking photographs of women.

5 In pairs, discuss the questions.

1 What photographs or pictures do you see every day?
2 What kind of pictures are they and what/who are the subjects?
3 Who is the best photographer or artist you know?

6 **CD·2.5** **MP3·49** Complete the table. Then listen, repeat and underline the stressed syllable in each word. In which cases does the word stress change syllable?

Country	Nationality
1 Brazil	Brazilian
2 Italy	_____
3 Egypt	_____
4 Mexico	_____
5 Hungary	_____
6 Poland	_____

7 Add six more countries and nationalities to the table in Exercise 6 and practise the pronunciation.

WORD STORE 3D

8 **CD·2.6** **MP3·50** Complete WORD STORE 3D with the words in the box. Then listen, check and repeat.

3.4 Reading

Matching

I can identify specific detail in film descriptions and reviews.

1 In pairs, talk about films. Use these phrases and the words in the box.

- I love … • I really like … • I quite like …
- I don't really like … • I can't stand …

action and adventure films   animations
crime films   documentaries   historical dramas
horror films   musicals   romantic comedies
science fiction or fantasy films   thrillers
war films   westerns

2 Read about the type of films five people like. What film would you recommend for each person?

1 **Simon, 17**
I like a good story and I particularly like factual films. I enjoy films that teach me something about people and the world. I don't like violence or blood.

2 **Paula, 16**
When I choose a film, I want it to be relaxing and entertaining. I don't want anything serious and I don't mind if the storyline is unoriginal. I like funny films with happy endings.

3 **Julia, 18**
I like films about relationships, but I'm not keen on a lot of the romantic comedies because they're so unrealistic. I quite like emotional films – films that make me laugh or cry.

4 **John, 16**
I hate boring films or anything too romantic. I like thrillers (but not very scary), dramas and crime stories with good acting and clever dialogue.

5 **Ben, 18**
I like films that make me forget real life – science fiction, fantasy or even horror. I love films with good special effects and lots of tension. I want to be scared!

EXAM FOCUS Matching

3 Read the descriptions again and the film reviews. Decide which film (A–F) would be the most suitable for each person (1–5).

1 Simon ☐
2 Paula ☐
3 Julia ☐
4 John ☐
5 Ben ☐

FILM CLUB FAVOURITES

CD·2.7 MP3·51

Sherlock Holmes

▶ This action-adventure film directed by Guy Ritchie takes place in London in 1891. Robert Downey Jr plays the role of Sherlock Holmes. He is one of the most interesting characters I've ever seen on screen. The special effects are amazing and the screenplay is excellent. It's fun, it's entertaining and Robert Downey Jr will hold your attention from beginning to end.

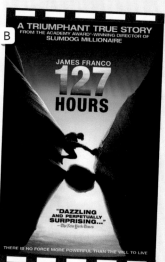

127 Hours

▶ This film is based on the true story of a mountain climber, Aron Ralston, who falls into a canyon in Utah. He can't get out of the canyon because his arm is under a rock. Over the next five days, he thinks about his life, his friends and his family. He wants to survive. After the fifth day, he cuts off his arm. It is an inspiring film and James Franco gives a brilliant performance as Aron Ralston.

The Proposal

▶ *The Proposal* is a romantic comedy that takes place in Alaska. The plot is predictable, but the dialogue is amusing and the lead actors give excellent performances. Sandra Bullock plays the role of the central character. She is Canadian and when her visa expires, she has twenty-four hours to leave the USA and the job she loves. Her American assistant, played by Ryan Reynolds, agrees to marry her and she promises him a promotion. This is an enjoyable film.

My Sister's Keeper

▶ This film is based on a novel by Jodi Picoult. The central character, Kate, has leukaemia. Her younger sister has numerous operations to help her sister survive. This is a moving film about what it means to be a good parent, a good sister, a good person. The acting is brilliant, with Cameron Diaz in the role of the mother. You'll need a big box of tissues!

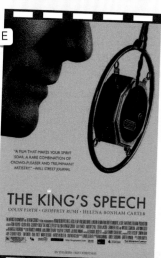

The King's Speech

▶ Everything about this award-winning historical drama is perfect: the screenplay, the costumes, the settings, the soundtrack and, of course, the wonderful performance by Colin Firth in the role of King George VI. The film is based on the true-life story of the King's speech impediment and his unusual friendship with his Australian speech therapist. A great film.

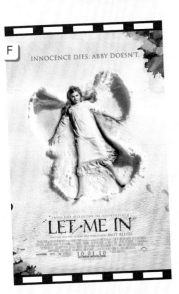

Let Me In

▶ This thriller is the story of a friendship between a lonely young boy and a strange pale girl. The girl has a mysterious secret. The filming, the music and the performances are perfect. In some scenes, the suspense will make you jump out of your seat. You won't forget it for a long time.

4 Match the words in blue in the descriptions with the underlined words with similar meanings in the reviews.

factual = true-life, true

5 Look at the highlighted synonyms of *good* that the writer uses to describe things in the reviews. Complete the table. Two words are used more than once.

Describing the ...	Synonyms of *good*
special effects	*amazing*
screenplay	_____ , _____
performance/acting	_____ , _____
	_____ , _____
film/drama	_____ , _____

6 Complete the sentences with one word in each gap.

1 In *Sherlock Holmes*, the _____ effects are amazing.
2 *127 Hours* takes _____ in Utah and is based _____ a novel by Aron Ralston.
3 In *The Proposal*, Sandra Bullock _____ the role of the central _____ .
4 In *My Sister's Keeper*, Cameron Diaz _____ a brilliant performance _____ the mother.
5 *The King's Speech* is an _____-winning film with Colin Firth in the role of King George VI.
6 *Let Me In* is a thriller that will _____ your attention from beginning to end.

7 Think of a film that you've seen for each of the following descriptions.

1 an award-winning film
2 a film that held your attention from beginning to end
3 a film based on a true story
4 a film with amazing special effects
5 a film that takes place in your country

8 Choose one of the films you thought of in Exercise 7. Then, in pairs, take turns to tell your partner about it. Talk about these things.

• type of film
• director
• actors
• setting
• plot
• things you liked/didn't like

WORD STORE 3E ⟩⟩⟩⟩⟩

9 CD·2.8 MP3·52 Look at WORD STORE 3E. Listen and repeat the adjectives. Then write them on the line according to how positive or negative they are.

3.5 Grammar

Comparative and superlative adjectives · *too* and *enough*

I can make comparisons.

1 `CD·2.9` `MP3·53` **In pairs, do the *Quick Culture Quiz*. Then listen and check.**

QUICK CULTURE QUIZ

True (T) or False (F)?

① Shakespeare's play *Romeo and Juliet* isn't as long as *Hamlet*. ☐

② Mariah Carey has a better vocal range than Christina Aguilera. ☐

③ The biggest music festival in the world is the Woodstock Festival in Poland. ☐

④ The Palace Museum in Beijing is busier than the Musée du Louvre in Paris. ☐

⑤ The *Harry Potter* films were more expensive to make than the *Pirates of the Caribbean* films. ☐

2 Read GRAMMAR FOCUS I. Then complete the examples with the comparative and superlative adjectives in blue in the quiz.

GRAMMAR FOCUS I

Comparative and superlative adjectives

	Comparative	Superlative
Short adjectives		
long	longer (than)	the longest
big	bigger (than)	¹_____
busy	²_____ (than)	the busiest
Long adjectives		
expensive	³_____ (than)	the most expensive
Irregular adjectives		
good	⁴_____ (than)	the best
bad	worse (than)	the worst
far	further (than)	the furthest

You use **not as + adjective + as** to make negative comparisons:

Romeo and Juliet isn't ⁵_____ long as *Hamlet*. =
Hamlet is longer than *Romeo and Juliet*.

3 Complete the sentences with *as*, *more* or *than*. Do you agree with the statements?

1 Music downloads are cheaper _____ CDs.
2 Jazz is not as popular _____ classical music.
3 Live music is _____ exciting than recorded music.
4 Lady Gaga is not _____ talented as Adele.
5 Male actors have more interesting roles _____ female actors.
6 The film is never as good _____ the book.

4 Complete the questions with the superlative form of the adjectives in brackets. Then, in pairs, ask and answer the questions.

What is:

1 _____ (bad) song you've ever heard?
2 _____ (great) band of all time?
3 _____ (exciting) place in your area?

Who is:

4 _____ (funny) comedian you've ever seen?
5 _____ (good) TV presenter in your country?
6 _____ (intelligent) person you know?

5 `CD·2.10` `MP3·54` **Listen to Andy and Chloe deciding what film to watch. Match actors 1–5 with opinions a–e.**

1 Tom Cruise ☐
2 Zac Efron ☐
3 Daniel Radcliffe ☐
4 Robert Pattinson ☐
5 Kristen Stewart ☐

a really small but gorgeous
b OK
c too short/not tall enough
d too serious
e perfect

6 Read GRAMMAR FOCUS II. Then complete the sentences with *too* or *not enough* and the adjectives in brackets.

GRAMMAR FOCUS II

too and *enough*

You use **too + adjective** or **not + adjective + enough** to show there is a problem with something.

Tom Cruise is too short. =
Tom Cruise is not tall enough.

1 I'm _____ (old) to watch X-rated films. You have to be eighteen. ☐
2 I don't go to the cinema much – tickets are _____ (expensive). ☐
3 I'm _____ (confident) to perform on the stage. ☐
4 I'm _____ (young) to remember music from the 1990s! ☐
5 I'm _____ (patient) to learn a musical instrument. ☐
6 I don't download films. My Internet connection is _____ (fast). ☐

7 Tick the sentences in Exercise 6 that are true for you. Then compare with a partner.

Grammar Focus page 114

3.6 Speaking

Describing a photo

I can describe a situation in a photo and speculate about what is happening.

1 In pairs, look at the photos and answer the questions.

    1 Who are the people?
    2 Where are they?
    3 What are they doing?

2 Complete sentences 1–3 in as many ways as possible with the adjectives in the box.

> bored   crowded   empty   excited
> famous   friendly   frightened   happy
> irritated   miserable   nervous   noisy
> proud   quiet   shy   tired   young

    1 (describing people)   He/She is …
    2 (describing feelings)   He/She is feeling …
    3 (describing places)   It is …

3 `CD·2.11` `MP3·55` Listen and decide which photo the speaker is describing. Give reasons for your answer.

4 `CD·2.11` `MP3·55` Complete the description with words and phrases from the SPEAKING FOCUS. Then listen again and check.

¹ _____ a famous author signing a book for a young boy. ² _____ there are book shelves, so ³ _____ they're in a bookshop. The author is a woman with blond hair. She's sitting behind a desk. ⁴ _____ friendly and she's looking at the boy. She's ⁵ _____ asking him what his name is so that she can write a personal message. The boy ⁶ _____ is wearing a blue top. I think he's about eight years old. He looks a bit shy, but ⁷ _____ he's very proud to meet the author of his favourite book. ⁸ _____ , I'd love to meet my favourite author.

SPEAKING FOCUS

Beginning a description
In this photo, I can see/there is/there are …
This photo shows …

Saying where (place)
There are …, so I think they're in a bookshop/art gallery/ at a concert, etc.

Saying where (in the photo)
in the background/in the middle/in the foreground
on the left/on the right
in front of/behind/next to

Speculating
He/She looks shy/bored/tired, etc.
She's probably …
Perhaps/Maybe/I imagine/I'm sure he's very proud.

Giving your opinion
I think/I don't think …
Personally, …
In my opinion, …

5 In pairs, take turns to describe the other two photos. Use the SPEAKING FOCUS to help you.

6 `CD·2.12` `MP3·56` Now listen to people describing photos B and C. Are the descriptions similar to yours? How are they different?

7 In pairs, follow the instructions and take turns to talk about music and art. Use the SPEAKING FOCUS to help you.

Student A: Ask Student B these questions:
- What kind of music do you enjoy listening to and who is your favourite band or singer?
- Describe a time when you saw live music.

Student B: Ask Student A the following questions:
- What kind of art do you like and why?
- Describe a time when you visited a gallery or museum.

An informal email/letter

I can write to someone and thank them, give news, express sympathy or invite them somewhere.

1 **What is the best or worst birthday present to give a teenage boy or girl? Discuss in pairs.**

2 **Complete Ryan's letter to his aunt and uncle with sentences A–G.**

A You must be very disappointed.
B It would be lovely to see you.
C I hope you're both well.
D I had a great time.
E Hope to see you at the family lunch.
F I think my painting is improving and I'm still hoping to go to art school one day.
G It was the best thing I've ever seen.

Dear Aunty Susan and Uncle Ron,

1_____ Thanks very much for the money for my birthday. I've bought some new paints and brushes.
2_____

I've just come back from my school trip to London.
3_____ We did some sightseeing and saw a fantastic photography exhibition at the Portrait Gallery. We also went to the theatre and saw a play called
War Horse. **4**_____

I'm sorry to hear that you've failed your driving test again, Aunty Susan. **5**_____ Do you think you'll take it a sixth time?

We're having a family lunch on 15 June. Would you like to come? **6**_____

Well, that's all for now. Thanks again for the present – it was very kind of you.

7_____

Love,
Ryan x

3 **What did Ryan do in his letter? Complete the sentences.**

1 He thanked his aunt and uncle for _____ .
2 He told them about _____ .
3 He was sorry about _____ .
4 He invited them to _____ .

4 Complete the WRITING FOCUS with the words in purple in Ryan's letter.

WRITING FOCUS

An informal email/letter

- Starting an email/a letter
  How are things with you?/¹ _I hope_ you're both well.

- Thanking somebody
  It was very kind of you to send me/² _____ very much for/Thanks again for …

- Giving recent news
  I must tell you about/³ _____ come back from …

- Expressing sympathy
  It's a shame/⁴ _____ to hear that …

- Inviting somebody
  I hope you can make it./⁵ _____ like to come?/
  It would be lovely to see you.

- Closing a letter/an email
  I must be going now./⁶ _____ for now./
  Look forward to seeing you./⁷ _____ to see you …

5 Complete Monica's email to her cousin Elisa with words from the WRITING FOCUS.

To: Elisa

Dear Elisa,

How are ¹_____ with you? It was very ²_____ of you to invite me to stay with you in Scotland. I had a fantastic time and really enjoyed meeting your friends.

I ³_____ tell you about my journey home. The weather was terrible and it was nearly midnight when my flight left! I started talking to a nice girl from my city and we are going to meet for coffee.

It's a ⁴_____ you can't come to visit me next month. Perhaps you can come in the summer instead. It's my eighteenth birthday in August and I'm having a big party. I hope you can ⁵_____ it.

I must be ⁶_____ now. Homework is waiting ☹

Look forward to ⁷_____ you in the summer I hope.

Bye 4 now,
Monica

---

6 Here are some situations where you need to write an email to someone. Will you need to thank (T), express sympathy (S), give news (N) or invite (I) in your email?

1 Your friend from Canada has sent you a book for your birthday. ☐

2 You're arranging to go out for a meal to celebrate your birthday. ☐

3 Your friend got low marks in his English exam. ☐

4 Your sister has just got married. ☐

5 Your friend helped you with your homework. ☐

7 Write two sentences for each of the emails in Exercise 6 using phrases from the WRITING FOCUS.

Writing task

You recently received a letter from a friend you met at a language school in London. Read part of his email and write your reply.

> I know you love music, so here's a link to my favourite music website: www.rockstuff.abc. I took my final English exam last month, but unfortunately, I failed! What's your news?
> I hope we can meet up soon.

A Write your letter in about 100 words. Include these points.

- Thank your friend for the link.
- Tell him what you liked best about the website.
- Tell him your news.
- Express sympathy for his exam result and say you're sure he'll pass next time.
- Invite him to come and see you.
- Tell him what you'll do together.

Useful language

- Thanks so much for sending …
- I liked … best.
- On Wednesday I went on a school trip.
- I had my exams last week and am still waiting for my results.
- I'm going to a party next Saturday.
- I'm sorry to hear about …
- I'm sure you will do better next time.
- Come and visit me!
- Why don't you visit me in the summer?

B Use the ideas in the WRITING FOCUS and the model to help you.

C Check.

✓ Have you addressed all the points in the task?

✓ Have you used phrases from the model, WRITING FOCUS and the Useful language box?

✓ Have you divided your letter into paragraphs?

✓ Have you used the correct spelling and punctuation?

VOCABULARY AND GRAMMAR

1 Choose the odd one out in each group.

1 documentary   western   opera   thriller
2 biography   book review   cookbook   fantasy novel
3 plot   gallery   museum   painting
4 album   sitcom   track   band
5 songwriter   chapter   playwright   poet
6 emotional   enjoyable   funny   fantasy

2 Complete the sentences with the correct form of the words in capitals.

1 My favourite _____ is Claude Monet. **ART**
2 The play at the theatre was really _____. **ENJOY**
3 J. K. Rowling is a very successful _____. **NOVEL**
4 She's a great _____. She always makes me laugh. **COMEDY**
5 It's the best _____ I've ever seen by a ballet dancer. **PERFORM**
6 I didn't like the film – the plot was _____. **ORIGINAL**

3 Use the prompts and the words in brackets to write sentences.

1 I / not do / my homework for tomorrow (yet)
_____

2 they / visit / Paris / so / they / not want / go / again (already)
_____

3 you / see / Quentin Tarantino's new film (yet)
_____

4 I / read / a very bad review of this crime story (just)
_____

5 Lottie / call / you? (yet)
_____

6 my brother / watch / this comedy / ten times (already)
_____

4 Complete the second sentence using the word in capitals so that it has a similar meaning to the first. Do not change the word in capitals.

1 I think Pink is more attractive than Lady Gaga. **AS**
I think Lady Gaga _____ Pink.
2 There's too much food on my plate. I'll never eat it all! **BIG**
This dinner _____ for me. I'll never eat it all!
3 My grade in Maths wasn't as good as my grade in Biology. **THAN**
My grade in Biology _____ my grade in Maths.
4 This is the most we have ever spent on a trip. **EXPENSIVE**
This is _____ we have ever been on.
5 I like really sweet tea. Can I have some more sugar, please? **NOT**
My tea _____. Can I have some more sugar, please?
6 There is more traffic between 5 and 7 p.m. than in any other part of the day. **BUSIEST**
_____ time for travelling is between 5 and 7 p.m.

LANGUAGE IN USE

5 Choose the correct answer, A, B or C.

1 A: We didn't go to the cinema ____.
  B: Why not?
    A yet   B since then   C last week
2 A: What a disappointing film!
  B: Yes, the ending was so ____.
    A entertaining   B moving   C predictable
3 A: Are you in this old school photo? I can't find you.
  B: I'm in the ____, behind everyone else.
    A background   B centre   C foreground
4 A: Have you heard anything about this play?
  B: Yes, I've read the online ____.
    A roles   B critics   C reviews
5 A: His latest novel is really boring.
  B: Yes, it is ____ books.
    A less boring than his previous   C the best of his
    B not as interesting as his other
6 A: What do you think of this story?
  B: ____
    A That sounds funny.   C What a funny story!
    B In my opinion, it's funny.

6 Read the text and choose the correct answer, A, B or C.

RUB MY NOSE AND GET GOOD LUCK

If you want to see attractive art, you don't necessarily need to visit an ¹_____ in an art gallery. In Bratislava, Slovakia, you can see bronze ²_____ in the street. There are several statues in the streets of Bratislava, but one, called *Man At Work*, is the most popular and gets lots of visitors. This ³_____ statue is of a man's head. The head is coming out of a hole in the ground. People say that if you touch the man's nose, you'll have good luck. Many people have ⁴_____ done this – you can see this because his nose is shinier ⁵_____ the rest of his head! *Man At Work* is so popular that it ⁶_____ in travel guides about the city.

1 A animation   B abstract painting   C exhibition
2 A sculptors   B sculptures   C portraits
3 A best-selling   B live   C amusing
4 A just   B yet   C already
5 A more   B than   C that
6 A has appeared   B used to appear   C appeared

7 **Read the texts and choose the correct answer, A, B or C.**

I can't believe I'm so scared. I'm a professional singer and I have performed on stage many times. I know my songs very well. In fact, I've never forgotten any lyrics. Why is it so difficult? But it's happening again. I don't want to go on stage and sing in front of thousands of people. I've tried breathing deeply and counting to a hundred very slowly, but nothing has helped.

Oh no! They've just announced my name!

1 The author talks about

  A preparing for a performance.

  B a health problem during a concert.

  C her feelings before appearing on stage.

The experience of a lifetime

One of the greatest operas, *Turandot*, by the Italian composer Giacomo Puccini, will be on at the State Opera. It is based on the story of Calaf, who falls in love with Princess Turandot. He wants to marry her, but first he must answer three difficult questions correctly or he will die. It's a very sad and emotional story.

* Saturday 19 October – Wednesday 23 October, for five performances only
* Daily at 7.30 p.m.
* Student discounts available

Limited number of tickets – book now!

---

2 The purpose of the text is to

  A give a review of a performance.

  B encourage readers to see a performance.

  C describe what readers will see at a performance.

The Monkeyz

I saw this band last Saturday at the Fun Day music festival. It was the longest concert I've ever attended. They played for four hours and sang all their biggest hits, as well as some tracks from their new album. There was something for everyone – faster dance tracks, slower songs and even some jazz.

The weather wasn't good. We had weeks of blue skies and sunshine, but that all changed on Saturday. The clouds moved in and all the fans got wet. But no one really cared because it was such a fantastic show.

<u>Comments (4)</u>

---

3 According to the author,

  A the weather didn't spoil the fun.

  B the concert was too long.

  C not everyone liked the songs.

8 **Look at the photos and choose the most suitable words from the box to describe them. Then, in pairs, take turns to describe the photos.**

> ambitious ballet room dancer easy little girl
> music pink professional singer teacher theatre

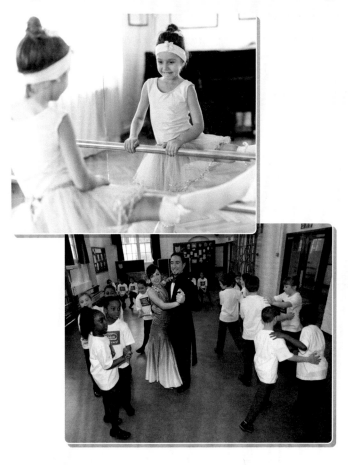

9 **Read the writing task below. Which of these sentences do you think are good advice about how to answer the task?**

  1 You shouldn't give or ask for lots of extra information.

  2 You should make sure you include all the points in the question.

  3 You can write more or less than forty-five words – the length isn't really important.

You have just come back from seeing a film that your friend Matt recommended. Write an email of about 35–45 words to Matt. In your email you should:

* thank him for recommending the film
* say what you thought about it
* invite him to go to the cinema with you next week.

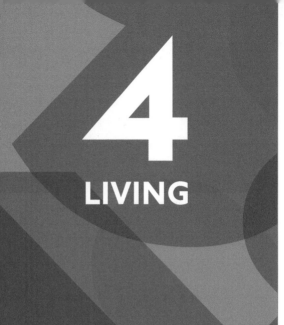

4
LIVING

Home is where the heart is.

A PROVERB

UNIT LANGUAGE AND SKILLS

Vocabulary:
• *Show what you know* – rooms and furniture
• houses and homes
• phrases with *make* and *do*
• adjective order
• places in the city and in the country

Grammar:
• Present Perfect with *for* and *since*
• Present Continuous, *be going to* and *will*

Listening:
• teenagers talking about their rooms

Reading:
• descriptions of different places

Speaking:
• making suggestions

Writing:
• a story

FOCUS EXTRA

• Grammar Focus page 115
• WORD STORE booklet pages 8–9
• Workbook pages 44–55 or MyEnglishLab

4.1 Vocabulary

Houses and homes • Phrases with *make* and *do*
I can describe houses and use phrases with make *and* do.

SHOW WHAT YOU KNOW

1   Think about your house and complete the task. You have five minutes.

   • List all the different rooms.
   • Put the rooms in order according to the time you spend in them.
     1 my bedroom (I spend most time in here.)
   • List at least six items you can find in each room.

2   In pairs, combine your lists. How many words for rooms and furniture did you think of altogether?

The HOBBIT HOUSE

Simon Dale didn't want to live in a 'mass-produced box' on a housing estate. So he made a brave decision. [5] He decided to build his own home in the countryside. He moved to rural Wales with his family and built a wooden eco-house. With the help of [10] his father-in-law, a builder, he moved into a cosy new home after only four months. It only cost £3,000 to build.

The Hobbit House, as local [15] people call it, is made of natural materials. Simon Dale and his father-in-law dug into the side of a hill and then used the mud and stone to make the [20] walls. The frame of the house and the floors are made from wood from the surrounding area. The design is open-plan. There is no central heating, [25] but there's a wood-burner and solar panels on the roof which provide power for lighting, music and computing. A skylight in the roof provides [30] lots of natural light and a pond in the front garden collects rainwater. Drinking water is from a nearby spring. There's a compost toilet and the fridge [35] stays cool thanks to air from under the ground. Simon Dale says, 'We try to live in harmony with the natural world.' He has certainly done his best to [40] achieve that.

3 In pairs, look at the photos, read the text and answer the questions.

    1 Why did Simon Dale build the Hobbit House?
    2 Where did he build it?
    3 How long did it take to build and how much did it cost?
    4 Where did they get the materials to build it?
    5 Where do they get heating, electricity, light and water from?
    6 How does Simon Dale say he wants to live?

4 In pairs, discuss what you like or don't like about the Hobbit House.

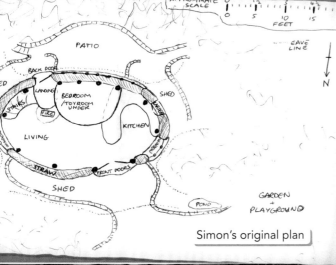

Simon's original plan

WORD STORE 4A ⟩⟩⟩

5 `CD·2.13` `MP3·57` Complete WORD STORE 4A with the words and phrases in red in the text. Then listen, check and repeat.

6 Replace the underlined phrases with words that have similar meanings from WORD STORE 4A.

    1 <u>detached house with only one floor</u> *bungalow*
    2 <u>house which is joined to my neighbour's house</u>
    3 house <u>on the edge of the city</u>
    4 <u>small traditional house</u> in a village
    5 modern house <u>in an area with other similar houses</u>
    6 flat that is <u>very warm and comfortable</u>

WORD STORE 4B ⟩⟩⟩

7 `CD·2.14` `MP3·58` Tick the items in WORD STORE 4B that you can see in the photos of the Hobbit House. Use your dictionary if necessary. Then listen and repeat.

8 Choose words and phrases from WORD STORES 4A and 4B and put them under these headings. Add your own ideas. Then compare with a partner.

My house	My dream house

WORD STORE 4C ⟩⟩⟩

9 `CD·2.15` `MP3·59` In pairs, think about the advantages and disadvantages of living in the Hobbit House. Then listen to three people talking about it. Do they mention any of your ideas?

10 `CD·2.16` `MP3·60` Complete WORD STORE 4C with the phrases in the box. Then listen, check and repeat.

> a noise   the cooking   a complaint
> the ironing   a mess   the gardening
> the housework   dinner   the shopping
> your bed   the washing   the washing-up

11 Complete the questions with the correct form of *make* or *do*.

    1 Did you _____ your bed this morning?
    2 Do your neighbours ever _____ a noise?
    3 Do you like _____ the washing-up?
    4 Who _____ the cooking in your house?
    5 Have you ever _____ dinner for somebody?
    6 Where does your family usually _____ the shopping?

12 In pairs, ask and answer the questions in Exercise 11.

4.2 Grammar

Present Perfect with *for* and *since*

I can talk about actions that started in the past and continue until now.

1 Tick the places where you have slept. What was the most unusual place? Discuss in pairs.

- in my bed ☐
- in a hotel ☐
- on a floor ☐
- on a train ☐
- on a couch ☐
- other ☐

2 Read *US TODAY*. What is couchsurfing? Would you like to do it? Why?/Why not?

US TODAY

We asked CS employee Dan about the world's largest travel community.

couchsurfing

What is it?
A worldwide travel network connecting travellers with people who offer free accommodation.

Who is it for?
People who don't want to stay in hotels, but want to meet local people and experience new cultures.

How much does it cost?
Nothing! It's free.

How long have you worked for CS?
I've been here since it started in 2004. I've worked with people from all over the world for more than ten years. Together, we want to create a global community.

3 Read the GRAMMAR FOCUS. Then complete the examples with the Present Perfect forms in blue in *US TODAY*.

GRAMMAR FOCUS

Present Perfect with *for* and *since*
You use the **Present Perfect** to talk about unfinished situations that started in the past and continue until now.

- You use **how long** to ask about the length of time until now.

  How long ¹_____ you _____ for CS?

- You use **since** when the answer is a point in time (e.g. *since 1998, since last week, since I was born*).

  I ²_____ here since it started in 2004.

- You use **for** when the answer is a period of time (e.g. *for six hours, for a few days, for a long time*).

  I ³_____ with people from all over the world for more than ten years.

4 **CD·2.17** **MP3·61** Choose *for* or *since* and complete the comments with the Present Perfect form of the verbs in brackets. Then listen and check.

Couchsurfer

I ¹'ve been (be) a member ²*for / since* three years now. ³*For / Since* I became a member, I ⁴_____ (stay) in thirty-two countries in different types of accommodation. I ⁵_____ (stay) in a luxury studio apartment in Manhattan, on a houseboat in Amsterdam and in a basement flat in London – all for free!

Host

I ⁶_____ (be) a couchsurfing host ⁷*for / since* two years now and I ⁸_____ (already/meet) more than thirty people. At the moment Miki is visiting from Tokyo. I ⁹_____ (only/know) her ¹⁰*for / since* a week, but I'm sure we'll remain friends. We have so much in common. Miki is happy too – she ¹¹_____ (study) English ¹²*for / since* ten years, but she ¹³_____ (never/have) the chance to speak with a native speaker before. When I show a guest around Oxford, I see my own city in a new way. For example, I ¹⁴_____ (not visit) the Natural History Museum ¹⁵*for / since* I was at primary school, but I'll go there with Miki. She ¹⁶_____ (be) here ¹⁷*for / since* nearly a week, but she ¹⁸_____ (not feel) homesick because she says I make her feel at home.

5 Complete the second sentence so that it has a similar meaning to the first. Use the verbs in brackets.

1 I met my best friend two years ago.
  I've known (know) my best friend ___for___ two years.

2 I joined this English class three months ago.
  I _____ (be) in this English class _____ three months.

3 My dad gave my mum this watch when she was forty.
  My mum _____ (have) this watch _____ she was forty.

4 I bought my last pair of trainers last Christmas.
  I _____ (not buy) any new trainers _____ last Christmas.

5 I had breakfast at 7 a.m.
  I _____ (not eat) anything _____ 7 a.m.

6 My dad was born in our house.
  My dad _____ (live) in our house _____ he was born.

6 Use the prompts to write sentences that are true for you. Use the Present Perfect and *since* or *for*.

1 I / know / (*name of your neighbour*) …
  I've known Barry for five years.

2 I / live in / (*name of your neighbourhood*) …

3 I / like / (*name of your favourite band*) …

4 I / have / (*make of your phone*) …

5 I / be interested in / (*name of a subject*) …

6 my dad / have / (*type of your dad's car*) …

7 In pairs, write questions about the sentences in Exercise 6. Then ask and answer the questions.

A: Who is your neighbour?   B: Barry.
A: How long have you known him?   B: For five years.

Grammar Focus page 115

4.3 Listening

Multiple choice

I can identify specific detail in short monologues.

1 In pairs, look at the photo and discuss how different or similar the bedroom is to your own rooms. Think about:

- **the size:** bigger/smaller, more/less spacious, the same
- **the decoration:** more/less modern, colour of walls/ curtains/carpet, posters, etc.
- **the furniture:** bookcase, bed, wardrobe, desk, etc.
- **other details:** more or less tidy, clothes, musical instruments, computer, etc.

EXAM FOCUS **Multiple choice**

2 `CD·2.18` `MP3·62` Listen to five people talking about their rooms. Choose the correct answer A, B or C for each speaker.

Speaker 1
Why does the speaker spend time in his room?
A to escape from the family
B to play loud computer games
C to chat to his brothers and sisters

Speaker 2
The speaker's sister
A often cleans their room.
B isn't home a lot.
C chats to the speaker until late.

Speaker 3
What do we learn about the speaker?
A She plays an instrument.
B She has lots of parties.
C She's very creative.

Speaker 4
Where does the speaker usually study?
A in his room
B in the kitchen
C in the sitting room

Speaker 5
The speaker's friends come round because
A they like her grandmother.
B they can play loud music.
C they play computer games with her parents.

3 In pairs, discuss which teenager's description is the most similar to your own situation.

4 `CD·2.19` `MP3·63` Listen to two teenagers talking about their most treasured possessions and complete the information.

DAFFYD

1 a laptop: has had it for _____ , a _____ present
2 a guitar: has had it for _____ , it belonged to his _____
3 a Welsh flag: feels _____ of being Welsh

KAREN

1 a collection of animals: has had them since she _____ , her favourite is _____
2 a bedside lamp: a present from her _____ , brought from _____
3 a collection of shells: souvenirs from _____ , she collected them since she _____

5 `CD·2.19` `MP3·63` Choose the correct prepositions and try to complete the sentences about Daffyd and Karen from memory. Then listen again and check.

1 Daffyd's _____ is *on / next* his desk.
2 His _____ is *on / in* the corner *next / next to* the bookcase.
3 His _____ is *onto / on* the wall *onto / above* his bed.
4 Karen's _____ is *on top of / on top* the wardrobe.
5 Karen's _____ is *on / in* her bedside table.
6 Her _____ is *in / on* the bottom shelf of her bookshelves, which are *opposite / in front* her bed.

6 In pairs, take turns to describe your own room. Talk about your most treasured possessions and say where they are.

PRONUNCIATION FOCUS

7 `CD·2.20` `MP3·64` Listen and repeat the words with long vowel sounds. Then write them in the correct column.

bar	blue	calm	cheap	dark
dirt	earth	floor	heat	lawn
porch	room	scene	view	work

1 /iː/	2 /uː/	3 /ɔː/	4 /ɜː/	5 /ɑː/
				bar

8 `CD·2.21` `MP3·65` Listen, check and repeat.

WORD STORE 4D

9 `CD·2.22` `MP3·66` Complete WORD STORE 4D. Use the adjectives in the box to finish the descriptions. Then listen, check and repeat.

4.4 Reading

Matching

I can find specific detail in an article.

1 Underline the things in the box that you can see in photos A–E.

> a canal   a canyon   golden sand
> a harbour   a monument   a mountain
> rainforest   a river   rocks   ruins
> shallow sea water   a statue

2 Read the texts and answer the questions.

1 How big and how old is the Grand Canyon?
2 What is the best way to visit the canyon today?
3 How many islands are there in Venice?
4 What's the most expensive way to visit Venice?
5 Where in Rio is the famous statue of Christ?
6 How do you get to the statue?
7 Where is the Great Barrier Reef?
8 Why is it a popular destination for scuba divers?
9 In which country is the Lost City of Petra?
10 How do tourists visit the city?

EXAM FOCUS Matching

3 Read the texts again and the descriptions below. Decide which location (A–E) would be the most suitable for each person (1–3) to visit.

1 Ethan wants to visit somewhere very old and a bit mysterious. He's interested in the natural world, in particular geology and rocks, but he doesn't like heights. He'd like to go somewhere he can walk round.

2 Jenny wants to go somewhere hot with her husband. She likes sunbathing and he likes water sports.

3 Gary and his girlfriend want to visit an exciting city where they can see lots of sights and beautiful old buildings. They don't want to pay for taxis or coach trips.

1 Ethan ☐   **2** Jenny ☐   **3** Gary ☐

---

4 Complete the questions with the words in blue in the texts.

1 Is there a building or monument that _____ your city?
2 Is your city a busy _____ centre?
3 Where are the rich _____ in your city?
4 How good is the public transport _____ ?
5 Which parts of your country _____ a lot of tourists?
6 Where can you see _____ views?

5 In pairs, ask and answer the questions in Exercise 4.

6 In pairs, complete the sentences to make them true for your country. Give reasons for your answers.

1 The most awesome natural wonder is …
2 The most impressive building is …
3 The most famous square is …
4 The most popular tourist destination is …
5 The most spectacular historic ruins are …

`CD·2.23` `MP3·67`

'Awesome' is how people describe the Grand Canyon! But words cannot describe it. You have to see it to believe it. The Grand Canyon in northwest Arizona, USA, is 446 kilometres long, 29 kilometres
5 wide and about 1,800 metres deep. Scientists believe the canyon is 17 million years old. It is not the deepest or the longest canyon in the world. However, it is probably the most beautiful. The rocks change colour depending on the time of day,
10 from red and orange to grey and ochre brown. The best view of the Grand Canyon is from a helicopter. But for a real adventure, you need to take a boat along the valley of the river Colorado.

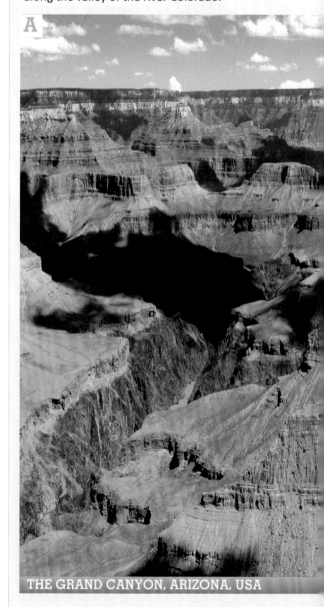

A

THE GRAND CANYON, ARIZONA, USA

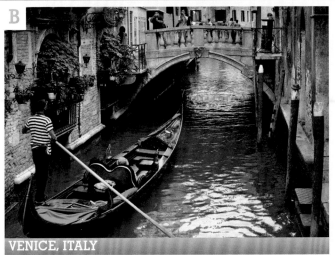
VENICE, ITALY

The 'floating city' in northeast Italy is famous for its unique
[15] beauty and wonderful architecture. The city consists of
around 117 islands and 409 bridges. You can walk through the
narrow streets for hours and then sit in a square and admire
the impressive buildings. St Mark's is the most famous square
and the central point of the city. **The public transport system**
[20] is fantastic. For example, the famous *vaporetto* (river bus)
only costs about 5 euros. It takes you all the way down the
Grand Canal. Alternatively, you can pay around 150 euros to
do the same trip on a gondola!

CHRIST THE REDEEMER, RIO DE JANEIRO, BRAZIL

The statue of Christ the Redeemer is 38 metres high and
[25] **dominates the city** of Rio de Janeiro. It is one of the
best-known sights of this lively city. When visitors go to the
top of the Corcovado mountain to visit the statue, they get
a breathtaking view of the city. From there you can see other
famous sights: the Sugar Loaf mountain, the Atlantic Ocean,
[30] the harbour and the long sandy beaches. As you drive up the
narrow road to the top of the mountain, you pass *favelas*
(slums), **rich neighbourhoods** and green rainforest.

THE GREAT BARRIER REEF, AUSTRALIA

It is one of the most amazing natural wonders of the world. It
is located in the Coral Sea and covers 2,600 kilometres along
[35] the northeast coast of Australia. It consists of around 3,000
coral reefs and hundreds of tropical islands. It is a popular
destination for scuba divers. They love the clear and shallow
sea water and all the different types of fish. The golden
sands of the tropical beaches **attract** about 1 million **tourists**
[40] each year.

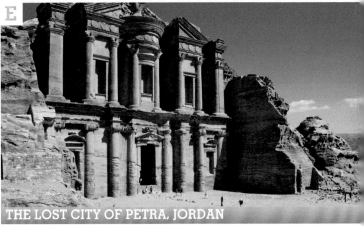
THE LOST CITY OF PETRA, JORDAN

The lost city of Petra is located in the rose-coloured
mountains of southwestern Jordan. This ancient city was
once **a busy trading centre** and the capital of the Nabataean
empire. It had a population of around 20,000. They made
[45] spectacular monuments from the pink limestone rock. The
city was 'lost' for centuries. Nobody knows exactly when or
why people left the city. Luckily, European travellers 'found'
it again in the nineteenth century. Today you can visit the
spectacular ruins on foot, on horseback or by camel.

---

7 Choose one of the places you thought of in Exercise 6
and write a paragraph.

*The most spectacular historic ruins in my country
are at Stonehenge. Stonehenge is an ancient
monument, but nobody knows exactly who built
it or why. The stones change colour depending on
the time of day. They are most beautiful when the
sun rises or sets. Stonehenge is a popular tourist
destination and millions of people come from all
over the world to visit these impressive ruins.*

WORD STORE 4E

8 CD•2.24 MP3•68 Complete WORD STORE 4E. Listen
and repeat the names of places in the city and in the
country. Then add them to the diagram according to
their distance from your school or city.

4.5 Grammar

Present Continuous, *be going to* and *will*

I can talk about future arrangements, intentions and spontaneous decisions.

1 **What makes a good party? In pairs, number these ideas in order of importance.**

decoration ☐ food and drink ☐ furniture ☐
lighting ☐ music ☐ people ☐ theme ☐

2 CD•2.25 MP3•69 **Read and listen to the conversation. Then answer the questions.**

1 Why is Tony having a party?
2 Where and when is he having it?
3 How is Luisa going to help?

Tony: I'm having a birthday party on the twenty-fifth. Can you come?

Luisa: That's next Saturday, right? Yes, that sounds great. Are you having it at home?

Tony: No, our apartment isn't big enough. I'm using my aunt and uncle's house. They're really nice – they say it's fine.

Luisa: That's kind of them – do they know how many friends you've got?

Tony: Not yet. I'm going to tell them later. We'll probably use the basement. It's huge.

Luisa: A basement? Are you going to decorate it?

Tony: I suppose so. I'm not very good at that sort of thing.

Luisa: Don't worry, I'll help you. What are you doing later?

Tony: I'm going to text everybody with the invitation now, but after that I'm free.

3 **Read the GRAMMAR FOCUS. Complete the examples with the future forms in blue in the conversation. Then underline more examples of each future form in the conversation.**

GRAMMAR FOCUS

Present Continuous, *be going to* and *will*

• You use the **Present Continuous** for future arrangements. You often mention a time, a date or a place.
  I ¹_____ a birthday party on the twenty-fifth.

• You use **be going to** for future intentions. You have already decided to do something and you tell people about it.
  I ²_____ tell them later.

• You use **will** for spontaneous decisions. You often use expressions like *I think I'll …, I'll probably …* and *Don't worry, I'll …*
  Don't worry, I ³_____ help you.

4 CD•2.26 MP3•70 **Read the conversation and choose the correct options. Then listen and check.**

Tony: Two of my friends ¹*are helping* / *will help* me prepare the room on Saturday afternoon. ²*We're going to hang / We'll hang* sheets on the walls and ceiling. Then ³*we're going to put / We're putting* coloured lights everywhere. ⁴*We'll have / We're having* a band and a DJ from eight to midnight. I've already booked them.

Aunt: OK, I think ⁵*I'll warn / I'm going to warn* the neighbours!

Tony: We've decided to have a fancy dress theme – everybody ⁶*will come / is coming* as their favourite film character.

Uncle: Oh good, I think ⁷*I'll come / I'm going to come* as Captain Jack Sparrow!

Aunt: No, ⁸*we'll go out / we're going out* to the theatre, remember? I told you yesterday.

Uncle: I know, I was joking. Now what are you ⁹*eating / going to eat*?

Tony: That's all arranged. Mum ¹⁰*will make / is making* some pizzas.

Aunt: And what about the cleaning the next day?

Tony: Oh, erm … don't worry, ¹¹*I'll do / I'm doing* that with my friend Luisa. She won't mind!

5 **Complete the email with the correct future form of the verbs in brackets.**

Hi Amy,

You know I ¹_____ (move) house next week. Well, I've decided that I ²_____ (have) a house-warming party in the new house. The theme is Superheroes, so I ³_____ (dress up) as Batman. You know my mum's a fantastic cook, so she ⁴_____ (make) four types of pizza. I think everybody ⁵_____ (like) that. I'm not sure about the music. I think I ⁶_____ (get) a DJ and ask him to play lots of dance music.

6 **Imagine you are responsible for organising an end-of-term party at your school. In pairs, follow the instructions to plan the party.**

• Make some decisions about location, food and drink, music, decoration, theme, etc.
• Write an email to the class to explain your ideas. Use all three future forms in your email.
• As a class, decide whose party ideas are best.

Grammar Focus page 115

Making suggestions

I can make and respond to suggestions.

1 Imagine you are visiting London. In pairs, discuss which of these activities you would like to do and why.

SIX OF THE BEST THINGS TO DO IN LONDON

London by speed boat
- Seven days a week, all year
- Suitable for all ages!
- £35 for fifty minutes

Shopping
- Oxford Street shops : Mon–Fri: 8.30 a.m.–9 p.m., Sun: 11.30 a.m.–6 p.m.
- Camden Market: clothes, music, souvenirs, 10 a.m.–6 p.m. daily

The London Eye
Get the best view of London!
- 10 a.m.–9 p.m. daily
- Adult: £19
  15 and under: £10

The London Dungeon
Prepare to be scared!
- ninety-minute tours: £20
- 10 a.m.–6 p.m., seven days a week

IMAX cinema
Watch the latest films in 3D for £15!
You'll feel like you're in the film!

Madame Tussaud's
Come and see the Royal Family!
- 9 a.m.–6 p.m. daily
- Adult: £30 – save fifty percent when you book online!

2 **CD·2.27** **MP3·71** Listen. What do Marcus and Ann decide to do? Which activities do they reject and why?

3 **CD·2.27** **MP3·71** Read the SPEAKING FOCUS. Then listen again and underline the phrases you hear.

SPEAKING FOCUS

Making suggestions
Do you fancy (going) …?
Let's (go) …
How about (going) …?
We could (go) …
(I think) we should (go) …
What about (going) …?
Why don't we (go) …?

Agreeing with suggestions
(That's a) good/great idea!
(That) sounds good/great!
Why not!

Disagreeing with suggestions
(I'm sorry,) I'm not keen on …
I don't really like …
I'd rather (go) …
I'm not sure about that.
Let's (go) … instead.

4 **CD·2.28** **MP3·72** Complete the conversation with words from the SPEAKING FOCUS. Then listen and check.

A: Do you fancy ¹_____ to the cinema tonight?

B: That's ²_____ good idea! What do you want to see?

A: The new film with Jennifer Aniston.

B: Oh no, I'm not ³_____ on romantic comedy. I'd ⁴_____ see an action film.

A: OK, let's see the new James Bond ⁵_____ .

B: Great. How ⁶_____ having a burger before we go?

A: Why ⁷_____ ! We ⁸_____ try that new burger bar in town.

5 You are planning a day out in Edinburgh. Look at the tourist information below. In pairs, follow the instructions to agree a plan for your day. Use the SPEAKING FOCUS to help you.

A: Suggest an activity for the morning.

B: Agree and suggest something for the afternoon.

A: Disagree and suggest something different for the afternoon.

B: Disagree and suggest something else for the afternoon.

A: Agree and suggest something for the evening.

B: Agree.

Scotland

National Museum of Scotland
10 a.m.–5 p.m.

Botanic Gardens
10 a.m.–6 p.m.

Climb a hill to get great views of the city
Two hours to climb up

Visit Edinburgh Castle
9.30 a.m.–5 p.m.

Comedy at Comedy Club
8.30 p.m.–midnight

Ghost tour: Dark secrets of Old Edinburgh
3 p.m.

Learn to do Scottish dancing
7 p.m.–midnight

Eat seafood in waterfront restaurants
7 p.m.–midnight

4.7 Writing

A story

I can write a story about an event on holiday.

1 In pairs, take turns to tell your partner the last three places you've been to on holiday and three places you'd like to go to in the future.

2 Choose one of the places you've been to and tell your partner something interesting that happened while you were there.

> I went to Paris. While we were there, a film company was making a film and we watched the actors. It was very interesting.

3 Read the story and choose the best title, A, B or C.

   A An interesting day on holiday
   B A holiday friend
   C A frightening event on holiday

We were on holiday near the sea and one morning I decided to take my dog, Betsy, for a walk.
I took the path to the beach because Betsy loves to go swimming. The water was much too cold for me!

When we got there, Betsy played in the water and I sat down to read my book. I completely forgot about Betsy.

Suddenly, I heard a cry and I looked up. There was a boy on the beach and he was pointing at something in the water. It was Betsy. She was in trouble.

The boy jumped into the water and swam out. When he came back, he had Betsy in his arms and he was smiling. She was all right!

The boy's name was Tommy and since then we've become great friends.

4 Cover the story. Try to remember the different events and note them down. Then read the story again and check the order in which they happened.

5 Complete the WRITING FOCUS with the words in purple in the story.

WRITING FOCUS

A story

- Set the scene.
  It was early in the morning./We were visiting my cousins./
  I was on my way to school./It was a lovely evening for a walk.
  [1] _____
- Use some short dramatic sentences:
  It was Betsy./[2]_____
- Use exclamation marks to show surprise or excitement.
  It was too cold for me!/[3]_____ /What a surprise!
- Use adverbs to add interest.
  suddenly/[4]_____
- Use linkers to join parts of sentences.
  and/but/so/[5]_____

6 Complete the sentences with your own ideas.

   1 I was asleep in bed when suddenly, …
   2 Although it was raining, we …
   3 We went to Spain because …
   4 We had just arrived at the airport when …
   5 While I was looking for our cases, …

7 Put the sentences in order to make a story.

- [1] Last summer I was on holiday in the countryside with my best friend, Jake.
- [ ] It finally did, but we were completely wet.
- [ ] After walking for three hours, we stopped for lunch.
- [ ] It got dark and started to rain heavily.
- [ ] We hid under a big tree and waited for the rain to stop.
- [ ] We were having lunch when suddenly, the weather changed.
- [ ] We couldn't wait to get back and have some warm tea and dry clothes.
- [ ] The weather was fantastic and we went hiking.
- [9] I will never go hiking again without checking the weather forecast first!

8 In pairs, read the opening sentence of a story and think of a story that could follow it. Use the questions to help you.

> When I got on the bus, it was very crowded and I couldn't find a seat.

1 Where were you?
2 When were you there?
3 Who were you with?
4 What was the weather like?
5 What happened?
6 What could you see?
7 What could you hear?
8 How did you feel?
9 What did you do next?
10 How did it end?

9 Use the questions in Exercise 7 to write a story ending with this sentence.

> At last it was over and I breathed a sigh of relief!

Writing task

Your teacher has asked you to write a story. Your story must begin with this sentence.

> I was sunbathing on the beach when something cold touched my back.

A Write your story in about 100 words. Remember to:

- give your story a title.
- make your story interesting for the reader.
- give your story a strong ending.

Useful language

- It was the first/second day of our holiday.
- When/While …
- Suddenly, …
- After that, …
- I was completely surprised!
- I finally realised …
- What a relief!/What a nightmare!
- In the end, …

B Use the ideas in the WRITING FOCUS and the model to help you.

C Check.

✓ Have you used the correct tenses to tell your story?
✓ Have you made it interesting?
✓ Have you divided your story into paragraphs?
✓ Have you used adverbs, adjectives and exclamations?
✓ Have you checked your spelling and punctuation?

VOCABULARY AND GRAMMAR

1 Complete the sentences with the words in the box. There are two extra words.

> accommodation   beach   bungalow   centre
> estate   heating   light   transport

1 Their house is cold – it doesn't have any central _____.
2 It's quicker to travel around the city by public _____ than by car.
3 What a bright room! There's so much natural _____.
4 My family didn't live in this house when I was young. I grew up on a housing _____.
5 Singapore is an important trading _____ in Asia. That's why the port there is so big.
6 I need a holiday! I'd love to just spend a week relaxing on a tropical _____.

2 Complete the sentences with the correct form of the words in capitals.

1 I love living in this _____. **NEIGHBOUR**
2 The Eiffel Tower is probably the most popular tourist _____ in Paris. **ATTRACT**
3 I bought the red sofa, not the blue one. I hope I've made the right _____! **DECIDE**
4 Our neighbours play loud music nearly every night. We've made several _____. **COMPLAIN**
5 The room was open-plan with _____ stairs leading up to the next floor. **WOOD**
6 I don't like _____. I plant lots of flowers, but they never grow! **GARDEN**

3 Complete the second sentence using the word in capitals so that it has a similar meaning to the first. Do not change the word in capitals.

1 They moved to Paris in 2013. **LIVED**
   They _____ 2013.
2 Liz became a doctor more than ten years ago. **WORKED**
   Liz _____ as a doctor for more than ten years.
3 They last saw Paul in January. **SINCE**
   They _____ January.
4 When did you first meet Karen? **KNOWN**
   How _____ Karen?
5 I stopped playing football six months ago. **FOR**
   I _____ six months.
6 When did you dye your hair red? **HAD**
   How _____ red hair?

4 Complete the sentences with the correct future forms of the verbs in brackets.

1 Are you moving house on Saturday? I _____ (help) you if you like.
2 I'm sorry I can't come. I _____ (work) this evening.
3 We _____ (meet) on Friday night, but we still don't know where exactly.
4 'Was that the doorbell?' 'Yes, I _____ (answer) it.'
5 'Shall we go out?' 'No, I _____ (do) the washing and the ironing this evening.'

LANGUAGE IN USE

5 Choose the correct answer, A, B or C.

1 A: What are your neighbours like?
   B: We haven't got any close neighbours. We live in a ____ house in the countryside.
   A terraced
   B semi-detached
   C detached

2 A: Let's go to the theatre on Friday.
   B: ____
   A: OK, let's see the new Batman film, then.
   A Sounds good.
   B I'd rather go to the theatre.
   C I'm not sure about that.

3 A: How long have you lived here?
   B: ____
   A In 2010.
   B Since 2010.
   C A few years ago.

4 A: Do you fancy going on the London Eye?
   B: ____
   A I'll never forget the views.
   B Good idea – the views are great.
   C In my opinion, the views are cool.

5 A: What's so special about their garden?
   B: It's very big. There's even a ____ with some fish in it.
   A path
   B porch
   C pond

6 A: Have you got any plans for the weekend?
   B: We've just decided that we ____ a fancy dress party.
   A are going to have
   B will have
   C are having

6 Choose the correct answer, A, B or C, to complete both sentences.

1 I'll ____ the dinner. What would you like?
   Can you tidy your room and ____ your bed, please?
   A do   B make   C choose
2 Don't be nervous in the exam. Just ____ your best.
   I'm too tired to ____ the shopping today.
   A make   B be   C do
3 I love my grandma'a house. I really feel ____ home there.
   My grandpa is good ____ repairing things.
   A in   B at   C to
4 Please use the ____ door to get to the garden.
   Will you bring me something ____ from your trip?
   A back   B return   C behind
5 The person on the left of the photo is my uncle. He's ____ next to my aunt.
   This is Mike's favourite place in the ____ room – next to the wood-burner.
   A right   B living   C sitting

LISTENING

7 CD•2.29 MP3•73 **Listen to a teacher talking to some students on a coach trip. Complete the sentences with a word or short phrase.**

1 The students are going to visit _____ House.
2 They may be able to see deer and wild _____ during their journey.
3 Arrival time is _____ .
4 During the tour of the house they will hear a _____ story about a member of the family that lived there.
5 The teacher advises the students to find a lovely _____ in the gardens.
6 The day trip will finish at _____ .

SPEAKING

8 A friend of yours is going on a beach holiday for two weeks. In pairs, talk about the things he or she will need there and decide which are the most important things to take.

WRITING

9 **Read the writing task. Number sentences a–d in the order you think they should appear in the blog entry.**

a Bath is not a very big city, but it's a lovely place.
b Unfortunately, we missed our train back to London.
c I would recommend visiting the Roman Baths.
d Last month we went on a class trip to Bath.

Recently you have been on a school trip in a big city in your country. Write a blog entry of about 100 words, sharing your impressions of the trip. In your blog entry you should:
• explain which city you visited and when
• give your opinion about the city, giving reasons
• recommend some sights to see there
• describe a problem you had on the trip and how it was resolved.

5
SCHOOL

Tell me and I forget, teach me and I may remember, involve me and I learn.

BENJAMIN FRANKLIN (1706–1790), A US PRESIDENT

UNIT LANGUAGE AND SKILLS

Vocabulary:
- *Show what you know* – school subjects
- phrasal verbs
- education
- phrases with *get*
- word families

Grammar:
- First Conditional
- relative clauses

Listening:
- a conversation about exams
- a talk about getting into university

Reading:
- a text on charity schools

Speaking:
- giving an opinion
- agreeing and disagreeing

Writing:
- an email/a letter of enquiry

FOCUS EXTRA

- Grammar Focus page 116
- WORD STORE booklet pages 10–11
- Workbook pages 56–67 or MyEnglishLab

5.1 Vocabulary

Education · Phrasal verbs · Phrases with *get*
I can talk about schools in different countries.

SHOW WHAT YOU KNOW

1   In pairs, discuss where you normally study the subjects in the box in your country. Put them under the appropriate heading. Some subjects may go in more than one group

> Architecture   Design and Technology   Engineering
> English   Geography   Law   Medicine   Music
> Physical Education (PE)   Reading   Science   Writing

primary school	secondary school	university

2   What other subjects do you study at secondary school? In pairs, talk about your favourite subjects and why you like them.

3   In a recent survey, Finland and South Korea came top of the list of the best state schools in the world. Look at the photos from the two countries. In pairs, discuss these points about them.

- the classrooms
- the students
- the atmosphere

4 Ji-min is a South Korean student. Read the text about her school day. Are the statements true (T) or false (F)?

1 Ji-min has to wear a school uniform. ☐
2 She wears trainers in school. ☐
3 She studies eleven subjects including PE, Music and Art. ☐
4 She wants to study English abroad. ☐
5 She always goes to bed before midnight. ☐

5 Replace the underlined words and phrases in the questions with the correct form of the phrasal verbs in red in the text. Then answer the questions.

1 What time does Ji-min <u>get out of bed</u>?
   What time does Ji-min get up?
2 <u>Is she friendly with</u> all her classmates?
3 Why doesn't she <u>see</u> her classmates outside school?
4 What does she <u>remove</u> and what does she <u>start wearing</u> when she gets to school?
5 Does she often <u>continue</u> studying after midnight?
6 What does she have to do to <u>get a place at</u> university?

Ji-min is a high school student in Seoul, South Korea. She gets up at 6.30 a.m., eats a quick breakfast of rice and seaweed soup, gets dressed and walks to school with her friends. She gets on
⁵ with all her <u>classmates</u>, but she doesn't meet up with them outside school because she's too busy with her studies.

Ji-min wears exactly the same clothes as the other girls in her school because school uniform is
¹⁰ <u>compulsory</u>. When she gets to school, she takes off her shoes and puts on a pair of slippers.

Ji-min has an extremely <u>demanding</u> timetable. She studies eleven subjects, but she doesn't have time for non-academic subjects, so she <u>has dropped</u> PE,
¹⁵ Music and Art. English is her favourite subject and she's hoping to go to Australia in the summer and <u>do a course</u> in English.

She has classes from 9 a.m. to 3 p.m. every day and after school she has extra lessons in a private
²⁰ academy. She has to do lots of Maths exercises and learn long lists of English vocabulary <u>by heart</u>. It can be quite boring, but she never <u>skips</u> a lesson because her parents pay a lot of money to send her to the academy. Sometimes she
²⁵ doesn't get home until after 10 p.m.

After dinner, she does her homework. When she has to <u>revise for</u> a test, she often carries on studying until 1 or 2 a.m. Of course, when it gets late, she gets tired, but she knows that if she wants to get
³⁰ into university and get a good job, she has to work hard, get good marks and <u>pass</u> all her exams. She wants to <u>do</u> English at university.

Go to **WORD STORE 5** page 11.

WORD STORE 5A ▶▶▶▶

6 `CD·2.30` `MP3·74` Complete WORD STORE 5A with the base form of the phrasal verbs in red in the text. Then listen, check and repeat.

7 Complete the sentences with phrasal verbs from Word Store 5A.

1 I _____ my big sister's friends. They all like me!
2 _____ your coat – it's hot it here.
3 Would you like to _____ me and my friends at the weekend, Jeff?
4 Boys, _____ your hats before you go out – it's cold outside!
5 What time do you _____ at the weekend, Fiona? Do you like staying in bed then?
6 Sally is hoping to _____ Manchester University next year to study History.

WORD STORE 5B ▶▶▶▶

8 `CD·2.31` `MP3·75` Listen to an interview with Beni, a Finnish student. Write three ways in which their school days are similar and four ways in which they are different.

9 `CD·2.32` `MP3·76` Complete WORD STORE 5B with the correct form of the underlined words and phrases in the text.

10 Do you prefer Ji-min's or Beni's school day? Discuss in pairs.

WORD STORE 5C ▶▶▶

11 `CD·2.33` `MP3·77` Complete WORD STORE 5C with the base form of the highlighted phrases with *get* from the text. Then listen, check and repeat.

12 Complete the sentences with the correct form of *get* and your own ideas. Then compare with a partner.

1 I usually _____ to school at _____ .
2 Yesterday I _____ home from school at _____ .
3 I rarely _____ good marks in _____ .
4 I think I'm _____ better at _____ .
5 I _____ tired if I study after _____ .
6 I'd like to _____ a job as a _____ .

5.2 Grammar

First Conditional

I can use the First Conditional to talk about the possible results of an action.

1 Read *UK TODAY*. What is a gap year? Would you like to do a gap year? Why?/Why not?

UK TODAY

Did you know that about ten percent of students in the UK do a gap year between leaving school and going to university or college?

What do they do?
• travel abroad   • go backpacking   • do voluntary work

Where do they go?
• Africa   • Southeast Asia
• Australia and New Zealand   • South America

How much does it cost?
usually about £4,000

2 [CD·2.34] [MP3·78] Look at the photo of Ricky's parents above and read the sentences. Who is in favour of Ricky doing a gap year and who is against? Listen and check.

3 Read the GRAMMAR FOCUS. Then complete the examples with the First Conditional forms in blue in Exercise 2.

GRAMMAR FOCUS

First Conditional

• You use the **First Conditional** to predict the future result of a possible action.

action	→	future result
***if* + Present Simple,**		***will/won't* + verb**

If he ¹_____ *to South America next year,*
he ²_____ *to university the year after.*
If he **doesn't go** *to university, he* **won't get** *a decent job.*

• You can put the *if* clause before or after the main clause.
*He***'ll waste** *a year if he* **goes** *travelling.*

4 [CD·2.34] [MP3·78] Match the sentence halves to make sentences from the conversation. Then listen again and check.

1 If Ricky doesn't go to university this year, ☐
2 He'll get a lot out of it ☐
3 He'll do bungee jumps and get a tattoo ☐
4 If he goes away on his own, ☐
5 If he doesn't do anything on his own, ☐

a if he does a gap year.
b he'll never go.
c he'll get into trouble.
d he'll never be independent.
e if he goes to South America.

If he **goes** to South America next year, he**'ll go** to university the year after.

He'll waste a ye[ar] if he goes travelli[ng]

5 [CD·2.35] [MP3·79] What other reasons might Ricky have for going to South America? Discuss. Then listen and check your ideas.

6 [CD·2.35] [MP3·79] Complete the sentences from Ricky and Emily's conversation. Then listen again and check.

1 He thinks if I _____ (go) travelling, I _____ (not go) to university when I come back.
2 If I _____ (tell) them the truth, they definitely _____ (not let) me go.
3 You _____ (not learn) any Spanish if you _____ (visit) her!
4 If my dad _____ (not agree), I _____ (not be) able to go.
5 If your mum _____ (think) it's a good idea, she _____ (convince) your dad.

7 In groups of three, use the prompts to role play a conversation about a gap year. Student A is the student, Student B is the positive parent and Student C is the negative parent.

A (student's wish)	B (positive parent)	C (negative parent)
1 live abroad	new culture	miss friends
2 join a band	have a lot of fun	no schoolwork
3 part-time job	earn money	get up early

A: I want to live abroad.

B: Great! If you live abroad, you'll learn about a new culture.

C: Oh dear! If you live abroad, you'll miss all your friends.

Grammar Focus page 116

True/False

I can identify specific detail in a conversation.

1 Read the tips for dealing with exam stress. Which tips do you usually follow? Can you add any more tips?

Get rid of exam stress!

- ☐ Create a revision schedule – and follow it!
- ☐ Don't get exhausted – get plenty of sleep.
- ☐ Study in a group from time to time.
- ☐ Be positive – imagine yourself passing the exam.
- ☐ Take regular breaks – do things you enjoy.
- ☐ Remember, it's only an exam. You won't die if you fail!

2 CD•2.36 MP3•80 Listen to Grace and Tom talking about exams. Tick the tips in Exercise 1 that Grace mentions.

3 Read statements 1–6 in the EXAM FOCUS. Match the underlined words and phrases with the words and phrases in the box.

alone	4	enjoy yourself	☐
marks	☐	learn by heart	☐
nervous	☐	relax	☐

EXAM FOCUS True/False

4 CD•2.36 MP3•80 Listen again. Are the statements true (T) or false (F)?

1 Tom wants to <u>memorise</u> fifty French verbs tonight. ☐

2 Tom doesn't usually get good <u>grades</u> at school. ☐

3 Grace thinks Tom will get sick if he doesn't <u>take it easy</u>. ☐

4 Grace thinks Tom should spend less time <u>on his own</u>. ☐

5 Grace doesn't get <u>stressed</u> about exams. ☐

6 Grace tells Tom to go out and <u>have a good time</u>. ☐

5 Do you have to take an entrance exam to get into university in your country? Read the information about British universities. Are the missing words nouns or numbers?

HOW TO GET A PLACE AT
University in Britain

1 Apply for a place at university when you're in your last year of secondary school: Year _____ .

2 You can apply to _____ universities.

3 To get into university, you have to get good _____ in three or four *A levels.

4 To get into Oxford or Cambridge university, you have to take an entrance _____ .

5 Last year _____ students applied for 400,000 university places.

6 You have to pay university tuition fees of up to £_____ a year.

*A levels = Advanced level exams. Students usually do A levels at eighteen in the UK.

6 CD•2.37 MP3•81 Listen and complete the text in Exercise 5.

PRONUNCIATION FOCUS

7 CD•2.38 MP3•82 Listen and choose the number you hear. Then listen again and repeat.

a	15.1	50.1	d	18.18	80.18
b	170	117	e	14,440	40,414
c	13,990	30,919	f	660,000	616,000

8 Write six similar numbers. Then, in pairs, take turns to dictate them to your partner. Check your partner's answers.

WORD STORE 5D 》》》》》

9 CD•2.39 MP3•83 Look at WORD STORE 5D. Listen and repeat the phrases with *get*. Then write example sentences with the phrases.

True/False

I can find specific details in an article.

Afghan girls at the secondary school in Afghanistan

The man who moves MOUNTAINS

by Louis Stevenson

CD•2.40 MP3•84

Greg Mortenson hates to be called a hero, but in the mountains of Pakistan and Afghanistan, that is what people call him. He has helped them to build more than sixty schools and this has changed the
⁵lives of many young people, especially the girls. But what first brought a white American man to this **remote** part of the world where tourists rarely go?

Greg Mortenson was born in the United States, but
¹⁰grew up in Africa, where his parents were teachers. His hobby was mountain climbing. He climbed his first mountain, Mount Kilimanjaro, when he was only eleven. Many years later, when his younger sister died suddenly, he decided to climb
¹⁵Pakistan's K2 in her memory. K2 is the second highest mountain in the world. He didn't reach the **summit** of K2 and after seventy-eight days at high altitude, he was exhausted. On his way back he got lost and eventually, unable to walk properly,
²⁰he **stumbled** into the tiny village of Korphe.

The villagers looked after him and nursed him back to health. He soon realised how poor these people were. When he asked to see the village school, they took him to the village square. But
²⁵there was no school – instead, the children were sitting on the ground outside, without a teacher, writing in the sand with sticks.

He could see that the children were thirsty for knowledge and were doing their best to learn,
³⁰even in such difficult conditions. So he promised to return and build a school for them.

Back in America he started a programme called Pennies for Pakistan. School children asked their friends and families to **donate** pennies and the
³⁵pennies became dollars. After three years of **fundraising**, he went back to Korphe.

The villagers were amazed when he **kept his promise** and built Korphe School for Girls. It was a simple building with eight classrooms and
⁴⁰a small playground. Most of the girls who attend the school will be the first **literate** women in their families. Their mothers never had the opportunity to learn to read and write. He explains that it is important to provide an education for girls. In the
⁴⁵developing world, girls often get married at the age of twelve and have children by fifteen. But if a girl stays in school, it makes a big difference to her life – she'll marry later, have fewer and healthier children; she can earn an income and **invest** in her
⁵⁰family. Greg Mortenson likes to quote an African proverb: 'If you educate a boy, you educate an individual. But if you educate a girl, you educate a community.'

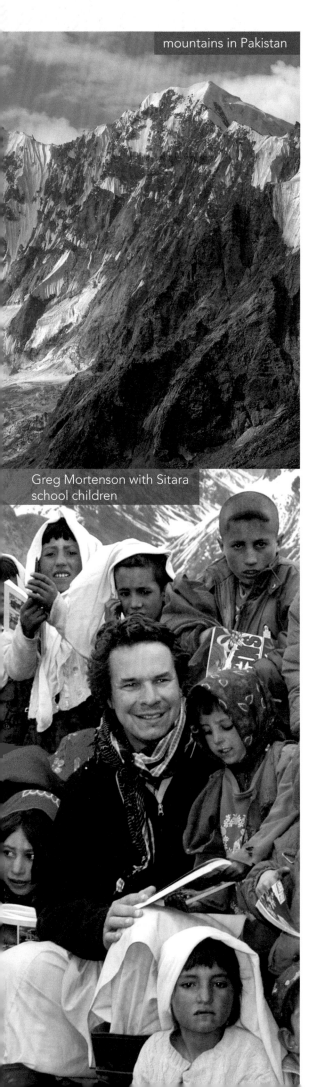

mountains in Pakistan

Greg Mortenson with Sitara school children

1 Look at the photos and the title of the text. Where do you think the people are and what do you think the text is about?

2 Read the text and check your ideas in Exercise 1. Why does Greg Mortenson think it is important to educate girls in developing countries?

3 Look at the words in blue in the text. Underline words or phrases around them that help you understand the meaning of those you don't know. For example:
   • Lines 6–8: But what first brought a white American man to this remote part of the world <u>where tourists rarely go</u>?
   • Lines 15–17: <u>K2 is the second highest mountain</u> in the world. He didn't <u>reach</u> the summit <u>of K2</u> ...

4 Match the words in blue in the text with the definitions.
   1 far away or isolated – _remote_
   2 top of a mountain – _summit_
   3 able to read – _____
   4 give money to charity – _____
   5 put money into – _____
   6 collecting money for a particular purpose – _____
   7 did what he said he would do – _____
   8 almost fell – _____

EXAM FOCUS True/False

5 Read the text again. Are statements 1–6 true (T) or false (F)?
   1 Greg Mortenson is a hero to people in the mountains of Pakistan and Afghanistan. ☐
   2 It took him seventy-eight days to climb to the top of K2. ☐
   3 He was very healthy when he first arrived in Korphe. ☐
   4 The people of Korphe were surprised when Greg came back. ☐
   5 Most of the mothers in Korphe can't read. ☐
   6 Greg thinks that if a girl stays in school, she'll have more children. ☐

6 CD·2.41 MP3·85 Listen to a conversation about how Pennies for Peace began. Complete the sentences with the numbers in the box. Then listen again and check.

1	6	100	580	1995
12,000		62,340	100,000	

   1 Greg Mortenson started the charity in _____ .
   2 He needed $_____ to build a school.
   3 He wrote _____ letters to famous people.
   4 He got _____ reply with a cheque for $_____ .
   5 His mother's elementary school collected _____ pennies in _____ weeks.
   6 The charity has collected more than $_____ .

7 Imagine you want to collect money for a charity at your school. In pairs, choose a charity and think of three ways to raise money for it.

   We can sell cakes at school.

WORD STORE 5E >>>>>>>>>

8 CD·2.42 MP3·86 Complete WORD STORE 5E. Add verbs to the table. Mark the stress. Then listen, check and repeat.

Relative clauses

I can use relative clauses to give more information.

1 Read an extract from *The British Students' Manifesto*. How is this school similar or different to your school?

> The school that we'd like is a school which is for everybody, with boys and girls who are from all backgrounds and abilities, a place where we don't compete against each other, but just do our best.

2 Read the GRAMMAR FOCUS. Then complete the rules with the relative pronouns in blue in the extract.

GRAMMAR FOCUS

Relative clauses

- You use ¹_____ or *that* for people.
- You use ²_____ or *that* for things.
- You use ³_____ to refer to a place.

The relative pronoun usually comes immediately after the person, thing or place it refers to. You can leave out the relative pronoun when it comes before a noun or a pronoun.

The school (that) we'd like is for everybody.

3 Read more of the *The British Students' Manifesto* and choose the correct options. Then underline the nouns in the text that each relative pronoun refers to.

4 Complete the definitions of words from the text with relative pronouns. Then tick the sentences where you can leave out the relative pronoun.

1 An *uncluttered* classroom is a classroom _____ is tidy with no unnecessary things in it. ☐
2 A *beanbag* is a large cushion _____ forms a comfortable shape when you sit on it. ☐
3 A person _____ *scrapes* their knees may get small cuts. ☐
4 *Chill out* is an informal expression _____ means 'relax'. ☐
5 *Blinds* are like curtains _____ you use to keep out the light. ☐
6 A *swipe card* is a plastic card _____ works like a key and lets you in or out. ☐
7 A *rigid* timetable is a timetable _____ you can't change. ☐
8 A *relevant* school is a school _____ lessons are directly connected with real life. ☐

5 In groups of three, prepare a group manifesto about your ideas for a perfect school. Think about:

- classrooms and study areas
- school uniforms
- gardens and sports grounds
- canteen
- equipment and technology

6 Present your group's manifesto to the rest of the class.

Grammar Focus page 116

The British Students' Manifesto

We, the school students of Britain, have a voice.

THIS IS WHAT WE SAY

The school that we'd like is:

A beautiful school ¹*where / that* the classrooms are uncluttered and the walls are brightly coloured.

A comfortable school with sofas and beanbags, cushions on the floors, tables ²*who / that* don't scrape our knees and quiet rooms ³*where / which* we can **chill** out.

A light school with huge windows ⁴*that / where* let the sunshine in and blinds ⁵*who / which* keep out the sun when we want to watch something on a screen.

A safe school with swipe cards for the school gate, anti-bully alarms, first aid classes and someone ⁶*where / that* we can talk to about our problems.

A flexible school without rigid timetables or exams, without compulsory homework, ⁷*where / who* we can follow our own interests and spend more time on the subjects ⁸*who / which* we enjoy.

A relevant school ⁹*who / where* we learn through experience, experiments and exploration, with field trips to historic sites and other places of interest.

A school which is for everybody, with boys and girls who are from all backgrounds and abilities, a place where we don't compete against each other, but just do our best.

The British Students' Manifesto was the result of a nationwide survey of over 15,000 students in England and Wales.

Giving an opinion · Agreeing and disagreeing

I can give opinions, and agree or disagree with other's opinions.

1 In pairs, think of three reasons why some students choose to leave school early and not go to university.

Ed   Lisa

2 [CD·2.43] [MP3·87] Listen to a conversation between Ed and Lisa. Look at the statements. Do Ed and Lisa agree (A) or disagree (D) about each statement?

	Ed	Lisa
1 Nick should leave school if he wants to be an actor.		
2 He doesn't need qualifications.		
3 He might need to get a proper job.		
4 Nick's good-looking and talented.		
5 He should do his degree first.		

3 [CD·2.43] [MP3·87] Listen again and number the expressions in the order you hear them.

SPEAKING FOCUS

Giving an opinion

I think he … ☐
I don't think it's … [1]
Personally, I think … ☐
I really believe … ☐
In my opinion, … ☐
If you ask me, … ☐

Agreeing

I couldn't agree more. ☐
That's a good point. ☐

Disagreeing politely

I see what you mean, but … ☐
That's true, but … ☐
I'm not so sure. ☐

Disagreeing

I totally disagree! ☐
Oh come on! That's nonsense. ☐

4 Choose the correct options.

1 A: What do you think about single-sex schools?
B: *I don't think / Personally, I think* they're a good idea. It isn't normal to separate boys and girls.

2 A: If you ask me, I think we get too much homework.
B: *I'm not so sure. / I couldn't agree more.* I never have time to do sport or relax in the evenings.

3 A: I don't think my pronunciation is very good.
B: *I really believe / I see what you mean, but* if you practise, I'm sure you'll improve.

4 A: I think the food in the school canteen is too expensive.
B: *Oh come on! That's nonsense. / That's a good point.* If you go to a restaurant in town, you'll pay much more.

5 A: In my opinion, it's a waste of time going to university – I want to get a job and earn some money.
B: *I totally disagree. / I couldn't agree more.* If you go to university, you'll get a much better job.

5 In pairs, discuss the subjects in the box.

> doing sport at school
> leaving school at sixteen
> having extra lessons after school
> wearing a uniform   doing a gap year

A: Ask what your partner thinks.
B: Give your opinion.
A: Agree or disagree and say why.

6 Your school has received a donation of €5,000. Photos A, B and C show three possible ways your school could spend the money. In pairs, follow the instructions and present your choice to the class. Use the SPEAKING FOCUS to help you.

- Choose the option which in your opinion is the best for the school.
- Support your choice with some reasons.
- Explain why you have rejected the other options.

I think the school should spend the money on computers because …
I don't think the school should choose option … because …

A
IT suite

B
gym

C
café

An email/A letter of enquiry

I can write a polite email/letter asking for information.

PADDINGTON ENGLISH SCHOOL

Central London location ideal for shops, art galleries and museums.

We offer English courses for all levels and all exams:

IELTS, TOEFL, CAMBRIDGE, PTE

Excellent teachers, competitive prices.

Contact us: call 00 44 208 44 44 44 or write to enquiry@paddingtonenglish.co.uk.

Dear Sir or Madam,

I am a seventeen-year-old Italian student and I am writing to enquire about doing an English course at your school next summer. I am particularly interested in doing the *Cambridge First* exam. I got good marks in my English exam this year and I think I am B2 level. Could you tell me how long I will need to study and how much it will cost?

I would also like to know if you can arrange accommodation for me. Could you tell me what kind of accommodation you provide and how much it costs?

Finally, I would be grateful if you could send me details of how to book a course and how to pay for it.

I look forward to hearing from you.

Yours faithfully,

Analisa Bargellini

---

1 You want to do an English course in the UK. Read the advertisement and write down three questions you would like to ask about the school.

2 Read Analisa's email. Did she ask any of the questions you wrote down?

3 Put the sentences summarising the email in the order they appear (1–3).

  a polite questions about the information you need ☐

  b what you would like the reader to do ☐

  c information about yourself and why you are writing the email ☐

4 Match sentences 1–4 to their more polite versions in the email.

  1 How long will I need to study and how much will it cost?

  _____

  2 Can you arrange accommodation for me?

  _____

  3 What kind of accommodation do you provide and how much does it cost?

  _____

  4 Please send me details of how to book a course.

  _____

5 Complete the indirect questions.

  1 Does your school have a canteen?
    Could you tell me _____ ?

  2 Can my friend stay in the same host family?
    I would like to know if _____ .

  3 How far is the school from the nearest tube station?
    Could you tell me _____ ?

  4 How many students are there in a class?
    I would like to know _____ .

6 Match these answers (a–d) with the questions (1–4) in Exercise 5.

  a There are about 8–10.

  b Yes, if there are enough rooms.

  c No, but there are a lot of cafés nearby.

  d It's about five minutes away.

7 Write indirect questions for these answers.

1 The school is about ten minutes from the town centre.
2 Yes, we have special exam courses for your level.
3 We arrange weekend trips for the students.
4 Yes, there are usually different nationalities in the same class.

8 Complete the WRITING FOCUS with the words in purple in the email.

WRITING FOCUS

An email/A letter of enquiry

- Start the email/letter with *Dear Mr* or *Dear Mrs* and the person's surname. If you don't know the person's name, use ¹*Dear Sir or Madam* .

- Don't use abbreviations or contractions. Use full forms: I would (not *I'd*)/² _____ (not *I'm*).

- Use polite expressions to:
  a ask for information:
   I would also like to know/³_____ …
  b ask somebody to do something for you:
   I would be grateful ⁴_____ …
  c say that you expect a reply:
   I look forward to ⁵_____ .

- Finish the email/letter with *Yours sincerely* if you know the name of the person you're writing to, or *Yours* ⁶_____ if you don't.

9 Change the note to make it more formal (parts underlined in green) and grammatically correct (parts underlined in red).

Hi Mr Jones,

I'm looking for a good language school. I'd like to know do you have courses in September.

I thank you if you could send me some information.

I am look forward for hear from you.

Bye for now,

Marcus

Writing task

You have seen this advertisement and want to study English at St John's School. Write an email of enquiry to the school.

St John's School

Study English in the beautiful,
peaceful village of Amberley.

Small groups, experienced staff,
excellent host-family accommodation.

For information about exams, fees and availability,
please call 00 44 543 43 32 21
or write to Mary Johnson at mary@stjohn.edu.

A Write your email in 80–130 words. Include these points.

- Give information about yourself and say why you are writing the email.
- Ask for information about taking an exam, the nearest town or city and public transport.
- Say what you would like the reader to do.
- Say that you expect a reply.

Useful language

- I am writing to enquire about …
- Could you please send me information about …
- Can you give me some additional information about …
- I look forward to your reply.

B Use the ideas in the WRITING FOCUS and the model to help you.

C Check.

✓ Have you used indirect questions?
✓ Have you started and closed the email with the correct phrases?
✓ Have you mentioned all the points in the question?
✓ Have you checked your spelling and punctuation?

VOCABULARY AND GRAMMAR

1 Complete the sentences with the correct form of the words in capitals.

1 We made a _____ to move to the suburbs. **DECIDE**
2 A good _____ can change your life. **EDUCATE**
3 I wasn't sure what he meant, so I asked him for an _____ . **EXPLAIN**
4 I'm going to do some _____ exercises tonight to practise before my English test tomorrow. **REVISE**
5 I've got a _____ of small rocks that I've brought back from holiday trips. **COLLECT**
6 She worked day and night and at the end of the week was close to _____ . **EXHAUST**

2 Complete the text with words which mean the same as the expressions in brackets. The first letter of each word is given.

We're ¹f_____ (collecting money) for children in ²r_____ (far away) areas of Afghanistan and Pakistan. We believe that every child in the world should have the ³o_____ (chance) to ⁴a_____ (go to) school. Help the children become ⁵l_____ (able to read and write). Ask everybody you know to ⁶d_____ (give) money to invest in schools and help these children do well in life.

3 Complete the First Conditional sentences with the correct form of the verbs in brackets.

1 If I _____ (get up) too late, I _____ (not get) to school on time.
2 If you _____ (not hurry), we _____ (miss) the bus.
3 _____ (your dad/get) angry if you _____ (not get) into university?
4 He _____ (not pass) his exams if he _____ (not revise) properly.
5 What _____ (he/do) if we _____ (use) his computer?
6 I _____ (not help) you with your Maths if you _____ (not help) me with my English.

4 Choose the correct answer, A, B or C.

1 Any student ____ hasn't finished their homework, please see me after the lesson.
  A who   B which   C where
2 This is the canteen ____ we eat our lunch.
  A that   B which   C where
3 Students ____ only revise the night before an exam don't usually do very well.
  A who   B which   C where
4 It was a gap year ____ seemed to last forever.
  A who   B that   C where
5 Oxford was the university ____ she did her degree.
  A who   B that   C where

LANGUAGE IN USE

5 Choose the option, A, B or C, which has the same meaning as the underlined phrase in each sentence.

1 I never avoid going to lessons.
  A drop   B leave   C skip
2 If you ask me, I think our school doesn't spend enough money on computers.
  A That's true, but   B In my opinion,   C I agree that
3 We have to learn fifty words by heart for our French test.
  A memorise   B explain   C revise
4 Uniforms are not compulsory at my school.
  A It is necessary to wear a uniform
  B You'll get into trouble if you don't wear a uniform
  C You don't have to wear a uniform
5 It's a single-sex school for ambitious boys that offers the best learning conditions.
  A which   B where   C who
6 A: I think that going to school every day is boring.
  B: That's true, but not all schools are the same.
  A I see what you mean   C That's complete nonsense
  B I couldn't agree more

6 Read the text and choose the correct answer, A, B or C.

www.myblog.abc

19 October

I'm in my final year of school and soon I'll have to make an important decision. My parents want me to apply ¹_____ a place at university, but my best friend is going to do a gap year and she wants me to go with her. She's going to travel to a developing country and teach children ²_____ can't read or write.

I like the idea of a gap year because I haven't decided what I want to do at university. Also, I'm tired of studying; I always get good ³_____ and I've never got into trouble at school. Now I want some freedom. I want to go to a place where I don't have to ⁴_____ exams or attend classes. And I'd really like the opportunity to learn something about the world.

Most of my classmates are going to go to university when they ⁵_____ school. I'm sure they'll have a lot of fun. But I think I'm ready for an adventure. If my parents ⁶_____, I'll go abroad for six months, and when I get home I'll be ready to continue my studies.

1 A for   B into   C in
2 A where   B which   C who
3 A marks   B fees   C points
4 A fail   B take   C drop
5 A take off   B leave   C go
6 A agree   B will agree   C are going to agree

7 Read the text and choose the correct answer, A, B, C or D.

Buy a lunch, save a life

A lot of school students probably don't think very much about their lunch. Perhaps they bring some sandwiches from home or maybe they go to the school canteen. However, in many developing countries around the world, students do not get lunch at all. Every year, 15 million children die of hunger. This shocking statistic is why the Really Good School Dinner programme started in 2009.

Many organisations ask people to donate some money for those in need. The idea behind the Really Good School Dinner programme is different but simple. Students in the UK buy a healthy meal from their school canteen. They pay for their meal and donate ten pence extra. So, if their lunch costs £2.50, they pay £2.60. This ten pence is enough to buy a whole meal for a child in another country.

This clever method of fundraising feeds poor children and also gives them an education. In some poor, remote areas, students have to work to earn enough money to buy food. If they receive a free meal, they do not have to work and can spend more time studying. Students that receive an education can then get a better job and help their families. It is amazing that a free lunch can pull whole communities out of poverty!

The Really Good School Dinner programme runs every February for one week. Since its beginning in 2009, students in the UK have raised over £28,000, which has bought more than 450,000 meals in the developing world. At the moment, over 300 schools are involved and more are joining each year. So far, the programme has helped children in Afghanistan and those affected by natural disasters such as the earthquake in Haiti in 2010 and the famine in East Africa in 2012.

1 According to the text, students in poor countries
  A buy lunch at the canteen.
  B don't usually eat.
  C bring something to eat from home.
  D don't worry about lunch.

2 How do students in the UK help poor children?
  A They donate nutritious meals.
  B They collect money and send it to poor countries.
  C They pay for a small part of a meal.
  D They give a small amount of money.

3 The programme is an excellent idea because
  A it is an easy way to make a better future.
  B it feeds all the members of a community.
  C it helps children get to know people in the UK.
  D it gives work to poor students.

4 How successful has the programme been?
  A UK students only raised money in 2009.
  B It has helped people in one area of the world.
  C More schools are becoming involved.
  D It raises over £28,000 every year.

5 In the text the author
  A explains why some children die of hunger.
  B informs readers about a way to reduce hunger.
  C describes different places where there is hunger.
  D shows how he helps poor, hungry children.

8 The photos show some students learning at school. In pairs, take turns to tell your partner what you can see in the photos.

I think they're doing a science experiment in photo A.

9 Now talk about how you use technology at school to help you learn.

10 Read the writing task. Think about photos you have taken and photos that you like.

You want to go on a popular photography course in England. Write an email to the course organiser. In your email you should:
- introduce yourself and say which course you're interested in
- tell them about your experience in photography
- ask for information about accommodation and payment.

6
WORKING LIFE

Choose a job you love and you will never have to work a day in your life.

CONFUCIUS (551–479 BC), A CHINESE PHILOSOPHER AND POLITICIAN

UNIT LANGUAGE AND SKILLS

Vocabulary:
• *Show what you know* – jobs
• *work* + prepositions
• collocations – terms and conditions
• confusing words – *job* vs *work*
• compound nouns
• phrasal verbs

Grammar:
• Second Conditional
• modal verbs for obligation and permission

Listening:
• a conversation about becoming an airline pilot

Reading:
• a text about a man who lived without money

Speaking:
• asking for and giving advice

Writing:
• an email/a letter of application

FOCUS EXTRA

• Grammar Focus page 117
• WORD STORE booklet pages 12–13
• Workbook pages 68–79 or MyEnglishLab

6.1 Vocabulary

work + prepositions • Terms and conditions • Confusing words – *job* vs *work*

I can talk about jobs and work.

SHOW WHAT YOU KNOW

1 In pairs, complete the jobs with the suffixes *-er, -or, -ian, -ist* or *-ant*.

build**er**	account__	doct__	electric__
flight attend__	hairdress__	shop assist__	swimming instruct__
reception__	scient__	politic__	plumb__

2 Which jobs would you like/not like to do? Why?

3 In pairs, look at the photos and read the job characteristics. Who do you think is happy (☺), OK (😐) or unhappy (☹) in their job? Why?

4 **CD·3.1 MP3·88** Listen and check your ideas. According to Lena and Albert, what is the secret of a happy job?

WHAT MAKES YOU HAPPY IN YOUR JOB?

What is the happiest job in the world? We want to find out what makes people happy in their work. Is it a big salary? A nice office? Or is it more than that?

We asked six people in different jobs what they like and what they don't like about their jobs.

Lena

a hairdresser
• works **long hours**
• is on her feet all day
• is **badly paid**
• makes people happy

Anna

a nurse
• works long hours
• does **shifts**
• helps people
• works in a team
• doesn't earn much

Real life

5 Match the people in Exercise 3 with the things they said.

1 I work for a construction company.

_____

2 I'm a plumber.

3 I work for Citibank.

_____

_____

4 I work in a large hospital.

5 I'm in IT.

_____

6 I work for my father.

_____

6 In pairs, talk about what you think would make *you* happy or unhappy in a job.

Martin

a builder

- does hard physical work
- works with his hands
- works outside
- gets/earns **low wages**
- does **overtime**

Eliza

a banker

- gets/earns a **high salary**
- gets **a pay rise** every year
- gets **a bonus**
- is responsible for a department
- gets very few **days off**

Albert

a plumber

- is **self-employed**
- works **flexible hours**
- works at the weekend
- deals with emergencies
- makes people happy

Justin

a computer programmer

- works **regular office hours**
- gets/earns **an average salary**
- gets **five weeks' paid holiday**
- works from home

Go to WORD STORE 6 page 13.

WORD STORE 6A

7 CD·3.2 MP3·89 Complete **WORD STORE 6A**. Add sentences from Exercise 5 as examples. Then listen, check and repeat.

8 Complete the sentences with prepositions. Then decide if they are true (T) or false (F).

1 Albert works _____ himself. ☐
2 Lena works _____ Microsoft. ☐
3 Eliza works _____ banking. ☐
4 Justin works _____ his brother. ☐
5 Anna works _____ the oil industry. ☐
6 Martin is _____ marketing. ☐

WORD STORE 6B

9 CD·3.3 MP3·90 Complete **WORD STORE 6B**. Complete the diagram with the words in red in the text. Then listen, check and repeat.

10 Choose the correct options.

1 Who *does / takes* shifts?
2 Who doesn't *take / work* many days off?
3 Who *earns / does* low wages?
4 Who *earns / does* overtime?
5 Who *gets / works* a bonus?
6 Who *works / takes* flexible hours?
7 Who *gets / works* a pay rise every year?
8 Who *does / is* self-employed?

11 Answer the questions in Exercise 10 about the people in the text.

WORD STORE 6C

12 CD·3.4 MP3·91 Complete **WORD STORE 6C** with *job* or *work*. Then listen, check and repeat.

13 Complete the questions with *job* or *work*. Then, in pairs, ask and answer the questions.

1 Do you have a part-time _____ ?
2 What time do most people start _____ in your country?
3 Have you ever applied for a holiday _____ ?
4 Would you like to _____ for a foreign company?
5 Do either of your parents _____ from home?
6 Do you know anybody who has a really good _____ ?

6.2 Grammar

Second Conditional

I can talk about imaginary situations.

1 In pairs, discuss how students can earn money in your country. Make a list of part-time jobs. Which jobs would you like/not like to do? Why?

2 Do the quiz. Choose the answers that are best for you and find out what your ideal part-time job is.

Your ideal part-time job

1 If I had a day off tomorrow, I'd spend it with a friend. We'd

A go swimming. **B** watch DVDs at home. **C** go shopping.

2 If I won the lottery, I'd give some money to a charity. I'd choose

A Free Sport for Everyone. **C** Love Eco Fashion.
B Save the Children.

3 If I had to describe myself in six words, it would be easy. I'd say

A I love walking by the sea. **C** I like spending time in shops.
B I want to help other people.

4 If I needed money, I'd get a part-time job

A in a sports centre. **B** at home. **C** in a shop.

5 If I was super rich, I'd live in a big house

A near a beach. **B** with all my family. **C** in the city centre.

What your answers mean

Mainly As = Your ideal part-time job is outside, possibly something connected with sport, e.g. a lifeguard or a skiing instructor.

Mainly Bs = You would be good at caring for people, e.g. a babysitter or a carer for elderly people.

Mainly Cs = Your ideal part-time job is in retail, e.g. a shop assistant or a beautician.

3 Read the GRAMMAR FOCUS. Then complete the examples with the Second Conditional forms in blue in the quiz.

GRAMMAR FOCUS

Second Conditional

- You use the **Second Conditional** to talk about the present or future result of an imaginary situation.

imaginary situation →	result
***If* + Past Simple,**	***would/wouldn't* + verb**

If I [1]_________ a day off tomorrow, I [2]_________ it with a friend.
(But I don't have a day off tomorrow, so I won't spend it with a friend.)

If I was super rich, I'd live in a big house.
(But I'm not super rich, so I don't live in a big house.)

Note:

- ***'d = would***
- ***If I/he/she/it were** …* is more formal than ***If I/he/she/it was** …*
  If he were rich, he wouldn't work. If I were you, I'd get a job.

4 Complete the Second Conditional sentences with the correct form of the verbs in brackets.

1 If everybody _________ (go) to university, nobody _________ (want) to do manual jobs.
2 There _________ (not be) so much traffic if more people _________ (work) from home.
3 Family relationships _________ (improve) if parents _________ (take) more time off work.
4 If people _________ (retire) at fifty, there _________ (be) more jobs for young people.
5 The world _________ (be) a better place if everybody _________ (have) a job.

5 Rewrite these real situations as imaginary situations. Use the Second Conditional.

1 I don't have a part-time job, so I don't earn any money.
2 I don't earn any money, so I don't go out.
3 I don't go out, so I don't meet new people.
4 I don't meet new people, so my life is boring.
5 My life is boring, so I'm not happy.
6 I'm not happy, so I need a part-time job.

6 Complete the gaps with the correct form of the verbs in brackets. Then finish the sentences to make them true for you.

1 If I _wanted_ (want) advice about getting a job, *I'd ask my uncle.*
2 If I _________ (need) to borrow money, I …
3 If I _________ (can) work anywhere in the world, I …
4 If I _________ (not have) a phone, I …
5 If I _________ (be) an animal, I …
6 If I _________ (not have to) study, I …
7 If today _________ (be) the last day of my life, I …

7 In pairs, write questions about the situations in Exercise 6. Then ask and answer the questions.

A: *If you wanted advice about getting a job, who would you ask?*
B: *I'd ask …*

Grammar Focus page 117

Multiple choice

I can identify specific detail in short conversations and monologues.

airline pilot

1 In pairs, look at the photos. What kind of person do you have to be to do these jobs? Use the adjectives in the box or your own ideas.

> ambitious   brave   caring   clever
> energetic   kind   practical   responsible
> sensible   serious

EXAM FOCUS Multiple choice

2 CD·3.5 MP3·92 Listen to three short recordings. Choose the correct picture (A, B or C) for each recording.

1 What is the woman's job?

A

B

C

2 Why did the girl's dad get a new job?

A

B

C

3 What do you need to do the woman's job well?

A

B

C

3 CD·3.6 MP3·93 Listen to a conversation between Sophie and her aunt. Are the statements true (T) or false (F)?

1 Aunt Mary doesn't want Sophie to become an airline pilot. ☐

2 Sophie hasn't been to university yet. ☐

3 Aunt Mary doesn't enjoy her job and wants to change. ☐

4 Aunt Mary is already a captain. ☐

5 Aunt Mary doesn't think it's a good career for women with children. ☐

childminder

electrician

4 In pairs, complete the sentences about airline pilots with the words in the box. Then think of one more job for each of the characteristics.

> degree   eyesight   home   off   people   training

Airline pilots:

1 must do long and expensive _____ .

2 need a university _____ .

3 have to get on well with _____ .

4 must have excellent _____ .

5 have to spend a lot of time away from _____ .

6 can't choose when they take time _____ .

PRONUNCIATION FOCUS

5 CD·3.7 MP3·94 Listen and repeat. Underline the stressed syllable in each word.

1 journalist   receptionist   specialist

2 beautician   electrician   musician

3 carpenter   instructor   interpreter

4 engineer   photographer   secretary

6 Which word in each group has one more syllable than the other words?

WORD STORE 6D ›››

7 CD·3.8 MP3·95 Complete WORD STORE 6D. Complete the diagram with the words in the box to make job titles. Use your dictionary if necessary. Then listen, check and repeat.

6.4 Reading

Multiple choice

I can understand the main points in short emails, notices and adverts.

1 In pairs, discuss these popular sayings about money. Which ones do you agree or disagree with?

 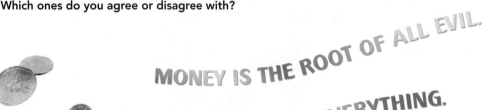 

MONEY IS THE ROOT OF ALL EVIL.

MONEY ISN'T EVERYTHING.

MONEY MAKES THE WORLD GO ROUND.

MONEY DOESN'T GROW ON TREES.

2 Read a text about a man who lived for a year without money. Which sayings do you think he would agree with?

3 In pairs, find at least six changes Boyle made to his lifestyle. Which changes would be possible or impossible for you? Why?

4 Read the text again. Are the statements true (T) or false (F)?

1 Mark Boyle <u>discovered</u> that he hated living without money.

2 He went to college in his <u>own country</u>, Ireland.

3 He wants people to offer their time, knowledge and <u>abilities</u> at a cheap price.

4 He <u>solved the problem</u> of how to manage the basics of life.

5 He lived in a tent, which <u>was given</u> to him for free.

6 He thinks that people <u>unnecessarily throw away</u> lots of food.

5 Find words or phrases in the text to replace the underlined words and phrases in Exercise 4.

1 discovered – *found out*

2 own country – _____

3 abilities – _____

4 solved the problem – _____

5 was given – _____

6 unnecessarily throw away – _____

6 Complete the sentences so they are true for you. Then compare with a partner.

1 My grandparents' native country is …

2 I'd like to learn or improve the following skills: …

3 I find it difficult to work out …

4 I think people waste a lot of …

5 If I don't know something, I find out the information by …

EXAM FOCUS Multiple choice

7 Read the three texts below and choose the correct answer, A, B or C.

1 A Angie sent the wrong website address.

 B Leo has read and likes the article.

 C Leo can't check the website address in Angie's email.

2 A People should take food to a main Food Bank.

 B People can give food inside supermarkets.

 C People should stop buying tins and pasta.

3 In the leaflet there is advice about

 A throwing less food away.

 B different types of energy.

 C how to pay energy bills.

1

To: Angie
From: Leo
Subject: Moneyless man article
Could you resend me the website for the article you recommended? I copied it down wrong and deleted your email! It sounds really interesting!

2

Instead of buying food you don't use, why don't you donate some tins and packets of pasta to our Food Bank for local people who need it? We collect at all supermarkets in the area. You'll find us just inside the main doors.

3

Take a leaflet to find out how YOU can waste less food and energy. Work out your daily energy bill using our easy calculations. You'll be amazed!

WORD STORE 6E

8  Complete WORD STORE 6E. Add *up* or *out* to make phrasal verbs from the article. Then listen, check and repeat.

Moneyless man

CD·3.9 MP3·96

Imagine living for a whole year without money: no cash, no credit cards, nothing. How would you manage? Where would you live? What would you eat? Businessman Mark Boyle did it and he found out that it wasn't so bad after all. In fact, he loved it.

So why did Mark Boyle decide to give up money?

The beginnings of 'Freeconomy'

Living without money was not his original plan. At college in his native Ireland he studied for a degree in Business. His plan was to get a good job and earn as much money as possible. But during his final year at college, he saw a film called *Gandhi* and heard the words that changed his life: 'Be the change you want to see in the world.'

The change that Boyle wanted to see in the world was for people to be less dependent on money. So he set up the Freeconomy Community. Its aim is for people to share their time, knowledge and skills without exchanging money. There are over 40,000 members of the community, in more than 160 different countries.

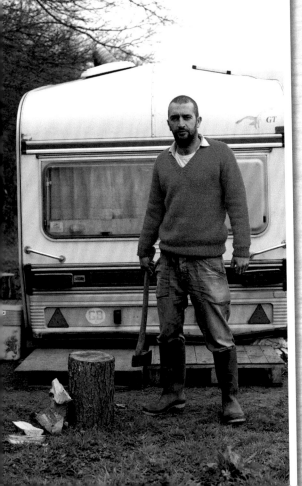

A year without cash

Then Boyle realised that if he wanted money to be less important to people, he should try to live without it. So he decided to live for a year without cash. He knew it wouldn't be easy, so he bought three things: a solar panel, a wood-fired stove and a bicycle. Then he worked out how to manage the basics of life: food, shelter, washing, transport and social life.

For food, he grew his own vegetables and picked wild fruit, leaves and nuts in the forest. He also found food in bins outside supermarkets.

For shelter, he lived in a caravan, which was donated by a member of the Freeconomy Community. He didn't have electricity, so he used candles in the evening and read books that he borrowed from the library.

For washing, he used a solar-powered shower. He cleaned his teeth using fennel seeds from the forest and a pack of toothbrushes that he found in a supermarket bin. His toilet was a hole in the ground and he used old newspapers as toilet paper.

He cycled everywhere and kept fit by doing push-ups every morning.

He didn't miss television at all: he found lots of ways to have fun without spending any money. He went to free art exhibitions, cinema nights and music events. He wrote a blog and answered emails on his solar-powered computer.

The Freeconomy philosophy

At the end of a year without money, Boyle felt fitter and happier than ever. This quote from his book entitled *The Moneyless Man* sums up his philosophy:

> **If we all had to grow our own food, we wouldn't waste forty percent of it as we do today. If we made our own tables and chairs, we wouldn't throw them out the moment we changed the interior décor. If we had to clean our own drinking water, we wouldn't contaminate it.**

6.5 Grammar

Modal verbs for obligation and permission

I can express obligation and permission.

1 In pairs, look at the saying and discuss what it means. What kind of jobs do you think it describes?

> **YOU DON'T HAVE TO BE CRAZY TO WORK HERE, BUT IT HELPS.**

2 CD·3.11 MP3·98 Listen to three people talking about their jobs. Choose the correct options.

1 Jonnie is in *the food industry / IT.*
2 Erica works for *a fashion magazine / a clothes shop.*
3 Sam works *in an office / from home.*

3 CD·3.11 MP3·98 Choose the correct options verb. Then listen again and check.

- He ¹*doesn't have to / has to* wear the company T-shirt.
- He ²*can / can't* eat at his desk.
- He ³*must / mustn't* take his laptop into the canteen.

1 Jonnie

- She ⁴*has to / doesn't have to* work very long hours.
- She ⁵*needs to / doesn't need to* wear designer clothes or a suit.

2 Erica

- He ⁶*needs to / doesn't need to* get up early.
- He ⁷*can / can't* go for a run when he wants a break.
- He ⁸*must / mustn't* remember to have a shave before his conference call tonight.

3 Sam

4 Read the GRAMMAR FOCUS. Then complete the table with the modal verbs in blue in Exercise 3.

GRAMMAR FOCUS

Modal verbs for obligation and permission

You use **must**, **need to**, **have to** and **can** to express obligation and permission.

Necessary	Not necessary	Permitted	Not permitted
• have to/ has to	• don't have to/ ² _____	• ³ _____	• can't
• need to/ ¹ _____	• don't need to/ doesn't need to/needn't		• ⁴ _____
• must			

Note:

You usually use **have to** (not *must*) and **can't** (not *mustn't*) to talk about rules or arrangements:

I have to (NOT ~~must~~) *work long hours.* BUT
I must (NOT ~~have to~~) *remember to shave.*

5 Complete the sentences with *mustn't* or *needn't*.

1 a You ___needn't___ rush – you've got plenty of time.
  b You ___mustn't___ rush – it's important to be 100 percent accurate.
2 a You _____ go – you can stay if you want.
  b You _____ go – we haven't finished yet.
3 a You _____ tell her – it's a secret between you and me.
  b You _____ tell her – she already knows everything.
4 a You _____ eat that – you can leave it if you want.
  b You _____ eat that – it's really bad for you.

6 Complete the questions with *have to* or *can*. Then write answers that are true for you.

1 _Do you have to_ wear a uniform?
2 _____ call your teachers by their first name?
3 _____ use your mobile phone in class?
4 _____ take end of term tests in each subject?
5 _____ change classrooms for each lesson?
6 _____ leave school before you are eighteen?

7 Write two sentences, one with *has to* and one with *doesn't have to* for each job. Use the phrases in the box.

> be fit   be good at Maths   have a degree
> have a driving licence   have good eyesight
> speak English   wear a uniform   work at the weekend

1 police officer
A police officer has to wear a uniform.
A police officer doesn't have to be good at Maths.
2 secondary school teacher
3 bus driver
4 airline pilot
5 accountant
6 tourist guide

8 Think of three people you know with different jobs and write sentences about their jobs, like the ones in Exercise 7. Then, in pairs, take turns to tell your partner about each person.

Grammar Focus page 117

6.6 Speaking

Asking for and giving advice

I can ask for and give advice about jobs and solving problems.

1 In pairs, read *UK TODAY* and discuss the questions.

1 What is work experience and why is it useful?
2 If you could do work experience, what would you do and why?

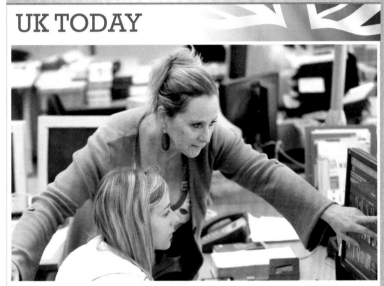

UK TODAY

Did you know that nearly all fifteen- or sixteen-year-old students in the UK do work experience before they leave school?

What is work experience?
• 1–3 weeks off school working full-time for a local employer.

What are the benefits of work experience?
• It teaches useful work skills.
• It makes you think about possible careers.
• It develops self-confidence and communication skills.

2 `CD·3.12` `MP3·99` Listen to Nick and Lisa talking about work experience. Are the statements true (T) or false (F)?

Lisa   Nick

1 Nick enjoyed doing work experience. ☐
2 He doesn't think you can learn much from other employees. ☐
3 He isn't sure that Lisa's father will accept her plans. ☐

3 `CD·3.12` `MP3·99` Listen again and tick the expressions you hear.

SPEAKING FOCUS

Asking for advice

What do you think I should do? ☐
Do you have any tips on how to …? ☐
Do you have any ideas about how to …? ☐

Giving advice

You should … ☐
I think you should … ☐
I don't think you should … ☐
Why don't you …? ☐
My best advice would be to … ☐
It's a good idea to … ☐
If I were you, I'd … ☐

Accepting advice

Thanks, that's really helpful. ☐
That's great advice. Thanks! ☐

Rejecting advice

I'm not sure that's a good idea. ☐

4 Match the sentence halves to make useful advice to somebody preparing for a job interview.

1 I think you should ☐
2 I don't think you should ☐
3 My best advice would ☐
4 It's a good idea ☐
5 If I were you, ☐

a be nervous.
b do some research.
c be to be on time.
d I'd just be yourself.
e to prepare some questions.

5 `CD·3.13` `MP3·100` Listen and check. Then listen and repeat.

6 Look at the statements and think about the advice you would give in each case. Make notes.

1 I want to stay fit.
2 It's my mother's birthday soon.
3 I need some new clothes but I haven't got any money.
4 I want to watch a good film.
5 I can't wake up in the mornings.

7 In pairs, follow the instructions.

Student A: Choose a problem from Exercise 6 and tell Student B about it.

Student B: Give Student A some advice. Use your notes from Exercise 6 and the SPEAKING FOCUS to help you.

79

6.7 Writing

An email/A letter of application
I can apply for a summer job.

1 Read the job advert and answer the questions.

1 What kind of job is it advertising?
2 Is it a permanent job?
3 Is it a well-paid job?
4 How old do you have to be to apply?
5 What characteristics should the candidate have?
6 What are the working hours?

ARE YOU LOOKING FOR A
summer job?

Johnson's Builders requires

an office helper – €10 per hour

Are you
sixteen or over? • reliable and hard-working?
friendly and willing to learn?
We offer
excellent conditions • flexible hours
a chance to learn office skills

No previous experience necessary!

---

2 If you saw this job advert in your local paper, would you be interested? Why?/Why not? Discuss in pairs.

3 Imagine you want to apply for the job. Tick five pieces of information you should include in your letter of application.

1 Say where you saw the advert. ☐
2 Say what you are doing now. ☐
3 Say how you intend to spend your salary. ☐
4 Give reasons why you are interested in the job. ☐
5 Mention your CV and any relevant work experience. ☐
6 Say why you liked or didn't like previous jobs. ☐
7 Say when you are available for an interview. ☐
8 Warn them not to call you at certain times. ☐

4 Read the letter and check your ideas in Exercise 2. Then cross out the three sentences in the letter which are not appropriate.

Dear Sir or Madam,

With reference to your advertisement in yesterday's *Devonshire Times*, I would like to apply for the position of part-time office helper. At the moment, I am in my final year at school and I will be available to start work from 1 June. I really need this job because I want to earn some money to go on holiday.

I am particularly interested in your company because I hope to study Architecture at university. I enclose my CV for your information. As you will see, I worked on a building site last summer. It was a bit hard, but I got a really good suntan.

I do not have much experience of office work, but I am a fast learner. I have good communication skills and I enjoy working as part of a team. For these reasons, I feel I would be a suitable candidate for the job you are advertising.

I can be available for interview at any time. I have listed my contact details on my CV. Please don't call me before ten o'clock in the morning.

I look forward to hearing from you.

Yours faithfully,

Richard Dawson

Richard Dawson

---

5 Complete the WRITING FOCUS with the words in purple in the letter.

WRITING FOCUS
An email/A letter of application
• Say where you saw the advert.
  I am writing in response to your advertisement in/
  With ¹_reference_ to your advertisement in …
• Say why you are writing.
  I am writing to express my interest in the position of/
  I would like to ²_____ the position of …
• Say what you are doing now.
  Currently, I am/At ³_____ , I am …
• Give reasons why you are interested in the job.
  I found your advertisement very interesting because/
  I am ⁴_____ your company because …
• Mention your CV and any relevant work experience.
  My experience includes/I worked for … as …/
  I ⁵_____ for your information. As you will see,
  I worked …
• Give reasons why you are suitable for the job.
  I would be a suitable candidate for the job because …/
  ⁶_____ , I feel I would be a suitable candidate
  for the job you are advertising.
• Say when you are available for an interview.
  I can be available for interview ⁷_____ .

6 Complete the sentences from a letter of application with phrases from the WRITING FOCUS.

1 I am writing with _____ on our school website.

2 I _____ interview after 17 July or any weekend.

3 My _____ working in a restaurant for two months last summer.

4 I _____ interesting because I would like to work outside.

5 I _____ candidate for the job because I learn very quickly.

6 I am writing to _____ the position of receptionist.

7 Read the advert and some sentences from different candidates. Are the people right (R) or wrong (W) for the job?

> # WILD WEST
> # SUMMER CAMPS
>
> require
>
> ## CAMP SUPERVISORS
>
> Do you love outdoor life and camping?
>
> We need friendly, outgoing young people with lots of energy and some knowledge of English.
>
> You must know how to swim.
>
> Experience with children and knowledge of first aid an advantage.
>
> **HAVE A GREAT SUMMER, IMPROVE YOUR ENGLISH AND EARN SOME MONEY AT THE SAME TIME!**
>
> Please apply to Ross Field, ross@wwsc.net.

1 I enjoy outdoor sports and games.

2 I got good results in my English exams.

3 I like the countryside, but I don't particularly like sleeping in tents!

4 I'd like a job in March or April.

5 I swim five times a week and I'm very fit.

6 I haven't worked with children before, but I think I'd be good at it.

7 I'm good at planning things, although I'm a bit shy with people.

Writing task

You have seen the advertisement in Exercise 7 in the *International Student Times* and want to apply for the job. Write a letter of application for the job.

A Write your letter in 80–130 words. Include these points.

- Say where you saw the advertisement.
- Say what you are doing now and give reasons why you are interested in the job.
- Mention your CV and any relevant work experience.
- Say when you are available for an interview.

B Use the ideas in the WRITING FOCUS and the model to help you.

C Check.

- ✓ Have you mentioned all the points in the question?
- ✓ Have you used the correct opening and closing for a formal letter?
- ✓ Have you used phrases from the WRITING FOCUS?
- ✓ Have you divided your letter into paragraphs?
- ✓ Have you used linking words where appropriate?
- ✓ Have you checked your grammar and spelling?

VOCABULARY AND GRAMMAR

1 Complete the sentences with words about work. The first letter of each word is given.

1 My sister is an **o**_____ **a**_____ . She answers phones and takes messages.
2 My dad is a **c**_____ . He loves working with wood.
3 My parents usually take some **t**_____ **o**_____ in the summer so we can all go on holiday together.
4 People who earn a **h**_____ **s**_____ should give more money to charity.
5 My brother has started a **p**_____-**t**_____ job in the evenings to earn some extra money.

2 Complete the sentences with the correct form of the words in capitals.

1 Once a year the company pays a bonus to its best _____ . **EMPLOY**
2 Tim is a _____ – he plays the guitar in a band. **MUSIC**
3 _____ work with their hands. They need to be fit and strong. **BUILD**
4 My sister is doing a course on make-up. She wants to become a _____ . **BEAUTY**
5 A taxi _____ has to know the city well. **DRIVE**

3 Complete the Second Conditional sentences with the correct form of the verbs in brackets.

1 If Tom _____ (earn) low wages, he _____ (look) for a new job.
2 If you _____ (can) work for any company, which company _____ (you/like) to work for?
3 If I _____ (be) you, I _____ (take) this job.
4 She _____ (give) lots of jobs to young people if she _____ (be) a successful businessperson.
5 If I _____ (wear) these glasses, everyone _____ (laugh) at me.

4 Complete the second sentence using the word in capitals so that it has a similar meaning to the first. Do not change the word in capitals.

1 I'll let you take an extra day off. **CAN**
   You _____ an extra day off.
2 Don't buy Zara a gift – we've sent her some flowers. **NEEDN'T**
   You _____ – we've sent her some flowers.
3 I mustn't forget my mum's birthday this year. **REMEMBER**
   I _____ my mum's birthday this year.
4 I have to get to work on time this morning. **LATE**
   I _____ for work this morning.
5 Go out for awalk – don't just study all day. **SHOULDN'T**
   Go out for a walk – you _____ all day.
6 Is it necessary to have a degree to be a computer programmer? **HAVE**
   _____ have a degree to be a computer programmer?

LANGUAGE IN USE

5 Choose the correct answer, A, B or C.

1 Alan _____ and he's tired in the evenings.
   A works with his hands   C work part-time
   B works short hours
2 I'm writing _____ the advertisement on your website.
   A because   B to apply for   C in response to
3 We could work in the garden if _____ sunny.
   A it was   B it will be   C it's
4 John is a lifeguard, but this summer he's going to work as a camp _____ .
   A carer   B babysitter   C supervisor
5 This is your desk, but you _____ come to the office every day – it's OK to work from home sometimes.
   A shouldn't   B needn't   C mustn't

6 Read the text and choose the correct answer, A, B, C or D.

JACOB'S DREAM JOB

Is it really possible to find your dream job? Jacob Wilder, nineteen, has done just that. Jacob has always loved music, so he was very happy when he got the opportunity to work ¹_____ a music company. It is three years later now and he works full-time as a music promoter.

'If I ²_____ choose any job in the world, it would be the job I have right now,' says Jacob. 'I am well-paid and the people I work with are great. Plus, I ³_____ dress smartly. I can wear what I want.'

There are disadvantages to his job, of course. Jacob needs to travel around the world. It is exciting, but also tiring and it means Jacob often works ⁴_____, sometimes until three or four o'clock in the morning.

At the age of nineteen, Jacob already has three years' work ⁵_____. But does he mind not going to university? 'Not really,' he says. 'I have worked hard, and I have my own car and my own flat. If I was at university, I ⁶_____ have all that now.'

1	A to	B for	C on
2	A will	B would	C could
3	A mustn't	B shouldn't	C don't have to
4	A shifts	B long hours	C from home
5	A experience	B travel	C education
6	A wouldn't	B don't	C won't

LISTENING

7 `CD•3.14` `MP3•101` **Listen to a conversation between a teenage girl and her uncle. Are the statements true (T) or false (F)?**

1 Leia only knows one male nurse. ☐
2 Jon's friends have always taken his profession seriously. ☐
3 Jon is satisfied with his salary. ☐
4 Sometimes Jon starts work at night. ☐
5 Jon has been promoted to nurse manager. ☐

WRITING

8 **You are going to write a story. Read the title of the story and think about what you are going to write. In pairs, discuss the questions.**

A TERRIBLE DAY AT WORK

1 What's your job?
2 When was the terrible day?
3 What happened first?
4 What happened next?
5 How did you feel?
6 Did you learn anything from this day? What?

9 **Write your story in about 100 words.**

SPEAKING

10 **Complete the questions with the words in the box. There are two extra words. Then, in pairs, ask and answer the questions.**

> boss   ever   kind   never   office   overtime

1 What _____ of job do you hope to get in the future? Why?
2 Have you _____ worked? Why?/Why not?
3 Would you like to work in an _____? Why?/Why not?
4 Do you think you could be a good _____? Why?/Why not?

11 **The photos show people in situations at work. In pairs, take turns to say what you can see in your photo. Then discuss the questions about each photo.**

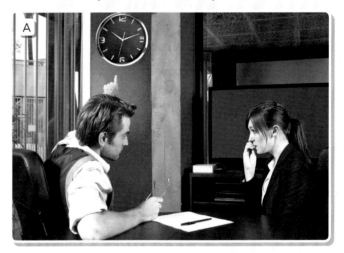

1 How is the woman in the photo feeling? Why?
2 What would you do if you were late for an important exam? Why?
3 Talk about a situation when you or someone you know were late for an important event.

1 In your opinion, why is the woman in the photo sleeping?
2 What would do you if you suddenly felt very tired/sleepy during a lesson?
3 Talk about a situation when you or someone you know felt bored during an important event.

7
SHOPPING

People who say money can't buy you happiness don't know where to go shopping.

ANONYMOUS

7.1 Vocabulary

Shops and services • Partitives • Shopping

I can talk about shops and shopping.

SHOW WHAT YOU KNOW

1 **Complete the sentences with the words in the box.**

> bread   clothes   meat   newspapers
> pet   shoe   toy   vegetables

1 You buy toys for your dog at a _____ shop.
2 You buy _____ at a butcher's.
3 You buy _____ at a newsagent's.
4 You buy _____ at a baker's.
5 You buy toys and games at a _____ shop.
6 You buy _____ at a greengrocer's.
7 You buy shoes and sandals at a _____ shop.
8 You buy shirts and skirts at a _____ shop.

2 **Look at the photos and read the text. What three things can you do in the Mall of America that you can't usually do in a shopping mall?**

3 **In pairs, discuss where you can do these things in your city.**

MALL OF AMERICA

THE MALL

THE CHAPEL

Shopping malls used to be indoor shopping centres, especially popular in the USA. But some of the biggest shopping malls around the world are much more than shopping centres – they're a way of life! Take the Mall of America in Bloomington, Minnesota. You can buy **trainers**, **toiletries**, **light bulbs** and **plants**, have a **manicure** before lunch and then you can have a ride in the **theme park**, watch hundreds of sharks in the **aquarium** or spend an afternoon at the **cinema**. Oh, and you can add 'get married' to your shopping list. There's even a **wedding chapel**!

4 CD·3.15 MP3·102 Listen to five people giving their opinion about shopping malls. Match speakers 1–5 with their opinions a–e.

ADVANTAGES

a ☐ It doesn't matter what the weather is like.
Parking is easy.
You don't need cash.

b ☐ There is something for everybody.

c ☐ You can spend all day there.
Everything is in the same place.

DISADVANTAGES

d ☐ Most things are too expensive.
All malls are the same.
There are too many designer shops.

e ☐ They take business away from small shops.
There are no windows in the restaurants.

5 In pairs, discuss your opinions about shopping malls. Which advantages or disadvantages in Exercise 4 do you agree with?

THE AQUARIUM

THE THEME PARK

Go to **WORD STORE 7** page 15.

WORD STORE 7A ►►►

6 CD·3.16 MP3·103 Complete WORD STORE 7A with the words in red in the text. Then listen, check and repeat.

7 Complete the questions with the correct form of the words from WORD STORE 7A. Then, in pairs, ask and answer the questions.

When was the last time you:
1 bought a pair of _____ ?
2 changed a _____ ?
3 had a scary ride in a _____ ?
4 bought some perfume or other expensive _____ ?
5 posted a parcel at the _____ ?
6 used a _____ to clean a rug or a carpet?

WORD STORE 7B ►►►

8 Speaker 1 in Exercise 4 talked about the advantages of a shopping mall. Complete her sentence with the words in the box. There are two extra words.

bottle   bunch   can   jar   packet   pair

'I can buy a ¹_____ of shampoo, a ²_____ of biscuits, a new ³_____ of skis and a ⁴_____ of flowers for my mum, all in the same place.'

9 CD·3.17 MP3·104 Complete WORD STORE 7B with the words in the box in Exercise 8. Then listen, check and repeat.

10 Complete WORD STORE 7B with the words in the box.

bananas   beans   crisps   mayonnaise
mineral water   scissors

WORD STORE 7C ►►►

11 CD·3.18 MP3·105 Complete WORD STORE 7C with the underlined phrases in the questions. Then listen, check and repeat.

1 Do you ever go window shopping? How often?
2 When do shops usually have a sale in your country?
3 When did you last buy something on special offer?
4 Where can you pick up a bargain? Name shops.
5 When was the last time you thought 'I'd love to buy that but I just can't afford it'?
6 If you don't keep your receipt, is it still possible to take something back to a shop and get a refund?

12 In pairs, ask and answer the questions in Exercise 11.

The Passive

I can use passive forms to talk about trade and processes.

1 In pairs, discuss the questions.

   1 Who usually does the shopping in your family?

   2 What food products do you and your family buy every week?

   3 Which of these things are important when you buy food?

     • the quality   • how it is produced

     • where it is produced   • a fair price

2 Read the text about Fairtrade. Why is it good for farmers, consumers and the environment?

WHAT IS FAIRTRADE?

Many of the products we buy in supermarkets are grown by farmers in developing countries. But often farmers aren't paid enough to make a living.

So the idea of 'fair trade' has been around for many years. When you see the Fairtrade Mark on a product, you know that the farmers have been paid a fair price for their crops. You also know that they have been given extra money –

the Fairtrade premium. This can be used by farmers to develop their businesses, invest in their communities or protect the environment.

In 1997, many organisations from different countries came together and one international Fairtrade organisation was formed. So far, the lives of approximately seven million people in developing countries have been improved by Fairtrade.

3 Read the GRAMMAR FOCUS. Then underline all the passive verb forms in the text.

GRAMMAR FOCUS

The Passive

You use passive forms when it isn't important to know (or you don't know) who performed the action. Passive verbs have the same tenses as active verbs.

The Passive: be + past participle

  + *Fairtrade products are grown in developing countries.*

  – *Fairtrade products aren't grown in developed countries.*

  ? *Where are Fairtrade products grown?*

4 Look at Exercise 2 again. Complete the examples below with the the passive forms in blue in the text.

Present Simple

Active

People don't pay farmers enough.

Passive

Farmers ¹_____ enough.

Past Simple

Active

In 1997, somebody formed one international Fairtrade organisation.

Passive

In 1997, one international Fairtrade organisation ²_____ .

Present Perfect

Active

Fairtrade has improved the lives of approximately seven million people in developing countries.

Passive

The lives of approximately seven million people in developing countries ³_____ by Fairtrade.

5 Read the text and choose the correct options.

Chocolate & Fairtrade

Last year more than one billion kilos of chocolate ¹*ate / was eaten* around the world. Chocolate ²*makes / is made* from the cacao plant. However, many cacao farmers ³*don't earn / aren't earned* enough money and ⁴*can't afford / can't be afforded* food, medicine or clean water. In Africa, a typical cacao grower ⁵*pays / is paid* less than a dollar a day. Now Fairtrade is helping farmers to get fair prices. Farming organisations ⁶*have set up / have been set up* in African countries and the extra money ⁷*invests / is invested* in projects such as drinking water.

6 Complete the sentences with the correct passive form of the verbs in brackets. Use the Present Simple, Past Simple or Present Perfect.

  1 My house _____ (build) fifty years ago.

  2 My name _____ (not pronounce) the same in English.

  3 My shoes _____ (make) in Italy.

  4 My school _____ (open) in the 1990s.

  5 I _____ (never/stop) by the police.

  6 Fairtrade products _____ (not sell) in my country.

  7 The new chocolate bar _____ (not introduce) yet.

  8 Rubbish _____ (collect) in our area every Wednesday and Friday.

Grammar Focus page 118

True/False

I can identify details in an interview.

1 In pairs, discuss the questions about presents.

   1 Have you ever given or received a present like the ones in the photos?

   2 What is the best or worst present you've ever received?

face cream

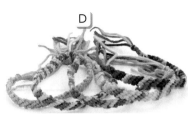
a friendship bracelet

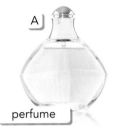
perfume

time in a recording studio

a bunch of flowers

a game console

a tablet

a purse

2 [CD·3.19] [MP3·106] Listen to a radio interview about buying presents. Which presents from the photos are suggested for each person?

   1 Isabelle's mum ☐

   2 Alexander's girlfriend ☐ , ☐

   3 Charlotte's classmate ☐

3 Read the statements in Exercise 4. Match the underlined phrases with these phrases from the interview.

can buy ☑2	cheer her up ☐
classmates ☐	is a question of ☐
it isn't the value of the present	
that matters ☐	

EXAM FOCUS True/False

4 [CD·3.19] [MP3·106] Listen again. Are statements 1–5 true (T) or false (F)?

   1 Amy thinks the ability to choose good presents <u>is a matter of</u> personality. ☐

   2 Amy thinks both men and women <u>are capable of buying</u> good presents. ☐

   3 Isabelle thinks her mother is upset about being forty, so she wants to <u>make her feel happier</u>. ☐

   4 Charlotte wants to buy a nice expensive gift for one of her <u>school friends</u>. ☐

   5 Amy says that <u>a successful present doesn't have to cost a lot of money</u>. ☐

5 Complete the advice with the verbs in the box. Which piece of advice is NOT given in the interview?

be	collect	do	don't spend	keep	spend

   1 _____ some research.

   2 _____ time thinking about the person.

   3 _____ careful when buying women's toiletries.

   4 _____ lots of money. It isn't necessary.

   5 _____ the receipt so you can take the present back.

   6 _____ money from friends to buy something really good.

6 In pairs, talk about the last time you bought a present for somebody. Think about these questions.

   1 Who was it for?   **4** Why did you buy it?

   2 What was the occasion?   **5** Where did you buy it?

   3 What did you buy?   **6** How much did it cost?

PRONUNCIATION FOCUS

7 [CD·3.20] [MP3·107] Listen and identify the silent letter in each word.

   1 recei(p)t   (p)sychology

   2 write   wrong

   3 debt   doubt

   4 island   aisle

   5 know   knife

   6 listen   castle

8 [CD·3.20] [MP3·107] Listen again and repeat.

WORD STORE 7D

9 [CD·3.21] [MP3·108] Complete WORD STORE 7D. Match the verbs and nouns in the boxes to make collocations. Then listen, check and repeat. Write an example sentence for each collocation.

Multiple choice

I can find specific detail in an article.

1 Look at the colour chart. In pairs, take turns to tell each other about these things.

- colours you like
- colours you don't like,
- colours you associate with the words in the box.

> ecology   elegance   energy
> fun   loyalty   passion   royalty
> young boys   young girls

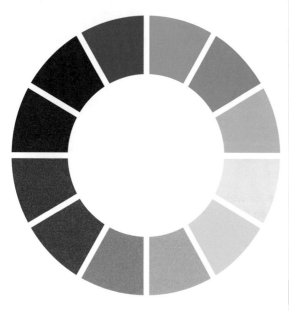

2 Read the text. Which colour associations are the same as your ideas in Exercise 1?

3 Match 1–6 with a–f to make questions.

1 What do you have to pay attention ☐
2 Which colour would you use to attract ☐
3 How can you get customers to trust you ☐
4 If you don't use purple with ☐
5 If you want to focus ☐
6 Why is it no ☐

a with their credit card details?
b care, what can happen?
c surprise that Amazon use the colour orange?
d to in today's market?
e on pre-teen girls, which colour is best?
f somebody's attention?

4 In pairs, discuss the questions in Exercise 3.

Colours and the consumer
by Tim Roberts

CD·3.22 **MP3·109**

In today's competitive market, shops need to pay attention to the colours they use to attract customers. All colours are associated with different emotions, so they have to choose them carefully. Here's a brief outline of the effect of
5 different colours on the typical consumer.

Red

Red is the colour of extremes and strong emotions: passion, danger and anger. It's associated with speed and excitement, so it's no surprise that red is the most popular colour for sports cars. It is the most noticeable colour in
10 the spectrum, so it's used for everything that wants to attract our attention in a hurry, such as warning signs on the road and fire engines. This is why you often see 'SALE' signs in red. The colour red makes your heart beat faster and attracts people who buy things on impulse.

Blue

15 Blue is the colour of security, loyalty and honesty. This is why it's used by so many banks. If blue is used on a website, customers will trust the site with their credit card details. Blue is a calm, relaxing colour, often used to attract careful customers rather than impulse buyers. When blue lighting was installed on the streets of Glasgow, crime fell dramatically.

20 Green

Green has always been the colour of growth and nature. Now it has become the symbol of ecology and the environment. This is why it's often used on food packaging. There are different shades of green and it's a colour that has to be chosen carefully. Light green is fresh and eco-friendly, while dark
25 green may be associated with negative emotions such as jealousy and greed. In western cultures, green is a lucky colour.

Purple

Since Roman times, purple has been associated with royalty. It suggests magic and mystery, wealth and luxury. Expensive anti-aging beauty products
30 are often packaged in purple, especially to attract the older and wealthier customers. Shops must use purple with care – it can easily look old-fashioned.

Yellow

Yellow is the colour of youth, happiness
35 and creativity. Bright and cheerful, yellow is
a colour that makes people feel energetic. If a shop
window has yellow in it, customers will be attracted to
the shop.

Pink

40 Pink is the colour of pre-teen girls. For products
that focus on this age group and gender, pink is the
colour that shops always choose. Pink suggests love,
friendship and kindness. While red is passionate, pink
is romantic and sweet.

45 ## Orange

Children love orange. It's fruity and fun. In shops it
may suggest that a product is economical or cheap.
It's no surprise that it's the colour of cheap airlines like
easyJet and the online bookstore Amazon.

50 ## Colour combinations

Red and yellow are used for logos by McDonald's,
Burger King and Kentucky Fried Chicken. It's difficult
to see this combination without thinking of fast food.
However, black and white suggest elegance and was
55 chosen by Chanel for their branding.

5 Read the text again. For questions 1–6, choose the correct answer, A, B, C or D.

1 Red is used for warning signs because it is the most
   A dangerous.
   B exciting.
   C visible.
   D impulsive.

2 What is people's attitude to the colour blue?
   A It makes them do things more carefully.
   B It makes them feel safe.
   C It makes them report crimes.
   D It makes them decide to buy things quickly.

3 Which colour is not associated with positive feelings?
   A light blue
   B dark green
   C purple
   D bright yellow

4 What do yellow, pink and orange have in common?
   A They appeal to younger people.
   B They have to be used carefully.
   C They are rarely used in advertising.
   D They are associated with happiness and fun.

5 An advert with red and yellow
   A makes you think of fast food.
   B can cause confusion.
   C is better than black and white.
   D helps customers understand your product.

6 This article is
   A a report on which colours consumers prefer.
   B one person's subjective opinion.
   C a summary of how colours can influence the consumer.
   D a guide for shops on how to improve their sales.

6 Choose the correct options. Then, in pairs, ask and answer the questions.

1 When was the last time you were in a *hurry / speed*?
2 Are you *a sudden / an impulse* buyer or do you plan your shopping?
3 What makes your heart *beat / hit* faster?
4 What sort of shops are you attracted *with / to*?
5 Do you think you are a *typical / usual* consumer?
6 How often do you eat *quick / fast* food?

7 In pairs, discuss the questions.

1 How many famous brands or logos can you think of?
2 What colours do they use?
3 Which logo do you think is the most recognisable?

WORD STORE 7E ⟫⟫⟫

8 CD•3.23 MP3•110 **Complete WORD STORE 7E. Add nouns to the table. Mark the stress. Then listen, check and repeat.**

7.5 Grammar

Quantifiers

I can understand countable and uncountable nouns and use appropriate quantifiers.

1 In pairs, discuss the questions.

    1 Which of these types of shoes have you got?
- pumps
- boots
- flip flops
- high heels
- sandals
- trainers

    2 Which are your favourite shoes? Why?

    3 When was the last time you bought a pair of shoes?

2 Read the text. What happens when you buy a pair of TOMS shoes?

Do you have **too many pairs** of shoes? **How many pairs** do you need? Most people have **a few pairs** of trainers, some smart shoes, a pair of boots and **some sandals**. But can you imagine living without **any shoes** at all?

Blake Mycoskie was shocked when he found out that **a lot of children** around the world were growing up without **any shoes**. So he set up a company called Shoes for Tomorrow (TOMS). Every time he sells a pair, he gives a pair of new shoes to a child in need. He doesn't have to do **much advertising** – when people hear about TOMS, they tell one another. Over the years, he's given **lots of shoes** to people in need – more than a million, in fact. TOMS has become the One for One™ company who give eyewear as well as shoes to people around the world. With **a little imagination** and **a lot of hard work**, Mycoskie has transformed the lives of a lot of people.

3 Look at the nouns and quantifiers in blue in Exercise 2. Which of the underlined nouns are countable and which are uncountable?

4 Read the GRAMMAR FOCUS and complete it with *countable* or *uncountable*.

GRAMMAR FOCUS

Quantifiers

You use different expressions to talk about quantity:

- With ¹_____ nouns you use:
  very few/a few/too many/how many?

- With ²_____ nouns you use:
  very little/a little/too much/how much?

- With both ³_____ and ⁴_____ nouns you use:
  any/some/a lot of/lots of

Note:
Usually, you use *a few*, *a little* or *some* in affirmative sentences and *many*, *much* or *any* in negative sentences and questions.

5 Read the text and choose the correct quantifiers.

FAQ

Q: How did TOMS begin?

A: When Blake Mycoskie was twenty-nine, he took ¹*a little / a few* time off work to go travelling. He met a charity worker, and she told him how ²*much / many* children in developing countries were without shoes. This gave Mycoskie an idea for a shoe company and a way to help ³*some / any* of these children.

Q: How ⁴*much / many* difference can a simple pair of shoes make to so ⁵*much / many* children's lives?

A: A pair of shoes can make ⁶*many / a lot of* difference to a child. Firstly, there are ⁷*lots of / a little* diseases in the soil and shoes protect children. Secondly, ⁸*very few / very little* schools allow children to attend classes without shoes. So shoes help children to get an education.

6 Complete the sentences with the correct Present Simple form of the verbs in brackets.

    1 There _____ (be) lots of shoe shops near here.

    2 A lot of people _____ (do) their shopping online.

    3 There _____ (be) a lot of pollution in our city.

    4 A lot of fast food _____ (be) bad for you.

    5 Lots of shops _____ (be) closed on Sundays.

    6 A lot of people in my country _____ (know) about TOMS.

7 Read REMEMBER THIS. Then rewrite the sentences in Exercise 6 replacing *a lot of/lots of* with *very little* or *very few*.

    1 There are very few shoe shops near here.

REMEMBER THIS

little money = not much money
few friends = not many friends
BUT
a little money = some money
a few friends = some friends

8 Make these sentences negative using *not much* or *not many*. On a typical school day, which sentence – affirmative or negative – is true for you?

    1 I eat a lot of bread. → I don't eat much bread.

    2 I send a lot of texts. → _____

    3 I drink a lot of water. → _____

    4 I do a lot of homework. → _____

    5 I spend a lot of money. → _____

    6 I talk to a lot of people. → _____

9 In pairs, ask and answer questions about your typical school day. Use *How much ...?* or *How many ...?* with the topics in Exercise 8 and the topics in the box.

> do exercise   get sleep   have lessons
> listen to music   spend time online   watch television

    A: How much bread do you eat?

    B: Lots. How about you?

    A: Very little. I don't like bread.

Grammar Focus page 118

7.6 Speaking

Shopping and making complaints
I can buy things in a shop and make complaints.

1 In pairs, talk about shopping in your area. Which shop is:
- the cheapest/most expensive?
- the most/least fashionable for clothes?
- the one with the most/least helpful shop assistants?

2 Match the customers' comments (a–g) with the situations (1–5).

a Get it. It really suits you.

b Oh no! They've sold out.

c They're on offer – buy one and get one free.

d I'm just looking, thanks.

e Look, it's half price!

f It's not exactly what I'm looking for.

g It's reduced from £50 to £19.99.

1 The item is on special offer. ☐ , ☐ , ☐
2 The colour and style are perfect. ☐
3 The item is not quite right for you. ☐
4 The item is out of stock. ☐
5 You don't want the shop assistant to bother you. ☐

3 [CD•3.24] [MP3•111] Look at the pictures and listen to two conversations. Which conversation are words a-h linked to? Write *1* or *2*.

a complain ☐   e ripped ☐
b dress ☐   f size 12 ☐
c receipt ☐   g zip ☐
d present ☐   h top ☐

4 [CD•3.24] [MP3•111] Complete the SPEAKING FOCUS with the words in the box. Then listen again and check.

> changing   fit   help   how
> looking   receipt   refund   size

SPEAKING FOCUS

Shopping for clothes

Shop assistant
- Can I ¹_____ you?
- Would you like to try it on?
- The ²_____ rooms are over there.
- ³_____ would you like to pay?
- Make sure you keep your receipt.

Customer
- Excuse me, I'm ⁴_____ for a top.
- I'm a ⁵_____ 10.
- Do you have this in a size 12, please?
- I'll take it.
- Cash, please./By credit card.
- If it doesn't ⁶_____ , can we get a refund?

Making complaints

Shop assistant
- What's wrong with it?
- Do you have your ⁷_____ ?
- We can exchange it for a new one.

Customer
- I bought this dress last week, but the zip doesn't work.
- I think it's faulty./It shrank./There's a hole in it./The colour ran.
- I'd like a ⁸_____ , please.

5 In pairs, follow the instructions to prepare a conversation. Use the SPEAKING FOCUS to help you.

Student A: You are a customer returning a faulty pair of jeans. Say when you bought the jeans and explain what is wrong with them (colour ran/they shrank).

Student B: You are a shop assistant. Ask Student B if he/she has a receipt. Suggest a solution to the problem (refund/repair/new pair of jeans).

6 Practise your conversation. Then act it out to the class.

Conversation 1

Conversation 2

7.7 Writing

An email/A letter of complaint
I can make a polite written complaint.

1 In pairs, tick any problems that you, your family or your friends have had when buying something. Tell your partner about them.

1 The product was past its sell-by date. ☐
2 It didn't work. ☐
3 It was broken or damaged. ☐
4 Some parts were missing. ☐
5 The service was bad. ☐
6 The delivery was late. ☐
7 The product was different from the description. ☐
8 It was the wrong product. ☐

2 Read email 1 and answer the questions.

1 Which problems from Exercise 1 did the customer have?
2 Is this a polite written complaint? Why?/Why not?

> **1**
>
> I can't believe you've sent me another pair of headphones that don't work. These headphones are rubbish! When I called about the first pair that didn't work, the person on the phone was very unhelpful. The second time, he was rude. I think he's in the wrong job – he shouldn't be in contact with the public. He needs to do a course in people skills.
>
> Anyway, he told me to write to the head office. I found that annoying, but I did it and you sent a replacement. Guess what – they're damaged and they don't work! I want my money back now – and I will never use your company again.
>
> Ronnie

3 Read the tips in the WRITING FOCUS. Which tips does email 1 *not* follow?

WRITING FOCUS

An email/A letter of complaint

- Open and close the email or letter politely.
- Give a reason for writing.
- Say what you bought and when.
- Explain the problem, giving details.
- Tell the reader what you expect them to do.
- Use polite language.
- Do not use contractions.

4 Read email 2. Underline examples for each of the tips in the WRITING FOCUS.

> **2**
>
> Dear Sir or Madam,
>
> I am writing to complain about the service provided by your company.
>
> I bought a pair of headphones (Model: SA-DIV-RED) from your website on 3 March. They arrived the next day, but when I tried them, they did not work, so I returned them to you on 5 March and you exchanged them. Unfortunately, the second pair you sent were the wrong model, so I emailed you again and sent them back one more time. I received a pair of headphones from you today, but when I unpacked them, I found they were damaged and they do not work.
>
> I am very disappointed with your service. I do not want another pair of headphones from your company. I would be grateful if you could send me a full refund for the headphones and the cost of sending them back to you three times.
>
> Yours faithfully,
>
> R. Barker

5 Complete the phrases in the Useful language box with the words in the box.

> afraid   complain   disappointed   grateful
> please   sir   unfortunately   yours

Useful language

1 Dear _____ or Madam,
2 I am writing to _____ about my new smartphone.
3 I am _____ I have a complaint to make.
4 _____ , the second phone you sent me did not work either.
5 I am very _____ with this phone.
6 I would be _____ if you could replace it.
7 Could you _____ refund my money?
8 _____ faithfully,

6 Rewrite the sentences so that they are polite.

1 I want the phone replaced!
2 This phone is useless!
3 I want a refund.
4 Your service is rubbish!

7 You have recently bought a product which doesn't work. Here are some notes you have started for the written complaint you want to make about the product. Add one or two sentences to each note. Use the phrases in the Useful language box.

To: Mr Jarvis
_____

Problem: new printer doesn't work
_____

Date bought: 15 February
_____

Previous complaint: emailed him ten days ago
_____

Action required: refund
_____

From:
_____

Writing task

Read the information and the message from a customer below, sent to an online music store. Imagine you are the customer and write an email of complaint to the store.

Contact	Customer Services	Returns	FAQ's

CONTACT US

Select a category: choose from the drop-down menu.

Please tell us the type of problem you are experiencing:

- My download won't complete.
- This is not the music I wanted.
- My file won't play.
- The quality of the sound is low.
- I deleted the file by mistake.

Comment

I want to complain about your service. I have tried to download Adele's album '21' three times this month, but every time the download has not completed. I've contacted you three times on 1, 8 and 17 April. I've been a loyal customer for two years and I've enjoyed the music I've bought each month from your site. But now I want a refund of my last month's subscription. Please close my account.

`SEND`

A Write your email in 80–130 words. Include these points.

- Give a reason for writing.
- Say what you bought and when you bought it.
- Explain the problem and give details.
- Tell the person what you expect them to do about the problem.

B Use the ideas in the WRITING FOCUS and the model to help you.

C Check.

- ✓ Have you included all the points in the question?
- ✓ Have you used polite language?
- ✓ Have you opened and closed your email correctly?
- ✓ Have you organised your email into paragraphs?
- ✓ Have you checked your grammar and spelling?

VOCABULARY AND GRAMMAR

1 Cross out the word in each group which cannot be used with the container.

1 a packet of   *tea / biscuits / cake / crisps*
2 a bunch of   *bananas / grapes / bread / flowers*
3 a pair of   *clothes / skis / scissors / jeans*
4 a bottle of   *water / jam / milk / shampoo*
5 a can of   *cola / tomatoes / beans / cheese*
6 a jar of   *jam / bananas / instant coffee / mayonnaise*

2 Complete the sentences with the correct form of the words in capitals.

1 Don't be _____ ! You've already had three cakes. **GREED**
2 _____ is an important quality. We all need friends we can depend on. **LOYAL**
3 I hope they'll _____ the prices in the sale. **REDUCTION**
4 Have you packed all your _____ ? What about toothpaste and shampoo? **TOILET**
5 There's far too much food _____ . I throw so much plastic away. **PACK**
6 This top is really pretty. Why don't you try it on in the _____ room? **CHANGE**

3 Complete the second sentence so that it has a similar meaning to the first.

1 They built the house in 2013.
The house _____ in 2013.
2 They didn't ask me any questions.
I _____ any questions.
3 They have sold over 1,000 bikes so far this year.
Over 1,000 bike bikes _____ so far this year.
4 You pronounce it the same way in English.
It _____ the same way in English.
5 He painted more than 100 pictures in this studio.
More than 100 pictures _____ in this studio.
6 When did they open their first shop?
When _____ ?

4 Choose the correct answer, A, B, C or D.

1 'How ____ purses do you own?' 'Just one.'
A any   B few   C much   D many
2 There are ____ different colours in that advert. It's difficult to read.
A a lot of   B lots   C a little   D lot
3 'I'm so hungry.' 'I have ____ biscuits in my bag. Would you like one?'
A very little   B a few   C too much   D any
4 I think I've eaten ____ chocolate. I feel sick.
A too many   B lots of   C too much   D a little
5 Do you need ____ help?
A a few   B very little   C many   D any
6 I'm sorry, I've got ____ money to give you.
A very little   B too many   C very few   D any

LANGUAGE IN USE

5 Choose the correct answer, A, B or C.

1 There _____ supermarkets in my neighbourhood.
A is little   B aren't much   C are few
2 If you haven't got money for an expensive jacket, you should try to ____ .
A pick up a bargain   C do some research
B have a sale
3 When Mary goes shopping, she ____ attention to prices.
A pays little   B never holds   C doesn't attract
4 Excuse me, I'm looking for a T-shirt. ____
A I'm 38.   B I'm a size 38.   C It's in a size 38.
5 If this dress doesn't fit, can I get a ____ ?
A receipt   B refund   C bonus

6 Read the text and choose the correct answer, A, B or C.

Kara's part-time job

Kara, eighteen, has an unusual part-time job. During the week she is a student at university, but at weekends she is a mystery shopper. What does this mean? One day she buys a bottle ¹____ perfume, another day she goes for a meal in a restaurant. She fills in a form about the shop or restaurant and a report ²____ to the company's office. This is how the shop or restaurant gets suggestions about how they could improve, to keep customers happy.

'It's the perfect job for me,' explains Kara. 'I love going shopping, even if it's just ³____ shopping. It's nice to eat in elegant restaurants from time to time as I don't have ⁴____ money for food.' Kara has to send her report within twenty-four hours and she ⁵____ at the end of each month.

Mystery Magic, the company that employs Kara, says mystery shoppers must be reliable, have a good memory and most importantly, they must be ⁶____ . 'Mystery shoppers must be fair,' explains one of the company's managers. 'If they tell a lie or exaggerate, we won't use them again.'

1 A with   B of   C full
2 A has sent   B sends   C is sent
3 A looking   B list   C window
4 A much   B many   C few
5 A must pay   B pays   C gets paid
6 A creative   B honest   C mysterious

READING

7 Read the text and choose the correct answer, A, B, C or D.

PINK

If you go shopping in any toy shop, you can see clearly the different games and toys for boys and girls: there are a lot of pink princesses and dolls on one side of the shop for girls; and dark-coloured cars, guns and soldiers for boys. Some bigger shops with toys may even have a separate pink floor for girls and a blue floor for boys. In fact, it is difficult to buy a toy for a girl that is not pink.

Some people think that a lot of pink is bad for girls. Also, Sue Palmer, author of *Toxic Childhood*, admits that she is very worried about this. She believes that most girls over the age of three are crazy about the colour. According to some psychologists, this happens for two reasons. Firstly, because most companies offer too many products in pink. But parents can be blamed too, as many think their little daughter looks cute in a pink outfit. Sue Palmer says that girls at this age cannot make rational decisions, but the pink can affect the choices and the decisions they will make in the future.

Some parents are concerned too – for example, Vanessa Holburn, thirty-two, who has two girls under the age of four. Their bedrooms are a sea of pink and Vanessa is not happy. 'Pink says that you are soft and gentle. Blue says that you are strong and powerful. I want my daughters to be strong and powerful. I'm worried that pink will not help them with that,' she says.

But not everyone thinks there's something wrong with pink. Grayson Turner is a father of three girls and he isn't worried at all. 'People forget that things change all the time,' he says. 'My girls used to love pink when they were little, but as they get older, they change.' Turner explains that his twelve-year-old daughter never wears pink clothes anymore. 'This love of pink is just a fashion and all fashions change,' he adds. 'It's only since the 1940s that people have started dressing girls in pink – before that it was a colour for boys.'

1 According to the text, toys for boys

   A are usually very similar to toys for girls.

   B cost about the same as toys for girls.

   C are as attractive as toys for girls.

   D are usually very different from toys for girls.

2 Vanessa Holburn thinks that boys' toys

   A should be soft and gentle.

   B help boys become strong.

   C aren't good for three-year-olds.

   D shouldn't be blue.

3 According to Grayson Turner,

   A parents should not worry so much about pink toys.

   B not all little girls love the colour pink.

   C pink has always been a popular colour.

   D his girls now prefer the colour blue.

4 The writer wants to

   A recommend a book by Sue Palmer.

   B make girls stop playing with pink toys.

   C present different opinions about the colour.

   D explain why parents should worry about the colour.

SPEAKING

8 Your sister is going to stay with an English teenage girl for the summer holidays. She wants to buy a present for the girl. In pairs, talk about the different presents she could buy and then decide which would be best.

WRITING

9 Match the products (1–4) with the possible problems (a–d). Then add one more problem for each product.

1 a box of chocolates ☐   **a** Some pages are missing.

2 a book ☐   **b** The sound quality is bad.

3 a pair of jeans ☐   **c** They are past their sell-by date.

4 an MP3 player ☐   **d** They shrank after the first wash.

10 Read the writing task and choose one of the products from Exercise 9 to write about.

You recently bought a product from an online shop. The shop had assured you that you would receive the product within two days, but you had to wait longer. When you opened the package, it turned out there was a problem with the product as well. Write an email of complaint to the online shop. Include these points.

* Explain what you bought and when.
* Complain about the delay in receiving the parcel.
* Describe the problem with the product.
* Suggest a way to solve the problem.

11 Write your email in 80–130 words.

8 SOCIETY

Ask not what your country can do for you; ask what you can do for your country.

JOHN FITZGERALD KENNEDY (1917–1963), A US PRESIDENT

UNIT LANGUAGE AND SKILLS

Vocabulary:
• *Show what you know* – politics
• crime and criminals; the justice system
• people involved in a crime case
• antonyms
• word families

Grammar:
• Past Perfect
• Reported Speech

Listening:
• an interview about lie-spotting

Reading:
• a text about the American Civil Rights Movement

Speaking:
• expressing and justifying an opinion

Writing:
• a reader's comment

FOCUS EXTRA

• Grammar Focus page 119
• WORD STORE booklet pages 16–17
• Workbook pages 92–103 or MyEnglishLab

8.1 Vocabulary

Politics • Crime • The justice system • Society
I can talk about crime and punishment.

SHOW WHAT YOU KNOW

1 Complete *UK TODAY* with the words in the box.

> capital   crime   elections   head
> minister   monarchy   population   United

UK TODAY

1 The <u>United</u> **Kingdom:** England, Wales, Scotland and Northern Ireland
2 _____ : 65 million
3 _____ **city:** London
4 **Political system:** constitutional _____
5 _____ **of state:** the Queen (of course!)
6 **Head of government:** the prime _____
7 **General** _____ : every five years
8 **Interesting fact:** Nobody is further than 120 km from the sea.
9 **Surprising fact:** It rains more in Milan than in London.
10 **Young people's worries:** youth unemployment, the environment, _____

2 Write a similar fact file for your own country.

3 Read the text and label the crimes in photos A–F with the words in red in the text.

4 Read the text again. Which crimes are growing, falling or staying the same in number?

5 Which of the crimes mentioned in the text are a problem in your country?

UK crime trends

In the past burglars used to break into houses to steal TVs and DVD players. But electronic goods are so cheap now that burglary has become less and less common.

Thieves are more interested in stealing small personal items like mobile phones and iPods that people carry with them. So there has been a fall in the number of house burglaries and robberies, but the number of muggings and mobile phone thefts has grown. Shoplifting and drug dealing crimes have grown, just like Internet crimes such as hacking and online piracy.

Murder rates haven't changed much and car crimes remain high: one in three reported crimes is a car theft. In the UK, a car is stolen every twenty-five seconds! Other crimes such as vandalism and arson have fallen.

WORD STORE 8A ❯❯❯❯❯

6 `CD·3.25` `MP3·112` Complete WORD STORE 8A with the base form of the words in red in the text. Then listen, check and repeat.

7 `CD·3.26` `MP3·113` Listen to six conversations and write the crime they refer to.

1 _____   3 _____   5 _____
2 _____   4 _____   6 _____

8 Imagine you have to report a crime. Choose the correct options.
1 Somebody has *robbed / stolen* my phone.
2 My apartment has been *stolen / burgled*.
3 Some youths have *set fire to / mugged* a shop.
4 My sister has been *vandalised / mugged*.
5 There's a man in my store. He's *shoplifting / burgling*.
6 My neighbour has just *murdered / stolen* his wife.

9 In pairs, discuss which three crimes in WORD STORE 8A are the most serious. Give reasons for your answers.

WORD STORE 8B ❯❯❯❯❯

10 Read two crime stories. Why are the crimes described as crazy?

CRIMINALS COMMIT CRAZY CRIMES

A suspect was arrested for robbing a jewellery store on Saturday afternoon. The suspect told police that he was **innocent**. He said that he couldn't be **guilty** of robbing the jewellery store because on Saturday afternoon he was breaking into a school and he had a witness to prove it. The police immediately arrested him for robbing the school. The **case** goes to court next month.

A thirty-year-old man was arrested for **vandalising a campsite**. In **court**, the judge heard how the police caught the criminal. 'It was easy,' the police officer said. 'There was no victim. We didn't have to interview any witnesses or collect any **evidence**. The man wrote his name on a wall!' The man was **sentenced** to three months in **prison**.

11 `CD·3.27` `MP3·114` Complete WORD STORE 8B with the words in red in the crime stories in Exercise 10. Then listen, check and repeat.

WORD STORE 8C ❯❯❯❯❯

12 `CD·3.28` `MP3·115` Complete WORD STORE 8C with the underlined words in the crime stories in Exercise 10. Then listen, check and repeat.

Past Perfect

I can use the Past Perfect to talk about past events.

1 Read the story. Does it have a happy ending?

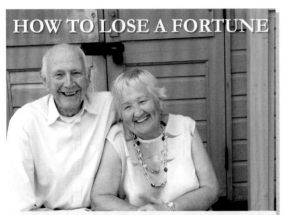

HOW TO LOSE A FORTUNE

An elderly man donated some things to a charity shop, including an old suitcase. He didn't know that his wife had hidden their life savings – over $100,000 – in a pocket inside the suitcase! He contacted the charity shop, but they had already sold the suitcase. Luckily, the shop found the buyers through their credit card details. However, the buyers had put the money into different bank accounts and, understandably, they didn't want to give it back. After a court case, which lasted several months, the elderly couple finally got their money back.

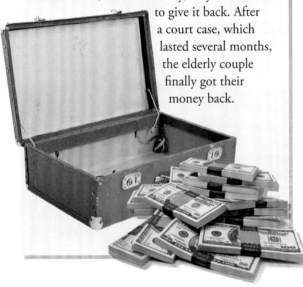

2 Read the story again and put the events a–g in chronological order 1–7.

a The old man donated the suitcase. ☐
b The old man's wife hid the money. ☐ 1
c The shop found the buyers. ☐
d The old man contacted the shop. ☐
e The elderly couple got their money back. ☐
f The shop sold the suitcase. ☐
g The buyers put the money into different bank accounts. ☐

3 Read the GRAMMAR FOCUS and answer the questions.

1 How do you form the Past Perfect?
2 When do you use it?

GRAMMAR FOCUS

Past Perfect

You use the **Past Perfect** to talk about the earlier of two actions in the past.

He contacted the shop, but they had already sold the suitcase.

past ←————————————————→ present

Past Perfect: had + past participle

+ *I had ('d) worked.*
– *He had not (hadn't) worked.*
? *Had they worked?*
  Yes, they had./No, they hadn't.

4 Underline all the examples of the Past Perfect in the text in Exercise 1.

5 Look at the sentence pairs. In each sentence, underline the action that happened first.

1 a When I got home yesterday, <u>my mum had made dinner</u>.
  b When I got home yesterday, my mum made dinner.
2 a When I got to school this morning, I had breakfast.
  b When I got to school this morning, I'd had breakfast.
3 a This lesson started when I arrived.
  b This lesson had started when I arrived.

6 Complete the sentences with the correct Past Simple or Past Perfect form of the verbs in brackets.

1 Dave suddenly _____ (remember) that he _____ (not lock) his apartment.
2 When the police _____ (arrive) at the house, the burglar _____ (disappear).
3 The police _____ (arrest) a man after they _____ (search) his apartment.
4 Julie _____ (not recognise) the suspect because he _____ (grow) a beard.
5 Sophie _____ (feel) nervous because she _____ (not appear) in court before.
6 The crime scene _____ (be) covered in water. What _____ (happen)?
7 When she _____ (get) home, the police _____ (already/call) her three times.
8 They _____ (live) there for many years before they _____ (find out) the terrible truth.

7 Look at the example and write six similar Past Perfect sentences about you. Use verb phrases from the box or your own ideas.

By the age of six, I had learnt how to swim.

> buy/get my first phone/laptop/bike
> go to the capital city/a foreign country/a live concert
> learn how to read/swim/ski

Grammar Focus page 119

Multiple choice

I can identify specific detail in an interview.

1 `CD•3.29` `MP3•116` **Complete the expressions about body language in the pictures with the words in the box. Then listen, check and repeat.**

> arms   eyebrows   eyes
> hair   nails   ~~something~~

1 stare at *something*

2 bite your _____

3 cross your _____

4 raise your _____

5 fiddle with your _____

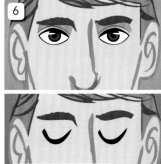

6 blink your _____

2 **Which types of body language from Exercise 1 do you think can show a person is lying? Discuss in pairs, giving reasons for your answers.**

3 `CD•3.30` `MP3•117` **Listen to an interview with expert 'lie spotter' Martin Johnson and answer the questions.**

1 Which type of body language from Exercise 1 shows that a person is lying?
2 What other things do liars do or say?
3 How many lies does an average person tell in a day?

EXAM FOCUS Multiple choice

4 `CD•3.30` `MP3•117` **Listen again. For questions 1–6, choose the correct answer, A, B or C.**

1 Martin Johnson became interested in the subject of lying when
  A he started working for the police.
  B he was at university.
  C he was in business.

2 A genuine smile affects
  A the sides of your mouth.
  B your whole face.
  C your eyes only.

3 Liars often
  A look you in the eyes for too long.
  B look at your mouth.
  C look out of the window.

4 What is also true about liars?
  A They don't give you much information.
  B They tell you about their home.
  C They give you too much detail.

5 Men and women
  A lie for different reasons.
  B are always honest about how they look.
  C never lie to teenagers.

6 Martin Johnson
  A isn't employed to identify serious lies.
  B has written a book about lying.
  C has got a very boring job.

5 **Write three things about you – two true and one false. In pairs, take turns to read the information to your partner. Can he/she spot which is a lie?**

PRONUNCIATION FOCUS

6 `CD•3.31` `MP3•118` **Listen and repeat.**

Diphthong	Example
1 /ɪə/	*ear*
2 /eɪ/	_____
3 /ʊə/	_____
4 /ɔɪ/	_____
5 /əʊ/	_____
6 /eə/	_____
7 /aɪ/	_____
8 /aʊ/	_____

7 `CD•3.32` `MP3•119` **Complete the table in Exercise 6 with the words in the box. Then listen, check and repeat.**

> ear   eye   face   hair
> mouth   nose   sure   voice

WORD STORE 8D ▶▶▶

8 `CD•3.33` `MP3•120` **Complete WORD STORE 8D. Add words to the table. Mark the stress. Then listen, check and repeat.**

8.4 Reading

True/False

I can find specific detail in an article.

1 Look at the pictures and complete the captions with the names in the box. Check the meaning of the underlined words in a dictionary.

> Abraham Lincoln   Africans   Barack Obama   Billie Holiday
> Martin Luther King   the Civil Rights Movement

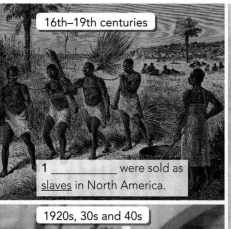

16th–19th centuries

1 _____ were sold as slaves in North America.

1920s, 30s and 40s

3 _____ and other famous black singers sang about racism.

1865

2 _____ ordered an end to slavery.

1950s and 60s

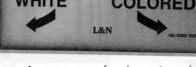

REST ROOMS
WHITE   COLORED
L&N

4 _____ fought against segregation.

1964

5 _____ got the Nobel Peace Prize for his work against racial discrimination.

2008

6 _____ became the first African American president of the USA.

2 CD•3.34 MP3•121 Listen to the beginning of a class presentation about Martin Luther King and check your answers to Exercise 1. Then answer the questions.

1 How long did slavery exist in North America?
2 Who led the Civil Rights Movement?
3 Why was the election of Barack Obama so significant?

3 Read the text about the American Civil Rights Movement. What happened on these dates?

> 1865   1870   1955
> 1963   1964   1968

EXAM FOCUS True/False

4 Read the text again. Are statements 1–6 true (T) or false (F)?

1 African Americans started fighting for their rights in 1955. ☐
2 Black American men were allowed to vote for the first time a few years after slavery ended. ☐
3 In the 1950s it was impossible for black and white people to sit together in a restaurant. ☐
4 Linda Brown couldn't go to her neighbourhood school because she wasn't white. ☐
5 Rosa Parks was arrested for sitting next to a white man on a bus. ☐
6 Martin Luther King made over 3,000 speeches in the thirteen-year period before his death. ☐

5 Match 1–6 with a–f to make compound nouns from the text. Then find an example sentence for each one in the text or write your own.

1 African ☐   a transport
2 civil ☐   b trade
3 human ☐   c rights
4 public ☐   d race
5 slave ☐   e Court
6 Supreme ☐   f American

African Americans became citizens of the USA after the end of slavery.

6 Do you think Martin Luther King's dream is now a reality anywhere in the world? Discuss in pairs.

WORD STORE 8E ▶▶▶▶▶

7 CD•3.36 MP3•123 Complete WORD STORE 8E with the appropriate nouns and verbs. Mark the stress. Then listen, check and repeat.

THE AMERICAN CIVIL RIGHTS MOVEMENT

CD·3.35 MP3·122

The African American Civil Rights Movement took place in the USA between 1955 and 1968. But African Americans had fought for freedom and justice for many years before that.

⁵ **The need for a Civil Rights Movement**

In 1865 Abraham Lincoln declared the end of slavery. After this African Americans became full citizens of the USA and in 1870 men were given the right to vote. However, in the first half of the twentieth century racism against the black ¹⁰community was a huge social problem. In the 1950s racial segregation still existed: black people couldn't attend the same schools as white people; black and white people were separated on trains and buses and in other public areas such as restaurants and movie theaters.

¹⁵**Two key events**

In the early 1950s in Kansas, a young black girl, Linda Brown, applied to a school near her house, but she wasn't accepted. Instead, she had to travel a long way to a black-only school. She became famous when her father fought against the local Board ²⁰of Education. Finally, the US Supreme Court agreed to stop segregation in public schools. Their victory helped all black children to get a better education.

In 1955 a forty-two-year-old black woman, Rosa Parks, sat near the front of a crowded bus in Alabama and refused to give up ²⁵her seat to a white man. Police were called and Rosa was put in prison. Rosa's actions inspired the black community to support the Civil Rights Movement. With Martin Luther King as their leader, they refused to use public transport for more than a year, until segregation on buses was stopped.

civil rights protests

Rosa Parks

³⁰**Dr. Martin Luther King Jr.**

Martin Luther King was one of the leaders of the Civil Rights Movement. He said, 'We are tired of being segregated and humiliated.'

He believed that all men and women, black or white, ³⁵are equal members of the human race. Between 1955 and 1968 he travelled over six million miles and made more than 3,000 speeches. In August 1963 he gave his famous 'I Have a Dream' speech at the Lincoln Memorial in Washington, D.C. Over ⁴⁰250,000 people heard him say:

> *I have a dream that my four little children will one day live in a nation where they will not be judged by the color of their skin, but by the content of* ⁴⁵ *their character. I have a dream today.*

In 1964 King was awarded the Nobel Peace Prize for his work to end racial discrimination. Tragically, on 4 April 1968 Martin Luther King was assassinated. He was thirty-nine years old.

Dr. Martin Luther King Jr. at the Lincoln Memorial

Reported Speech

I can report what other people have said.

1 Read this true story and write what happened at these times.

- yesterday
- five years ago
- two weeks ago
- before that

Mystery German forest boy

Yesterday a boy walked out of a German forest. He spoke fluent English and broken German. He told the police that his first name was Ray and he was probably fifteen. He said his father had died two weeks ago and he had buried him in the forest. He also told them that he had lived in the forest for about five years, but he couldn't remember anything about his life before that. The police told reporters that Berlin Youth Services were looking after him until they could find out his identity.

2 Compare these direct statements with the reported statements in blue in the text. What changes have been made to the verb forms and pronouns?

1 'My first name is Ray and I'm probably fifteen.'
2 'My father died two weeks ago.'
3 'I've lived in the forest for about five years.'
4 'I can't remember anything.'
5 'Berlin Youth Services are looking after him.'

3 Read the GRAMMAR FOCUS. Then complete the examples with the correct verb forms.

GRAMMAR FOCUS

Reported Speech

In Reported Speech verb forms and pronouns change depending on the context.

Direct Speech	→	Reported Speech
Present Simple	→	**Past Simple**
'I work,' she said.		*She said she worked.*
Present Continuous	→	**Past Continuous**
'He's working,' we said.		*We said he ¹_____ .*
Present Perfect	→	**Past Perfect**
'We've worked,' he said.		*He said they ²_____ .*
Past Simple	→	**Past Perfect**
'She worked,' they said.		*They said she ³_____ .*

REMEMBER THIS

say (that)
He said his father had died two weeks ago.
tell somebody (that)
He told the police (that) his first name was Ray.

4 Six months later, the Berlin police were interviewed about Ray. Report their statements. Begin with *They said ... .*

1 'We looked everywhere for information about Ray.'
   They said they had looked everywhere for information about Ray.
2 'We put a photo of him in newspapers around Europe.'
3 'His school friends in Holland saw the photo and contacted us.'
4 'We now know that Ray's real name is Robin van Helsum.'
5 'He is going back home very soon.'
6 'His lies have cost the German police over £20,000.'

5 Choose the correct options.

1 My teacher *said / told* me I wasn't concentrating.
2 He *said / told* I looked tired.
3 I *said / told* him that I hadn't slept very well.
4 I *said / told* I had watched a really scary film.
5 I *said / told* him that was why I hadn't done my homework.
6 He *said / told* I'd used that excuse before!

6 Rewrite the sentences in Exercise 5 in Direct Speech.

1 *'You aren't concentrating.'*

7 In pairs, take turns to tell your partner five true things about you. Choose from the box or use your own ideas.

> I am/am not tired.
> I can/can't snowboard.
> I like/don't like politics.
> I've been/haven't been to London.
> I'm going out/not going out tonight.
> I watched/didn't watch TV last night.

8 How many facts can you remember about your partner? Report what he/she said.

A: *You said you could snowboard.*
B: *Yes, that's right.*
A: *You said you liked politics.*
B: *No, I said I didn't like politics.*

Grammar Focus page 119

8.6 Speaking

Expressing and justifying an opinion

I can choose from options and justify my choice.

1 Do you think this anti-drugs poster is effective? In pairs, discuss which of these ideas could be effective in an anti-drug campaign.

- shocking images of drug addicts
- information and facts about the effects of drugs
- information and facts about prison sentences

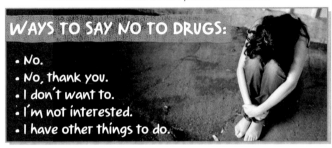

WAYS TO SAY NO TO DRUGS:
- No.
- No, thank you.
- I don't want to.
- I'm not interested.
- I have other things to do.

2 CD·3.37 MP3·124 Listen to Anna and David discussing anti-drugs posters. Who prefers a poster with facts and who prefers one with images?

3 CD·3.37 MP3·124 Read the SPEAKING FOCUS and complete the conversation. Then listen again and check.

A: Have you seen the new anti-drugs poster at the bus stop?

D: No. What's it like?

A: The poster ¹ _shows_ a woman's face. Her skin is white and spotty and her eyes are dead.

D: Do you think it's a good poster?

A: Well, on the one ² _____ , it looks shocking, but on the other ³ _____ , it doesn't look real. I don't ⁴ _____ it very convincing.

D: Hm, I know what you mean. I don't ⁵ _____ posters like that ⁶ _____ they're only shocking the first time you see them. I ⁷ _____ posters that give some information and statistics. I ⁸ _____ it's important to know that you can go to prison for a long time if you use illegal drugs!

A: I ⁹ _____ think statistics are ¹⁰ _____ good as a shocking image. I think the ¹¹ _____ disadvantage of statistics is that you have to stop and read them. Most people don't have time.

D: That's true. The best poster I've seen was a photo of a young guy in prison. He was sentenced to ten years for dealing drugs. To ¹² _____ mind, that was more shocking than a girl's face because it was a true story.

SPEAKING FOCUS

Describing a picture

The poster shows …

On the one hand, …, but on the other hand, …

Justifying your choice and rejecting other options

✓ I prefer …

✗ I don't like … because …

✗ I don't find it very convincing/interesting/shocking, etc.

Giving your opinion

To my mind, …   I think it's important to …

I think the main advantage/disadvantage is that …

I don't think … is/are as good/useful/effective, etc. as …

4 CD·3.38 MP3·125 Look at the posters. What message do they have in common? Listen and number them in the order you hear about them.

A

B

C

5 Your school is organising a campaign about mobile phone theft and the students are going to help choose a poster for it. In pairs, talk about the posters above and decide which would work best for the campaign. Follow the instructions below and use the SPEAKING FOCUS to help you. Then present your choice to the class.

- Say why you like or don't like the posters.
- Say which you think would be best and why.

8.7 Writing

A reader's comment

I can give and support my opinion in writing.

1 Look at the photo. In pairs, talk about graffiti. Is it vandalism or art?

2 Read the article from a news website. How does the writer answer the question in the title?

Newsfocus: daily discussion

Graffiti: Street art or crime?

Yesterday five members of a graffiti gang were sentenced to eighteen months in prison for damaging public property. The judge said that the damage had cost the government at least £1 million. The question must be asked about the people who spray graffiti: are they artists or vandals?

Personally, I believe that street art is a form of art. However, it is illegal to paint on public or private property without permission. Local councils spend millions of pounds each year cleaning graffiti and this means that taxes go up.

For this reason, I agree that the gang of graffiti artists should get prison sentences. When the judge sent the graffiti artists to prison, he gave a clear message to other graffiti artists: you think you are expressing yourself, but you are also committing a crime, and what is more, you could go to prison.

Join the daily discussion and tell us what you think in our *Readers' comments* section below.

daisy345 says: Thank you for your excellent article. I found it interesting because it shows that street art …

3 Complete the WRITING FOCUS with the linkers in purple in the article.

WRITING FOCUS

A reader's comment

When you give your opinion in a piece of writing such as a reader's comment, use linkers to:

- give an opinion: I think that/[1]*Personally, I believe that* …

- add further points: In fact/I also agree that/ I also think that/[2]_____ , …

- give an opposite opinion: On the other hand, I strongly disagree /[3]_____ , …

- conclude: Therefore /So/That's why/ [4]_____ …

4 Read and complete the reader's comment on the article in Exercise 2 with phrases from the WRITING FOCUS. The first letter of each word is given.

daisy345 says: Thank you for your excellent article. I found it interesting because it shows that street art can be called 'vandalism' or 'free expression', depending on your point of view.

[1]P*ersonally*, I b_____ t_____ street art is a form of art. [2]I_____ f_____ , there are some famous street artists who sell their work for a lot of money. I also [3]a_____ t_____ people who do graffiti are committing a crime. On the one hand, I think they should be punished. On [4]t_____ o_____ h_____ , I strongly disagree with your opinion that they should go to prison. These people are not dangerous criminals. They have vandalised public property and [5]t_____ they should clean the graffiti and do community service.

5 Read the reader's comment again and answer the questions.

1 Which two opinions do both writers agree on?
2 Which opinion do they disagree about?
3 Who do you agree with? Why?

6 Match opinions 1–3 with the follow-up sentences a–c.

1 Personally, I believe that people who throw litter in the streets are committing a crime.
2 I strongly disagree with those who say that people who take drugs should go to prison for a long time.
3 I really think that rich people who don't pay their taxes should spend a long time doing some work for their community.

a What is more, I think they should give half their money to charity!
b In my opinion it's the people who *sell* them that should go to prison.
c For this reason, I think they should pay a big fine and have to pick up dirty bags every day for a month.

7 Read the titles for discussion articles below. Write two sentences giving your opinion on each one. Use these phrases.

- Personally, I believe that …
- I strongly disagree that …
- That's true. However, …
- I also think that …
- I agree that …

A
Newsfocus: daily discussion
Hacking isn't a real crime.

B
Newsfocus: daily discussion
Pickpockets should be sent to prison.

C
Newsfocus: daily discussion
Everyone downloads music and films now; it isn't a problem.

Writing task

You have just read the article below on a news website. Write a reader's comment for the website.

Newsfocus: daily discussion
Celebrity shoplifting: crime or illness?

Yesterday a judge sentenced a Hollywood star to six months in prison for stealing jewellery worth $5,000. The celebrity could easily afford to buy the necklace, so the question must be asked: is she a criminal or is she sick?

Personally, I believe that rich people who steal from shops are sick. Shoplifting is like a drug for these people. However, shoplifting is a crime and therefore the celebrity broke the law.

For this reason, I think the judge made the right decision.

> Join the daily discussion and tell us what you think in our *Readers' comments* section below.

A Write your comment in 80–130 words. Include these points.

- Give your opinion on the article.
- Say what you agree with and why.
- Say what you disagree with and why.
- Write your conclusion.

Useful language

- I found the article interesting/boring/controversial.
- I strongly believe that … because …
- Contrary to what was said in the article, I think that …
- I agree/disagree with the opinion in the article.
- Another reason why I disagree/agree is that …

B Use the ideas in the WRITING FOCUS and the model to help you.

C Check.

✓ Have you included all the points in the question?
✓ Have you used linkers from the WRITING FOCUS?
✓ Have you divided your comment into paragraphs?
✓ Have you checked your grammar and spelling?

FOCUS REVIEW 8

VOCABULARY AND GRAMMAR

1 Choose the correct options.

1 The thief *robbed / mugged / stole* my wallet.
2 The police have collected an important piece of *identity / evidence / truth*: a knife covered in blood.
3 Lots of young people don't have jobs and the level of *racism / unemployment / sexism* is still increasing.
4 The *head / capital / major* city of France is Paris.
5 Don't *bite / fiddle / blink* your nails! It's disgusting.
6 A *witness / police officer / judge* decides on sentences in court.

2 Complete the sentences with the correct form of the words in capitals.

1 The _____ tried to hide the DVD under his coat, but a police officer saw him. **SHOPLIFT**
2 Tom faced total _____ when Fern told all their friends about his lies. **HUMILIATE**
3 The _____ got a four-year sentence for setting fire to the department store. **ARSON**
4 Racial _____ is still a big problem in many countries today. **DISCRIMINATE**
5 If you have ever downloaded music illegally, you have committed online _____. **PIRATE**

3 Complete the second sentence so that it has a similar meaning to the first.

1 The police officer chased the criminal for ten minutes, then he caught him.
The police officer _____ the criminal for ten minutes before he _____ him.
2 The thief burgled the flat, then escaped through an open window.
After the thief _____ the flat, she _____ through an open window.
3 Someone stole my purse before I got home.
When I _____ home, I realised that somebody _____ my purse.
4 He spent a year in prison, then his sentence ended.
He _____ a year in prison by the time his sentence _____.
5 Marie robbed ten banks before she was arrested.
Marie _____ after she _____ ten banks.

4 Report the statements.

1 'I feel ill,' said Eva.
Eva said _____.
2 'I've contacted the police, Jon,' said Reece.
Reece told Jon that _____.
3 'I found the weapon in the kitchen,' said the detective.
The detective said _____.
4 'I'm waiting for the court case to end, Tim,' said Jo.
Jo told Tim that _____.
5 'I didn't go out last night,' she said.
She said _____.

LANGUAGE IN USE

5 Choose the correct answer, A, B or C.

1 A: Is the new anti-drugs campaign any good?
B: ____ it's not clear what they want to say.
A To my mind, C On the other hand,
B The main advantage is that
2 A: What will happen if the court decides he ____?
B: He will be able to go home freely.
A has committed a crime C is not guilty
B might be a suspect
3 A: Have the police caught the bank robber?
B: Well, yesterday they said that they ____ the robber for three weeks! Can you believe it?
A haven't seen B didn't see C hadn't seen
4 A: I don't think that community service is a good form of punishment.
B: Why not? I think it's ____ a prison sentence.
A as effective as C less useful than
B important to get
5 A: Did you ask him about the robbery?
B: Yes, but he didn't ____ me the truth. He lied as usual.
A say B tell C speak
6 A: Why did you phone the police?
B: Because when I got back home from Fiji, I realised someone ____ into my house during my holiday.
A broke B was breaking C had broken

6 Choose the correct option, A, B or C, to complete both sentences.

1 Burglars ____ into shops and houses.
People who ____ the law should be punished.
A enter B break C commit
2 I can't read this ____. His handwriting is difficult to read.
The prime minister got a two-year ____ for corruption.
A letter B decision C sentence
3 I'm sure she'll just ____ her arms and get really angry when she hears the news.
To get to the police station, you have to ____ the bridge and then turn left.
A cross B follow C raise
4 She could swim ____ the age of three.
It's common to judge people ____ the way they look.
A before B at C by
5 Her case has just gone ____ court.
He was arrested for setting fire ____ ten cars.
A to B in C for

LISTENING

7 `CD·3.39` `MP3·126` **Listen to six extracts from a conversation and choose the correct answer, A, B or C.**

1 The conversation takes place
  A at the man's house.
  B in a garage.
  C at a police station.
2 The speaker is
  A a police officer.
  B a professional musician.
  C a radio presenter.
3 How will the boy get home?
  A by bus
  B by car
  C on foot
4 The woman is
  A explaining something.
  B criticising someone.
  C asking people to do something.
5 How many young people are unemployed?
  A forty-nine percent
  B six percent
  C twenty-five percent
6 The text does *not* mention
  A when the criminal robbed the bank.
  B where the police found the criminal.
  C what the criminal stole.

SPEAKING

8 **Match the two halves of the questions. Then, in pairs, ask and answer the questions.**

1 Would you like to work as ☐
2 Do you like reading ☐
3 What qualities do you need ☐
4 What would you do ☐

a to be a judge? Why?
b crime stories? Why?/Why not?
c if you lost your mobile phone?
d a police officer? Why?/Why not?

9 **In pairs, discuss and choose the best poster for a campaign against crimes on teenagers.**

Say **NO** to cyberbullying

BEWARE OF PICKPOCKETS

10 **In pairs, discuss these questions.**

1 What can you do to prevent being a victim of crime?
2 Do you think that people feel safer when they see a lot of police officers in the streets? Why?/Why not?
3 What would you do if you suspected that someone was breaking into your house at night?
4 Do you think secondary school students should learn about the law? Why?/Why not?

WRITING

11 **Read the writing task. Tick three points from the list that you might include in your story. Then add one more idea of your own.**

• where and when Grace saw the photo
• how long she had to wait to catch the bus
• how she followed the boy when he got off the bus
• why she phoned someone on her mobile

Your teacher has asked you to write a story. Your story must begin with this sentence:

Grace was on the bus and she saw a young boy just like the photo on the news.

12 **Write your story in about 100 words.**

GRAMMAR FOCUS

0.1 Present Simple and Present Continuous

Present Simple

We use the Present Simple to talk about:
- states and permanent situations:
  *Maria **likes** swimming.*
- regular activities:
  *We often **visit** my aunt.*

Affirmative		Negative	
I/You/ We/ They	work.	I/You/ We/ They	don't (do not) work.
He/ She/It	works.	He/ She/It	doesn't (does not)

Yes/No questions		Short answers
Do	I/you/we/ they	work?	Yes, I/you/we/they do. No, I/you/we/they don't.
Does	he/she/it		Yes, he/she/it does. No, he/she/it doesn't.

Wh- questions			
What	do	I/you/we/they	like?
	does	he/she/it	

SPELLING RULES – THIRD PERSON SINGULAR
- general rule: infinitive + -s, e.g. *enjoy – enjoys*
- verbs ending in a consonant and -y: y + -ies, e.g. *study – studies*
- verbs *do* and *go* as well as verbs ending in -ss, -x, -ch, -sh: + -es, e.g. *do – does, go – goes, wash – washes*
- *have: has*

Common time expressions used with the Present Simple:
- *always*
- *regularly*
- *usually*
- *often*
- *sometimes*
- *never*
- *every day/week/month*

Present Continuous

We use the Present Continuous to talk about actions happening at the moment of speaking:
*It's **raining** again.*

Affirmative			Negative		
I	am		I	'm not (am not)	
You/We/ They	are	playing.	You/We/ They	aren't (are not)	playing.
He/She/It	is		He/She/ It	isn't (is not)	

Yes/No questions			Short answers
Am	I		Yes, I am. No, I'm not.
Are	you/we/ they	playing?	Yes, you/we/they are. No, you/we/they aren't.
Is	he/she/it		Yes, he/she/it is. No, he/she/it isn't.

Wh- questions			
Where	am	I	going?
	is	he/she/it	
	are	you/we/they	

SPELLING RULES – -ING FORM
- general rule: infinitive + -ing, e.g. *walk – walking*
- verbs ending in a consonant + -e: e + -ing, e.g. *write – writing*
- one-syllable verbs ending in one vowel + one consonant: double the consonant + -ing, e.g. *run – running*

Common time expressions used with the Present Continuous:
- *at the moment*
- *now*
- *today*
- *this morning/afternoon*
- *this year*
- *these days*
- *at present*

0.2–0.3 Past Simple

We use the Past Simple to talk about actions which started and finished in the past. We often say when they happened:
*John and I **were** at the same school.*
*My dad **went** to a concert yesterday.*

The Past Simple of *be* is *was/were*.

Affirmative			Negative		
I/He/She/It	was	at home.	I/He/She/It	wasn't (was not)	at home.
You/We/They	were		You/We/They	weren't (were not)	

Yes/No questions			Short answers
Was	I/he/she/it	at home?	Yes, I/he/she/it was. No, I/he/she/it wasn't.
Were	you/we/they		Yes, you/we/they were. No, you/we/they weren't.

Wh- questions			
Why	was	I/he/she/it	at home?
	were	you/we/they	

In questions and negatives we use the auxiliary verb **did**.

Affirmative		Negative		
I/You/He/She/It/We/They	played.	I/You/He/She/It/We/They	didn't (did not)	play.

Yes/No questions			Short answers
Did	I/you/he/she/it/we/they	play?	Yes, I/you/he/she/it/we/they did. No, I/you/he/she/it/we/they didn't.

Wh- questions			
What	did	I/you/he/she/it/we/they	play?

SPELLING RULES – PAST SIMPLE FORM

Regular verbs
* general rule: infinitive + -ed, e.g. *help – helped*
* verbs ending in -e: + -d, e.g. *love – loved*
* verbs ending in a consonant + y: -ied, e.g. *try – tried*
* verbs ending in one vowel + one consonant: double the consonant + -ed, e.g. *stop – stopped*

Irregular verbs
For a list of irregular verbs, see Word store page 23.

Common time expressions used with the Past Simple:
* *yesterday*
* *yesterday moring/afternoon/evening*
* *ast night/week/month/year*
* *two days/weeks/months/years ago*
* *in May/2012*

0.4 Present Perfect

We use the Present Perfect to talk about actions which finished in the past, but we don't know or it is not important exactly when they happened:
*My friend **has bought** a new bag.*
***Have** you ever **been** camping alone?*

We form the Present Perfect with the auxiliary verb **have/has** and the past participle of the main verb.

Affirmative			Negative		
I/You/We/They	've (have)	finished.	I/You/We/They	haven't (have not)	finished.
He/She/It	's (has)		He/She/It	hasn't (has not)	

Yes/No questions			Short answers
Have	I/you/we/they	finished?	Yes, I/you/we/they have. No, I/you/we/they haven't.
Has	he/she/it		Yes, he/she/it has. No, he/she/it hasn't.

Wh- questions			
What	have	I/you/we/they	done?
	has	he/she/it	

SPELLING RULES – PAST PARTICIPLE FORM

Regular verbs
The past participle form of regular verbs is the same as the Past Simple form.

Irregular verbs
For a list of irregular verbs, see Word store page 23.

GRAMMAR FOCUS

0.5 | be going to

We use **be going to** + **infinitive** for
- intentions and plans:
  *My dad **is going to buy** a new car.*
- predictions about the future based on what we know and can see now:
  *Look at the sky. It's **going to rain.***

Affirmative			Negative		
I	am		I	'm not (am not)	
You/We/They	are	going to fall.	You/We/They	aren't (are not)	going to fall.
He/She/It	is		He/She/It	isn't (is not)	

Yes/No questions			Short answers
Am	I		Yes, I am. No, I'm not.
Are	you/we/they	going to fall?	Yes, you/we/they are. No, you/we/they aren't.
Is	he/she/it		Yes, he/she/it is. No, he/she/it isn't.

Wh- questions				
Where	am	I	going to	fall?
	is	he/she/it		
	are	you/we/they		

0.6 | will for predictions

We use **will** + **infinitive** for predictions about the future based on our opinions, intuition or experience:
*I think people **will travel** to Mars.*

If we want to say that an event will not happen in the future, we use *I don't think + will*:
*I **don't think** cars **will fly**.*

Affirmative			Negative		
I/You/He/She/It/We/They	will	travel.	I/You/He/She/It/We/They	won't (will not)	travel.

Yes/No questions			Short answers
Will	I/you/he/she/it/we/they	travel?	Yes, I/you/he/she/it/we/they will. No, I/you/he/she/it/we/they won't.

Wh- questions			
Where	will	I/you/he/she/it/we/they	travel?

0.7 must, have to and should

- We use **must** or **have to** to express obligation or necessity.
- We use **must** to refer to something the speaker feels is necessary or important:
  *I **must** go home now.*
- We use **have to** to refer to something that is necessary because of a rule or law, or because someone else says so:
  *Triathletes **have to** get up early.*
- We use **mustn't** to express prohibition:
  *You **mustn't** smoke.*
- We use **should**/**shouldn't** to give advice or say what we think is a good idea:
  *Max **should** train more.*
  *You **shouldn't** eat so many sweets.*

0.8 Countable and uncountable nouns • Articles

Nouns can be countable or uncountable.

Countable nouns
- have both singular and plural forms:
  *This **banana** is very sweet.*
  ***Bananas** are very sweet.*
- are used with articles (*a/an* or *the*), numbers or *some* (in affirmative sentences) and *any* (in questions and negatives):
  a sandwich, the sandwich, the sandwiches, two sandwiches
  *Are there **any sandwiches**?   There are **some sandwiches**.*

SPELLING RULES – PLURAL NOUNS
- general rule: noun + -s, e.g. *animal – animals*
- nouns ending in -s, -ss, -x, -sh, -ch or -o: + -es,
  e.g. *bus – buses, sandwich – sandwiches*
- nouns ending in a consonant + -y: -y̶ + -ies,
  e.g. *lady – ladies, strawberry – strawberries*
- irregular nouns, e.g. *person – people,
  child – children, man – men, woman – women*

Uncountable nouns
- have no plural form:
  ***Milk** is very healthy.*
- are used with the definite article *the*, *some* (in affimative sentences) or *any* (in questions and negatives). We do not use uncountable nouns with *a/an* or numbers:
  butter, the butter, a butter, one butter
  *Is there **any butter**?   There's is **some butter**.*

Indefinite article: *a/an*
We use **a/an** with singular countable nouns when:
- we talk about something for the first time:
  *There's **a café** and **a pub** on this street.*
- we talk about something that is an example of a certain category:
  *My dad is **a** great **cook**.*

Definite article: *the*
We use **the** with singular, plural and uncountable nouns:
- to talk about something we have mentioned before:
  *There's a café and a pub on this street. Let's go to **the café**.*
- to talk about something that is unique:
  *The **sun** is shining.*

No article
We do not use an article when we talk about things in general:
***Life** is beautiful.*
***Melons** are larger than **oranges**.*

GRAMMAR FOCUS

1.2 Present tenses – question forms

We form *yes/no* questions and *wh-* questions in different ways, depending on what we are asking about: the subject or the object of a sentence. In subject questions, we do not use an auxiliary verb. Look at the tables below for questions in the Present Simple, the Present Continuous and the Present Perfect.

Present Simple

Yes/No questions		
Do	I/you/we/they	speak English?
Does	he/she/it	

Wh- questions			
What	do	I/you/we/they	speak?
languages	does	he/she/it	

Subject questions	
Who	speaks English?

Present Continuous and Present Perfect

Yes/No questions		
Am	I	
Are	you/we/they	working now?
Is	he/she/it	
Have	I/you/we/they	
Has	he/she/it	swum in a river?

Wh- questions			
	am	I	
What	is	he/she/it	doing?
	are	you/we/they	
	have	I/you/we/they	
What	has	he/she/it	done?

Subject questions	
Who	is working now?
Who	has swum in a river?

Notice the position of the preposition in *wh-* questions with verbs followed by a preposition, e.g. *listen to music*.

What does Emily listen **to**?

1 **Write questions about the underlined information.**

1 My grandparents give money to <u>a charity</u>.

_____

2 <u>Tina</u> has tried Japanese food.

_____

3 I'm dreaming about <u>my winter holiday in the Alps</u>.

_____

4 My best friend lives <u>in Frankfurt</u>.

_____

5 Jo has visited <u>Poland, Russia and Slovakia</u>.

_____

6 <u>Jim</u> is watching a comedy at the moment.

_____

1.5 Verb + -ing or verb + to-infinitive?

We use the *-ing* form after these verbs: *can't stand, consider, don't mind, enjoy, hate, like, love, miss, prefer, spend* (time):

I **hate wearing** a suit and a tie.

We use the *to-infinitive* after these verbs: *agree, can't afford, choose, decide, hope, manage, need, pretend, refuse, want, would like, would prefer.*

I **can't afford to buy** this jacket.

1 **Complete the sentences with the correct form of the verbs in brackets.**

1 I don't mind _____ (get up) early.

2 Karen spends a lot of time _____ (chat) online.

3 We refuse _____ (eat) meat or fish.

4 I always agree _____ (help) my brother with his homework.

5 They hope _____ (get) a job in the media.

6 I can't stand _____ (wait) in queues.

7 Peter wants _____ (be) like Steve Jobs.

8 Sue has decided _____ (lend) me her new dress.

9 You should avoid _____ (eat) fast food.

10 Does Angela enjoy _____ (work) in a hospital?

11 A lot of people can't afford _____ (eat) in a restaurant every day.

12 I'm considering _____ (become) a volunteer.

13 When are you coming back? I really need _____ (see) you.

14 In the winter I always miss _____ (swim) in the sea.

15 Most of my friends prefer _____ (wear) jeans to sweatpants.

16 I would prefer _____ (stay) at home tonight if you don't mind.

17 Rob really hates _____ (tidy) his room.

18 Amy works for a charity – she loves _____ (help) people in need.

19 We mananged _____ (finish) our project on time.

20 Peter likes _____ (work) in a team.

2.2 Past Continuous and Past Simple

We use the Past Continuous:
- to describe a background scene in a story or in a description of a main event:

  *At 7 a.m. Doug **was having** breakfast. He **was sitting** at the table and he **was drinking** his coffee.*
- to talk about an action that was in progress when another action took place (for the shorter action, which happened while the longer one was in progress, we use the Past Simple):

  *When he **was finishing** his breakfast, Meg **came** into the kitchen.*

Affirmative			Negative		
I/He/She/It	was	watching TV.	I/He/She/It	wasn't (was not)	watching TV.
You/We/They	were		You/We/They	weren't (were not)	

Yes/No questions			Short answers
Was	I/he/she/it	watching TV?	Yes, I/he/she/it was. No, I/he/she/it wasn't.
Were	you/we/they		Yes, you/we/they were. No, you/we/they weren't.

Wh- questions				Subject questions		
What	was	I/he/she/it	watching?	Who	was	watching TV?
	were	you/we/they				

1 Choose the correct options.

1 I *lay / was lying* on the beach when suddenly it *started / was starting* raining.

2 What *did you do / were you doing* when I *called / was calling* you at four o'clock this afternoon?

3 The first time I *was seeing / saw* my boyfriend, he *danced / was dancing* at a party.

4 We *were having / had* lunch when the phone *was ringing / rang*.

5 It was a beautiful morning. I *left / was leaving* home to go to work. Suddenly, the postman *was knocking / knocked* on the front door.

6 When my mother *drove / was driving* to work yesterday, she *saw / was seeing* her old friend from school.

7 Molly *was breaking / broke* her leg when she *climbed / was climbing* a tree.

8 *Was Susan studying / Did Susan study* at 8 p.m. yesterday?

2.5 used to

We use **used to** to talk about past states or actions which happened regularly in the past but do not happen anymore.
*I **used to play** tennis a lot.* (I don't play anymore or I don't play very often.)
*He **didn't use to be** so unkind.* (But he's different now.)

When we talk about single actions that happened only once or that did not happen regularly, we use the Past Simple, not *used to*.
*In high school we **went** to the mountains two or three times.*

Affirmative			Negative		
I/You/He/She/It/We/They	used to	swim.	I/You/He/She/It/We/They	didn't use (did not use) to	swim.

Yes/No questions			Short answers
Did	I/you/he/she/it/we/they	use to swim?	Yes, I/you/he/she/it/we/they did. No, I/you/he/she/it/we/they didn't.

Wh- questions			Subject questions		
Where	did	I/you/he/she/it/we/they use to swim?	Who	used to	swim?

1 Complete the sentences with the correct form of *used to* and the verbs in brackets.

1 Kim _____ (be) much more confident about herself.

2 _____ (our neighbours/live) abroad before they moved here?

3 My boyfriend's friends _____ (not like) me.

4 _____ (your brother/play) the piano when he was your age?

5 _____ (you/have) a mobile phone when you were very little?

2 Write sentences from the prompts. Use *used to* where possible. If *used to* is not possible, use the Past Simple.

1 I / go / to the cinema / with my grandparents / every week

_____

2 we / not have / mobile phones or computers

_____

3 my family / move / to San Francisco / last year

_____

4 I / get / a digital watch / for my seventh birthday

_____

5 a poet / live / in that house

_____

GRAMMAR FOCUS

3.2 Present Perfect with *just, already, (not) yet* and Past Simple

We use the Present Perfect to talk about actions which happened and finished in the past, but we do not know when exacly or it is not important:
I **have read** many biographies and autobiographies.
(It's not important when I did it.)

Common time expressions used with the Present Perfect:
* **ever** – used in questions:
  Have you **ever** been to an art galery?
* **never** – used in negative sentences:
  My grandparents have **never** left England.
* **since then**:
  She won The X Factor in 2006. **Since then** she has sold millions of albums.
* **already** and **just** – used mainly in affirmative sentences:
  I have **already** seen this film.
  They have **just** left.
* **yet** – used in negative sentences and questions and always at the end of the sentence:
  I haven't seen her **yet**.
  Has she written any songs **yet**?

If we want to say when something happened, we use the Past Simple. We also use the Past Simple in questions with *when*.
She **won** a Grammy in 2009.
When **did** you **see** Blur play live?

1 Complete the sentences with the Present Perfect or Past Simple form of the verbs in brackets.

1 A: _____ (you/ever/be) to the opera?
  B: Yes. I _____ (go) last month. I _____
  (see) Madama Butterfly by Puccini.
2 Claire Richards _____ (write) many crime stories.
  She _____ (write) her latest crime story in 2014.
3 Look, Pierre _____ (just/upload) some videos.
4 My favourite singer _____ (release) his new single last week, but I _____ (not hear) it yet.
5 Emily _____ (already/buy) a birthday present for her mum.
6 A: _____ (you/do) your homework yet?
  B: Yes, I _____ (finish) an hour ago.

3.5 Comparative and superlative adjectives • *too* and *enough*

* We use the comparative form of adjectives and the word *than* to compare two people or things:
  Daniel Craig is **taller than** Zac Efron.
* To compare two people or things, we can also use the structure: (*not*) as + adjective + *as*:
  Rupert Grint is **not as famous as** Daniel Radcliffe.
* We use the superlative form of adjectives to show that a person or thing has the higest degree of a certain quality (compared to at least two other people or things):
  Sean Connery is **the tallest**.

Adjectives		Comparative	Superlative
one-syllable	young nice hot	younger nicer hotter	the youngest the nicest the hottest
one- and two-syllable ending in -y	pretty dry	prettier drier	the prettiest the driest
two-syllable or longer	attractive difficult	more attractive more difficult	the most attractive the most difficult
irregular	good bad far	better worse further	the best the worst the furthest

We use **too** + adjective or **not** + adjective + **enough** to talk about a degree of a quality. **Too** means 'more than you need or want'. **Not enough** means 'less than you need or want'.
You're **too young** to watch this film.
The comedian was **not funny enough**.

1 Complete the sentences with the correct form of the adjectives in brackets.

1 New York is _____ (modern) than Barcelona.
2 January is _____ (cold) month of the year.
3 Katy Perry is not as _____ (popular) as Miley Cyrus.
4 This is the _____ (bad) film I've ever seen.
5 My younger brother is _____ (tall) than me.
6 My English isn't as _____ (good) as my German.

4.2 Present Perfect with *for* and *since*

We use the Present Perfect to talk about states and actions that started in the past and still continue. We often use the words **since** and **for** when we use the Present Perfect in this way.

- **Since** refers to a moment or point in time when the activity started:
  since 2000/Monday/last summer/my birthday
- **For** refers to a time period between a time in the past and now.
  for five minutes/two weeks/a long time/ages

*My parents **have had** this house **since** 1990.*
*I **have known** Carol **for** ten years.*

***How long** have you lived in this house?*

1 Look at today's date and time and complete the table with the correct time expressions.

since		for
1 since December	=	
2 since Saturday	=	
3	=	for forty-five minutes
4 since breakfast	=	
5	=	for twenty-seven years
6	=	for five weeks
7 since I started school	=	

2 Write questions with *How long ...?* Then write two answers to each question with *since* and *for*. Use your general knowledge or check the answers at the bottom of the page.

1 the USA / independent?

_____ ?
_____ .
_____ .

2 the UK / be / in the European Union?

_____ ?
_____ .
_____ .

3 Peter Jackson / work / as a film director?

_____ ?
_____ .
_____ .

4 people / travel / in space?

_____ ?
_____ .
_____ .

Answers: **1** 1776 **2** 1973 **3** 1976 **4** 1961

4.5 Present Continuous, *be going to* and *will*

- We use the Present Continuous for fixed arrangements:
  *I can't go shopping tomorrow at five. I**'m playing** tennis with Joy. (I've already made an arrangement with Joy.)*
- We use *be going to* + infinitive to talk about intentions or plans:
  ***Are** you **going to invite** your aunt to the party?*
- We use *will* + infinitive for decisions made at the moment of speaking. We often use *I think* with *will*:
  *I think I**'ll ask** Luke for help.*

1 Complete the sentences with the correct future form of the verbs in brackets.

1 Mum _____ (see) the dentist this afternoon.
2 It's my birthday next month, but I _____ (not have) a party.
3 Brrr, it's cold in here! I think I _____ (turn) the heating on.
4 What _____ (you/do) later? Do you want to go for a coffee?
5 My cousin _____ (get married) in May.
6 Sorry, I can't talk now. I _____ (call) you back later.
7 **A:** These bags are so heavy.
  B: I _____ (carry) them for you.
8 _____ (you/study) in London or in Brighton?

2 What are these people saying? Choose the best options.

1 a customer at a café:
  I'll have / 'm having a big glass of orange juice, please.
2 someone who was invited to a picnic on Saturday:
  I can't come. My uncle *will paint / is going to paint* his house and *I'll help / I'm going to help* him.
3 someone who's just heard about uncle Bob's problem:
  What? Uncle Bob *will paint / is going to paint* his house all by himself on Saturday? *I'll help / I'm helping* him!
4 a businesswoman talking about her plans for the new year: *I'm going to help / I'm helping* some African charities this year.

GRAMMAR FOCUS

5.2 First Conditional

We use First Conditional sentences to talk about the possible results of an action. First Conditional sentences refer to the future:

If I tell them the truth, they **won't believe** me.

We use the Present Simple in the *if*-clause, which describes the condition. We use a future form, usually *will/won't*, in the clause describing the result.

We put a comma at the end of the *if*-clause if it comes first in the sentence.

If + Present Simple, (condition)	*will/won't + infinitive* (result)
If he works hard,	**he will pass** his exams.
will/won't + infinitive (result)	*if + Present Simple* (condition)
He will pass his exams	**if he works** hard.

1 Choose the correct options.

1 If Joe *passes / will pass* all his exams, his parents *buy / will buy* him a car.
2 My teacher *doesn't / won't* mind if I *finish / will finish* my essay tomorrow.
3 If Ella *doesn't / won't* find a job this year, she *does / will do* voluntary work to get experience.
4 They *miss / will miss* all their friends if they *choose / will choose* to go abroad.
5 If the school uniform *is / will be* compulsory next year, we *have / will have* to wear it.
6 If John *drops / will drop* PE and Art, he *has / will have* more time for academic subjects.
7 *Will you help / Do you help* me with my homework if I *have / will have* a problem?
8 Sandra *doesn't do / won't* do a gap year if she *doesn't collect / won't collect* some money.

2 Complete the sentences to make them true for you.

1 I will get a place at university if …
2 If I don't get a place at university, I …
3 If my timetable is very demanding next year, …
4 I won't get good marks if …
5 If I don't get a good job, …
6 I will move house if …
7 I will travel round the world if …
8 If I get stressed about my next exams, I …
9 I will do voluntary work if …
10 If I have more free time next week, I …

5.5 Relative clauses

In defining relative clauses (which give essential information about a person, thing or place) we use the following relative pronouns:

* *who* and *that* to talk about people:
  *This is the teacher **who/that** teaches my class.*
* *which* and *that* to talk about things:
  *Is this the laptop **which/that** you ordered?*
* *where* to talk about places:
  *We're going to visit the school **where** my mum taught for twenty years.*

The relative pronouns *who*, *which* and *that* usually come after the noun they refer to.

We can omit the relative pronouns *who*, *which* and *that* if they are followed by a personal pronoun or noun.

1 Add the relative pronouns *who*, *where* or *which* in the correct place in the sentences.

1 We live in a town doesn't have a university.
2 Do you know the boy is dancing with Molly?
3 Sam used to live in a country the schools are very good.
4 This is the teacher teaches my sister.
5 A levels are exams you take at the age of eighteen.
6 Bath is a small town has many historic sites.
7 What is the school subject you like best?
8 I go to a school uniforms are compulsory.
9 Is this the girl lives in the house opposite yours?
10 France is the country Susan loves the most.

2 Join the sentences using relative clauses.

1 There is a nice café. We can go there.
   _____

2 I know a boy. He speaks perfect Chinese.
   _____

3 McDonald's is a restaurant. It sells hamburgers.
   _____

4 I'm sure you'll find a job. You're going to love it.
   _____

5 My cousin knows lots of websites. You can play online games there.
   _____

6 Tina is a great sportswoman. She never gives up.
   _____

7 *Titanic* is a film. I've seen it about ten times.
   _____

8 This is the man. I saw him in front of the jeweller's.
   _____

6.2 Second Conditional

We use Second Conditional sentences to talk about:
* imaginary situations in the present:
  *If I **were** rich, I **would live** in a huge house.*
* improbable events in the future:
  *If he **left** home earlier, he **would never be** late for work.*

We use the Past Simple in the *if*-clause and *would/wouldn't* in the clause describing the result.

We put a comma at the end of the *if*-clause if it comes first in the sentence.

If + Past Simple, (condition)	would/wouldn't + infinitive (result)
If Sue **knew** Italian,	she**'d apply** for this job.

would/wouldn't + infinitive (result)	if + Past Simple (condition)
Sue **would apply** for this job	**if** she **knew** Italian.

In Second Conditional sentences we use *was* or *were* after *I, he, she* and *it. Were* is more formal.

Remember to use *were* in *If I were you*:

If I were you, I would tell him the truth.

1 Complete the Second Conditional sentences with the correct form of the verbs in brackets.

1 If everybody _____ (go) to university, nobody _____ (want) to do hard physical work.
2 Buses _____ (not be) so crowded if more people _____ (work) from home.
3 If people _____ (not apply) for low-paid jobs, salaries _____ (go) up.
4 Family relationships _____ (improve) if parents _____ (spend) more time with their children.
5 You _____ (be) happier if you _____ (have) an interesting and well-paid job.
6 If I _____ (be) you, I _____ (go) and see a doctor.
7 Her grades _____ (be) better if she _____ (study) harder.
8 _____ (you/take) that job, if they _____ (offer) it to you?

6.5 Modal verbs for obligation and permission

To express obligation or necessity, we use:
* **must**, especially when we refer to something the speaker feels is necessary:
  *I **must** talk to her right now. (I feel this is necessary.)*
* **have to**, especially when we refer to something that is necessary because of a rule or law:
  *My brother **has to** wear a suit to work. (These are the rules.)*
* **need to**:
  *Neil often **needs to** do overtime.*

To express lack of obligation or necessity, we use:
* **don't have to**:
  *A teacher **doesn't have to** do physical work.*
* **don't need to/needn't**:
  *You **needn't** come to the office. You can work from home.*
  *You **don't need to** write the essay again.*

To say what is allowed, we use **can**:
*Journalists **can** work flexible hours.*

To say what is not allowed, we use:
* **can't**:
  *I **can't** leave the office during office hours.*
* **mustn't**:
  *You **mustn't** check your private email at work.*

1 Choose the correct options.

1 A: It is a formal meeting?
  B: No, you *must / don't need to / can* wear a tie.
2 A: Can I smoke in here?
  B: I'm afraid you can't. You *need to / needn't / mustn't* smoke anywhere inside this building.
3 A: What's wrong? You look stressed.
  B: I am. I *can / needn't / have to* finish all this work before the end of the week. There's so much of it!
4 A: Mr Long, I'd like to take the day off tomorrow.
  B: Sorry, I'm afraid you *don't need to / must / can't*. We're too busy in the office tomorrow.
5 A: You look worried. What's wrong?
  B: I have a meeting with my boss today. I *needn't / need to / don't need to* get to work on time. Otherwise, I'll lose my job.
6 A: Why can't Sarah come with us?
  B: She *need to / has to / can* prepare a presentation for her boss.

117

GRAMMAR FOCUS

7.2 The Passive

We use the Passive when the action is more important than the person who performs it. If we want to add information about the person (the agent), we use the word **by**:
*This shopping mall **is visited by** about 50,000 people every day.*
*How many languages **are spoken** in the USA?*

We form the Passive with the correct tense of *be* and the past participle.

Tense	Examples
Present Simple	*Tea **is grown** in India.* *Cars **are** not **repaired** here.* *Where **are** the tickets **sold**?*
Past Simple	*I **was offered** a job.* *These tablets **were** not **produced** in China.* *Where **was** our car **made**?*
Present Perfect	*The house in High Street **has been sold**.* *We **have** not **been informed** about the change.* ***Has** he **been invited** to Kerry's wedding?*
Modal verbs	*Conditions **must be improved**.* *Parcels **can be sent** at the post office.* *Do the rooms **need to be cleaned** every day?*

1 Put the words in the correct order to make sentences.

1 be / music / the iTunes store / downloaded / from / can

_____

2 organically / plants / farm / on / are / our / grown

_____

3 uniforms / are / by / in England / worn / all schoolchildren?

_____

4 have / since 1988 / been / these shoes / produced

_____

5 son / month / is / given / presents / their / every

_____

6 cinema / opened / a new / has / in my street

_____

7 in / switched off / all phones / must / the the library / be

_____

8 made / this jam / by / was / my grandmother

_____

7.5 Quantifiers

To talk about quantities, we use the following quantifiers:

Countable nouns	Uncountable nouns
How many? ***How many** friends have you got?*	How much? ***How much** money have you got?*
(very) few *I've got (**very**) **few** friends.*	(very) little *I've got (**very**) **little** money.*
a few *I've got **a few** friends.*	a little *I've got **a little** money.*
some *I've got **some** friends.*	some *I've got **some** money.*
many *Have you got **many** friends?* *I haven't got **many** friends.*	much *Have you got **much** money?* *I haven't got **much** money.*
a lot of/lots of *I've got **a lot of/lots of** friends.*	a lot of/lots of *I've got **a lot of/lots of** money.*
too many *I've got **too many** friends.*	too much *I've got **too much** money.*
any *Have you got **any** friends?*	any *Have you got **any** money?*
any *I haven't got **any** friends.*	any *I haven't got **any** money.*

1 Complete the conversation with the quantifiers in the box.

> any   how many   little   lot of   some (x2)   too much

Pia: Thanks for inviting me to your party, Sam. You've got a ¹_____ presents! ²_____ do you think you've got?

Sam: Maybe ten or twelve. And my parents gave me ³_____ money. Here, try ⁴_____ birthday cake. It's really delicious.

Pia: Oh, thanks, I'll have just a ⁵_____ , please. I've already eaten quite a lot. Have you got ⁶_____ orange juice?

Sam: Yes, I bought 20 litres. I think we have ⁷_____ .

8.2 Past Perfect

We use the Past Perfect to talk about the earliest of two or more events in the past. The action expressed in the Past Perfect happened before the action expressed in the Past Simple:

*When the police caught the thief, he **had** already **stolen** five computers.* (The theft happened before the police caught the thief.)

Notice how the Past Perfect changes the meaning of these sentences:

*The children **went** to sleep when we came.* (First we came and then the children went to sleep.)
*The children **had gone** to sleep when we came.* (The children were asleep when we came.)

We often use **by** with the Past Perfect, e.g. *by the age of six, by the time I was six, by 1978*:
***By** the time I was six, I had learnt to read.*

Affirmative			Negative		
I/You/He/ She/It/ We/ They	had	watched TV.	I/You/He/ She/It/ We/They	hadn't (had not)	watched TV.

Yes/No questions			Short answers
Had	I/you/he/ she/it/we/ they	watched TV?	Yes, I/you/he/she/it/ we/they had. No, I/you/he/she/it/ we/they hadn't.

Wh- questions				Subject questions		
What	had	I/you/he/ she/it/we/ they	watched?	Who	had	watched TV?

1 Join the sentences. Use the Past Perfect and the Past Simple in each sentence.

1 The thieves escaped abroad. Then a detective found out about it.
   A detective _____ .

2 The suspect was released from prison. Then new evidence was found.
   When new evidence _____ .

3 The robbers drove away in a black jeep. The police knew about it.
   The police _____ that _____ .

4 The mugger took my mobile phone. I couldn't call the police.
   I _____ because _____ .

8.5 Reported Speech

To report what other people said, we can quote their actual words (Direct Speech) or use Reported Speech:

Direct Speech
*'We **are looking** for the criminal.'*
*They said, 'We **are looking** for the criminal.'*

Reported Speech
In Reported Speech we often use *say (that)* and *tell sb (that)*:
'The party is great.' → *She **said** (**that**) the party was great.*
'I forgot to lock the front door.' → *He **told me** (**that**) he had forgotten to lock the front door.*

We also change tenses, pronouns and determiners in Reported Speech.

Tenses

Direct Speech	→	Reported Speech
Present Simple Sam: 'I work.' 'Sue doesn't work.'	→	**Past Simple** Sam said (that) he worked. Sam said (that) Sue didn't work.
Present Continuous Sam: 'I'm working.' 'Sue isn't working.'	→	**Past Continuous** Sam said (that) he was working. Sam said (that) Sue wasn't working.
Present Perfect Sam: 'I've worked.' 'Sue hasn't worked.'	→	**Past Perfect** Sam said (that) he had worked. Sam said (that) Sue hadn't worked.
Past Simple Sam: 'I worked.' 'Sue didn't work.'	→	**Past Perfect** Sam said (that) he had worked. Sam said (that) Sue hadn't worked.
can Sam: 'I can work.' 'Sue can't work.'	→	**could** Sam said (that) he could work. Sam said (that) Sue couldn't work.

Pronouns and determiners
*'**My** brother has bought a new car.'* → *She said that **her** brother had bought a new car.*

1 Report what the witnesses told the police.

1 'We saw the burglars in the office,' said Mrs Reid.
   Mrs Reid told _____ .

2 'I have never been witness to a crime before,' said Mr Ross.
   Mr Ross said _____ .

3 'I feel very frightened,' said Miss Hill.
   Miss Hill said _____ .

4 'I'm still shaking,' added Miss Hill.
   Miss Hill added _____ .

5 'I can't stop thinking about the burglary,' said Mrs Reid.
   Mrs Reid said _____ .

6 'I haven't been to the office since the burglary,' added Mrs Reid.
   Mrs Reid added _____ .

Personality

able to /'eɪbəl tə/
adorable /ə'dɔːrəbəl/
ambitious /æm'bɪʃəs/
arrogant /'ærəgənt/
bad-tempered /ˌbæd 'tempəd/
boring /'bɔːrɪŋ/
brave /breɪv/
bravery /'breɪvəri/
caring /'keərɪŋ/
cheerful /'tʃɪəfəl/
clever /'klevə/
confident /'kɒnfədənt/
cooperative /kəʊ'ɒpərətɪv/
cowardly /'kaʊədli/
crazy /'kreɪzi/
dishonest /dɪs'ɒnəst/
disloyal /dɪs'lɔɪəl/
dull /dʌl/
emotional /ɪ'məʊʃənəl/
energetic /ˌenə'dʒetɪk/
enthusiastic /ɪnˌθjuːzi'æstɪk/
experienced /ɪk'spɪəriənst/
fair /feə/
fit /fɪt/
friendly /'frendli/
funny /'fʌni/
generosity /ˌdʒenə'rɒsəti/
generous /'dʒenərəs/
good at /'gʊd ət/
grumpy /'grʌmpi/
hard-working /ˌhaːd 'wɜːkɪŋ/
helpful /'helpfəl/
honest /'ɒnəst/
inexperienced /ˌɪnɪk'spɪəriənst/
insensitive /ɪn'sensətɪv/
interesting /'ɪntrəstɪŋ/
irresponsible /ˌɪrɪ'spɒnsəbəl/
kind /kaɪnd/
laziness /'leɪzɪnəs/
lazy /'leɪzi/
loyal to /'lɔɪəl tə/
loyalty /'lɔɪəlti/
mean /miːn/
miserable /'mɪzərəbəl/
modest /'mɒdəst/
modesty /'mɒdəsti/
negative about /'negətɪv əˌbaʊt/
optimistic /ˌɒptə'mɪstɪk/
outgoing /ˌaʊt'gəʊɪŋ/
pessimistic /ˌpesə'mɪstɪk/
popular /'pɒpjələ/
positive /'pɒzətɪv/
responsibility /rɪˌspɒnsə'bɪləti/
responsible for /rɪ'spɒnsəbəl fə/
selfish /'selfɪʃ/
sensible /'sensəbəl/
sensitive to /'sensətɪv tə/
serious /'sɪəriəs/
shy /ʃaɪ/
sociable /'səʊʃəbəl/
stupid /'stjuːpəd/
successful /sək'sesfəl/
uncommunicative /ˌʌnkə'mjuːnɪkətɪv/
uncooperative /ˌʌnkəʊ'ɒpərətɪv/
unfair /ˌʌn'feə/
unfit /ʌn'fɪt/
unhelpful /ʌn'helpfəl/
unkind /ˌʌn'kaɪnd/
unpopular /ʌn'pɒpjələ/
unsuccessful /ˌʌnsək'sesfəl/

Feelings and emotions

bad mood /ˌbæd 'muːd/
crazy about /'kreɪzi əˌbaʊt/
disappointed with /ˌdɪsə'pɔɪntəd wɪð/
inspired by /ɪn'spaɪəd baɪ/
interested in /'ɪntrəstəd ɪn/
involved in /ɪn'vɒlvd ɪn/
keen on /'kiːn ɒn/
obsessed with /əb'sest wɪð/
passionate about /'pæʃənət əˌbaʊt/
serious about /'sɪəriəs əˌbaʊt/

Clothes

casual clothes /ˌkæʒuəl 'kləʊðz/
designer clothes /dɪ'zaɪnə kləʊðz/
hoodie /'hʊdi/
jacket /'dʒækət/
skinny jeans /ˌskɪni 'dʒiːnz/
suit /suːt/
sweatpants /'swetpænts/
tie /taɪ/
uniform /'juːnəfɔːm/
winter coat /ˌwɪntə 'kəʊt/

Other

adapt to /ə'dæpt tə/
admire /əd'maɪə/
argue /'aːgjuː/
avoid /ə'vɔɪd/
can't afford /ˌkaːnt ə'fɔːd/
can't stand doing /ˌkaːnt stænd 'duːɪŋ/
care about /'keə əˌbaʊt/
charity /'tʃærəti/
developing country /dɪˌveləpɪŋ 'kʌntri/
elderly /'eldəli/
experience /ɪk'spɪəriəns/
get a job /ˌget ə 'dʒɒb/
have sth in common /hæv ˌsʌmθɪŋ ɪn 'kɒmən/
healthy /'helθi/
homeless /'həʊmləs/
housework /'haʊswɜːk/
human rights /ˌhjuːmən 'raɪts/
identity /aɪ'dentəti/
impress /ɪm'pres/
inspire /ɪn'spaɪə/
make a good impression /meɪk ə gʊd ɪm'preʃən/
opportunity /ˌɒpə'tjuːnəti/
peace /piːs/
priority /praɪ'ɒrɪti/
prison /'prɪzən/
refuse to do sth /rɪ'fjuːz tə duː ˌsʌmθɪŋ/
role model /'rəʊl ˌmɒdl/
spend money on /ˌspend 'mʌni ɒn/
spend time /spend 'taɪm/
stereotype /'steriətaɪp/
survey /'sɜːveɪ/
take risks /ˌteɪk 'rɪsks/
team-player /'tiːm ˌpleɪə/
unhealthy /ʌn'helθi/
voluntary work /'vɒləntəri wɜːk/
volunteer /ˌvɒlən'tɪə/

Inventions

antibiotics /ˌæntibaɪˈɒtɪks/
camera /ˈkæmərə/
communications satellite /kəˌmjuːnɪˈkeɪʃənz ˌsætəlaɪt/
credit card /ˈkredət kɑːd/
GPS /ˌdʒiː piː ˈes/
jet engine /ˈdʒet ˌendʒən/
mobile phone /ˌməʊbaɪl ˈfəʊn/
nuclear power /ˌnjuːkllə ˈpaʊə/
radar /ˈreɪdɑː/
refrigerator /rɪˈfrɪdʒəreɪtə/
robot /ˈrəʊbɒt/
television /ˈteləˌvɪʒən/
washing machine /ˈwɒʃɪŋ məˌʃiːn/

Computers and phones

attach a photo /əˌtætʃ ə ˈfəʊtəʊ/
battery /ˈbætəri/
blog /blɒg/
broadband /ˈbrɔːdbænd/
click on (an icon) /ˌklɪk ɒn (ən ˈaɪkɒn)/
crash /kræʃ/
desktop computer /ˌdesktɒp kəmˈpjuːtə/
digital /ˈdɪdʒətl/
document /ˈdɒkjəmənt/
download music /ˌdaʊnˌləʊd ˈmjuːzɪk/
e-book /ˈiː bʊk/
e-ink /ˈiː ɪŋk/
electronic /ˌelɪkˈtrɒnɪk/
email /ˈiː meɪl/
follow sb on Twitter /ˌfɒləʊ ˌsʌmbədi ɒn ˈtwɪtə/
go dead /ˌgəʊ ˈded/
go online /ˌgəʊ ɒnˈlaɪn/
hang up /ˌhæŋ ˈʌp/
icon /ˈaɪkɒn/
Internet server /ˈɪntənet ˌsɜːvə/
keyboard /ˈkiːbɔːd/
laptop /ˈlæptɒp/
log on /ˌlɒg ˈɒn/
menu /ˈmenjuː/
mouse /maʊs/
open a document /ˌəʊpən ə ˈdɒkjəmənt/
password /ˈpɑːswɜːd/
scanner /ˈskænə/
screen /skriːn/
scroll up/down /ˌskrəʊl ˈʌp/ˈdaʊn/
search engine /ˈsɜːtʃ ˌendʒən/
social networking site /ˈsəʊʃəl ˈnetwɜːkɪŋ saɪt/
switch on /ˌswɪtʃ ˈɒn/
text message /ˈtekst ˌmesɪdʒ/
tweet /twiːt/
update your profile /ʌpˌdeɪt jɔː ˈprəʊfaɪl/
username /ˈjuːzəneɪm/
virus /ˈvaɪərəs/
visit a website /ˌvɪzət ə ˈwebsaɪt/

Science

analyse /ˈænəlaɪz/
analysis /əˈnæləsəs/
archaeologist /ˌɑːkiˈɒlədʒɪst/
archaeology /ˌɑːkiˈɒlədʒi/
chemicals /ˈkemɪkəlz/
chemist /ˈkeməst/
chemistry /ˈkeməstri/
collect evidence /kəˌlekt ˈevədəns/
data /ˈdeɪtə/
discover /dɪsˈkʌvə/
discovery /dɪsˈkʌvəri/
do experiments /ˌduː ɪkˈsperɪmənts/
do research /ˌduː rɪˈsɜːtʃ/
ecologist /ɪˈkɒlədʒəst/
ecology /ɪˈkɒlədʒi/
engineer /ˌendʒəˈnɪə/

environment /ɪnˈvaɪrənmənt/
evolution /ˌiːvəˈluːʃən/
evolve /ɪˈvɒlv/
exploration /ˌekspləˈreɪʃən/
explore /ɪkˈsplɔː/
find a cure /ˌfaɪnd ə ˈkjʊə/
geologist /dʒiˈɒlədʒɪst/
geology /dʒiˈɒlədʒi/
global warming /ˌgləʊbəl ˈwɔːmɪŋ/
imagination /ɪˌmædʒəˈneɪʃən/
imagine /ɪˈmædʒən/
make a discovery /ˌmeɪk ə dɪsˈkʌvəri/
(marine) biologist /(məˈriːn) baɪˈɒlədʒəst/
(marine) biology /(məˈriːn) baɪˈɒlədʒi/
mathematician /ˌmæθəməˈtɪʃən/
mathematics /ˌmæθəˈmætɪks/
nature /ˈneɪtʃə/
observation /ˌɒbzəˈveɪʃən/
observe /əbˈzɜːv/
oxygen /ˈɒksɪdʒən/
physicist /ˈfɪzəsəst/
physics /ˈfɪzɪks/
preservation /ˌprezəˈveɪʃən/
preserve /prɪˈzɜːv/
protect /prəˈtekt/
protection /prəˈtekʃən/
researcher /rɪˈsɜːtʃə/
science /ˈsaɪəns/
scientist /ˈsaɪəntəst/
solution /səˈluːʃən/
solve /sɒlv/
technology /tekˈnɒlədʒi/

Space exploration

astronaut /ˈæstrənɔːt/
astronomy /əˈstrɒnəmi/
atmosphere /ˈætməsfɪə/
black hole /ˌblæk ˈhəʊl/
capsule /ˈkæpsjuːl/
commander /kəˈmɑːndə/
explosion /ɪkˈspləʊʒən/
fuel tank /ˈfjuːəl tæŋk/
gravity /ˈgrævəti/
hatch /hætʃ/
launch /lɔːntʃ/
mission control /ˌmɪʃən kənˈtrəʊl/
moon /muːn/
on board /ɒn ˈbɔːd/
orbit /ˈɔːbət/
parachute /ˈpærəʃuːt/
planet /ˈplænət/
space /speɪs/
spacecraft /ˈspeɪs-krɑːft/
splash down /ˌsplæʃ ˈdaʊn/

Other

breathe a sigh of relief /ˌbriːð ə saɪ əv rɪˈliːf/
carry out /ˌkæri ˈaʊt/
cheer /tʃɪə/
come up with /ˌkʌm ˈʌp wɪð/
figure out /ˌfɪgər ˈaʊt/
find a solution /ˌfaɪnd ə səˈluːʃən/
fix a problem /ˌfɪks ə ˈprɒbləm/
follow events /ˌfɒləʊ ɪˈvents/
get home /ˌget ˈhəʊm/
go crazy /ˌgəʊ ˈkreɪzi/
on duty /ɒn ˈdjuːti/
raise your hand /ˌreɪz jɔː ˈhænd/
run out /ˌrʌn ˈaʊt/
spend hours /ˌspend ˈaʊəz/

Art

abstract /'æbstrækt/
art gallery /'ɑːt ˌgæləri/
artist /'ɑːtɪst/
black and white /ˌblæk ənd 'waɪt/
brush /brʌʃ/
colour /'kʌlə/
exhibition /ˌeksə'bɪʃən/
landscape /'lændskeɪp/
museum /mju:'ziəm/
(oil) painting /('ɔɪl) ˌpeɪntɪŋ/
paint /peɪnt/
painter /'peɪntə/
photo/photograph /'fəʊtəʊ/'fəʊtəgrɑːf/
photographer /fə'tɒgrəfə/
photography /fə'tɒgrəfi/
portrait /'pɔːtrət/
sculptor /'skʌlptə/
sculpture /'skʌlptʃə/
street art /'striːt ˌɑːt/
street artist /'striːt ˌɑːtɪst/
studio /'stjuːdiəʊ/

Types of books and films

action film /'ækʃən fɪlm/
adaptation /ˌædæp'teɪʃən/
adventure film /əd'ventʃə fɪlm/
autobiography /ˌɔːtəbaɪ'ɒgrəfi/
biography /baɪ'ɒgrəfi/
classic /'klæsɪk/
comedy /'kɒmədi/
cookbook /'kʊkbʊk/
crime story/film /'kraɪm ˌstɔːri/fɪlm/
documentary /ˌdɒkjə'mentəri/
drama /'drɑːmə/
encyclopedia /ɪnˌsaɪklə'piːdiə/
fairy tale /'feəri teɪl/
fantasy novel/film /'fæntəsi ˌnɒvəl/ˌfɪlm/
ghost story /'gəʊst ˌstɔːri/
historical drama /hɪˌstɒrɪkəl 'drɑːmə/
horror /'hɒrə/
musical /'mjuːzɪkəl/
novel /'nɒvəl/
play /pleɪ/
poetry /'pəʊətri/
romantic comedy /rəʊˌmæntɪk 'kɒmədi/
romantic fiction /rəʊˌmæntɪk 'fɪkʃən/
science fiction novel/film /ˌsaɪəns 'fɪkʃən ˌnɒvəl/ˌfɪlm/
short story /ˌʃɔːt 'stɔːri/
thriller /'θrɪlə/
travel guide /'trævəl gaɪd/
war film /'wɔː fɪlm/
western /'westən/

Film, theatre, books

act /ækt/
acting /'æktɪŋ/
animation /ˌænə'meɪʃən/
author /'ɔːθə/
award-winning /ə'wɔːd ˌwɪnɪŋ/
based on /'beɪst ɒn/
best-seller /ˌbest'selə/
book/film review /'bʊk/'fɪlm rɪˌvjuː/
camera /'kæmərə/
central character /ˌsentrəl 'kærəktə/
chapter /'tʃæptə/
costume /'kɒstjʊm/
dialogue /'daɪəlɒg/
direct /də'rekt/
filming /'fɪlmɪŋ/
give a good performance as ... /gɪv ə ˌgʊd pə'fɔːməns əz/
hold your attention /ˌhəʊld jɔːr ə'tenʃən/
lead actor /ˌliːd 'æktə/
literary critic /ˌlɪtərəri 'krɪtɪk/
movie /'muːvi/
novelist /'nɒvəlɪst/
perform /pə'fɔːm/

performance /pə'fɔːməns/
play the role of ... /ˌpleɪ ðə 'rəʊl əv/
playwright /'pleɪraɪt/
plot /plɒt/
poem /'pəʊɪm/
poet /'pəʊət/
producer /prə'djuːsə/
scene /siːn/
screenplay/script /'skriːnpleɪ/skrɪpt/
scriptwriter /'skrɪptˌraɪtə/
setting /'setɪŋ/
soundtrack /'saʊndtræk/
special effects /ˌspeʃəl ə'fekts/
stage /steɪdʒ/
storyline /'stɔːrilaɪn/
suspense /sə'spens/
take place in /ˌteɪk 'pleɪs ɪn/
tension /'tenʃən/
verse /vɜːs/
violence /'vaɪələns/
writer /'raɪtə/
X-rated /'eks ˌreɪtəd/

Music

album /'ælbəm/
band /bænd/
classical music /ˌklæsɪkəl 'mjuːzɪk/
composer /kəm'pəʊzə/
hit /hɪt/
instrument /'ɪnstrəmənt/
jazz /dʒæz/
live /laɪv/
music award /'mjuːzɪk əˌwɔːd/
music festival /'mjuːzɪk ˌfestəvəl/
opera /'ɒpərə/
piano /pi'ænəʊ/
singer /'sɪŋə/
song /sɒŋ/
songwriter /'sɒŋˌraɪtə/
symphony /'sɪmfəni/
the charts /ðə 'tʃɑːts/
track /træk/
vocal range /ˌvəʊkəl 'reɪndʒ/

TV and media

comedian /kə'miːdiən/
episode /'epəsəʊd/
journalist /'dʒɜːnələst/
newspaper article /'njuːsˌpeɪpə ˌɑːtɪkəl/
report /rɪ'pɔːt/
sitcom /'sɪtkɒm/
TV presenter /ˌtiː 'viː prɪˌzentə/

Description

amazing /ə'meɪzɪŋ/
amusing /ə'mjuːzɪŋ/
boring /'bɔːrɪŋ/
brilliant /'brɪliənt/
emotional /ɪ'məʊʃənəl/
enjoyable /ɪn'dʒɔɪəbəl/
entertaining /ˌentə'teɪnɪŋ/
excellent /'eksələnt/
factual /'fæktʃuəl/
funny /'fʌni/
great /greɪt/
inspiring /ɪn'spaɪərɪŋ/
moving /'muːvɪŋ/
perfect /'pɜːfekt/
predictable /prɪ'dɪktəbəl/
relaxing /rɪ'læksɪŋ/
true-life /ˌtruː 'laɪf/
unoriginal /ˌʌnə'rɪdʒɪnəl/
unrealistic /ˌʌnrɪə'lɪstɪk/
wonderful /'wʌndəfə/

Types of houses

bungalow /'bʌŋgələʊ/
cottage /'kɒtɪdʒ/
detached house /dɪˌtætʃt 'haʊs/
eco-house /'iːkəʊ haʊs/
flat /flæt/
houseboat /'haʊsbəʊt/
semi-detached house /ˌsemidɪˌtætʃt 'haʊs/
studio apartment /ˌstjuːdiəʊ ə'pɑːtmənt/
terraced house /ˌterəst 'haʊs/

Location

in a village /ˌɪn ə 'vɪlɪdʒ/
in the city centre /ˌɪn ðə ˌsɪti 'sentə/
in the countryside /ˌɪn ðə 'kʌntrisaɪd/
in the suburbs /ˌɪn ðə 'sʌbɜːbz/
near the sea /ˌnɪə ðə 'siː/
on a housing estate /ɒn ə 'haʊzɪŋ ɪˌsteɪt/
on the edge of the city /ˌɒn ði 'edʒ əv ðə 'sɪti/

Building materials

brick /brɪk/
concrete /'kɒŋkriːt/
mud /mʌd/
stone /stəʊn/
wood /wʊd/

Description

comfortable /'kʌmftəbəl/
cosy /'kəʊzi/
lots of natural light /lɒts əv ˌnætʃərəl 'laɪt/
modern /'mɒdn/
open-plan /ˌəʊpən 'plæn/
spacious /'speɪʃəs/
traditional /trə'dɪʃənəl/

Inside a house

basement /'beɪsmənt/
bedside table /ˌbedsaɪd 'teɪbəl/
bookcase /'bʊk-keɪs/
bookshelf /'bʊkʃelf/
carpet /'kɑːpət/
ceiling /'siːlɪŋ/
central heating /ˌsentrəl 'hiːtɪŋ/
cooker /'kʊkə/
couch /kaʊtʃ/
cupboard /'kʌbəd/
duvet /'duːveɪ/
electricity /ɪˌlek'trɪsəti/
floor /flɔː/
floorboard /'flɔːbɔːd/
fridge /frɪdʒ/
kitchen sink /ˌkɪtʃən 'sɪŋk/
lamp /læmp/
shelf /ʃelf/
single bed /ˌsɪŋgəl 'bed/
sofa /'səʊfə/
stairs /steəz/
toilet /'tɔɪlət/
wardrobe /'wɔːdrəʊb/
windowsill /'wɪndəʊˌsɪl/
wood-burner /'wʊd ˌbɜːnə/
worktop /'wɜːk tɒp/

Outside a house

back door /ˌbæk 'dɔː/
balcony /'bælkəni/
front door /ˌfrʌnt 'dɔː/
garage /'gærɪdʒ/
path /pɑːθ/
patio /'pætiəʊ/
pond /pɒnd/
porch /pɔːtʃ/
roof /ruːf/
shed /ʃed/
sky-light /'skaɪlaɪt/
solar panel /ˌsəʊlə 'pænl/
stone wall /ˌstəʊn 'wɔːl/

Places in the city and in the country

beach /biːtʃ/
bridge /brɪdʒ/
canal /kə'næl/
canyon /'kænjən/
castle /'kɑːsəl/
coast /kəʊst/
harbour /'hɑːbə/
hill /hɪl/
island /'aɪlənd/
monument /'mɒnjəmənt/
mountain /'maʊntən/
rainforest /'reɪnfɒrəst/
reef /riːf/
river /'rɪvə/
rock /rɒk/
ruins /'ruːənz/
slums /slʌmz/
square /skweə/
statue /'stætʃuː/
temple /'tempəl/
valley /'væli/

Tourism

a must /ə 'mʌst/
accommodation /əˌkɒmə'deɪʃən/
attract tourists /əˌtrækt 'tʊərɪsts/
attraction /ə'trækʃən/
breathtaking view /ˌbreθteɪkɪŋ 'vjuː/
entertainment /ˌentə'teɪnmənt/
historic site /hɪˌstɒrɪk 'saɪt/
host /həʊst/
local speciality /ˌləʊkəl ˌspeʃi'æləti/
nightlife /'naɪtlaɪf/
sights /saɪts/
tourist destination /'tʊərəst destəˌneɪʃən/

Phrases with make and do

do the cooking /ˌduː ðə 'kʊkɪŋ/
do the gardening /ˌduː ðə 'gɑːdnɪŋ/
do the housework /ˌduː ðə 'haʊswɜːk/
do the ironing /ˌduː ði 'aɪənɪŋ/
do the shopping /ˌduː ðə 'ʃɒpɪŋ/
do the washing /ˌduː ðə 'wɒʃɪŋ/
do the washing-up /ˌduː ðə ˌwɒʃɪŋ 'ʌp/
do your best /ˌduː jɔː 'best/
do your homework /ˌduː jɔː 'həʊmwɜːk/
make a complaint /ˌmeɪk ə kəm'pleɪnt/
make a decision /ˌmeɪk ə dɪ'sɪʒən/
make a mess /ˌmeɪk ə 'mes/
make a noise /ˌmeɪk ə 'nɔɪz/
make dinner /ˌmeɪk 'dɪnə/
make your bed /ˌmeɪk jɔː 'bed/

Other

architecture /'ɑːkətektʃə/
awesome /'ɔːsəm/
busy /'bɪzi/
dominate /'dɒməneɪt/
house-warming party /'haʊswɔːmɪŋ ˌpɑːti/
impressive /ɪm'presɪv/
move (house) /ˌmuːv ('haʊs)/
narrow /'nærəʊ/
natural wonder /ˌnætʃərəl 'wʌndə/
neighbour /'neɪbə/
neighbourhood /'neɪbəhʊd/
population /ˌpɒpjə'leɪʃən/
public transport system /ˌpʌblɪk 'trænspɔːt ˌsɪstəm/
selection /sə'lekʃən/
shallow /'ʃæləʊ/
spectacular /spek'tækjələ/
teddy bear /'tedi beə/
trading centre /'treɪdɪŋ ˌsentə/

Subjects and courses

Architecture /'ɑːkətektʃə/
Art /ɑːt/
Art History /'ɑːt ˌhɪstəri/
Design and Technology /dɪˌzaɪn ənd tekˈnɒlədʒi/
Engineering /ˌendʒəˈnɪərɪŋ/
English /'ɪŋglɪʃ/
Geography /dʒiˈɒgrəfi/
Law /lɔː/
Maths /mæθs/
Medicine /'medsən/
Music /'mjuːzɪk/
Physical Education (PE) /ˌfɪzɪkəl ˌedjʊˈkeɪʃən (ˌpiːˈiː)/
Reading /'riːdɪŋ/
Science /'saɪəns/
Writing /'raɪtɪŋ/

School

A levels /'eɪ ˌlevəlz/
ability /əˈbɪləti/
attend a school /əˌtend ə ˈskuːl/
bully /'bʊli/
canteen /kænˈtiːn/
classmate /'klɑːsmeɪt/
classroom /'klɑːsrʊm/
compulsory /kəmˈpʌlsəri/
demanding /dɪˈmɑːndɪŋ/
discipline /'dɪsəplən/
do a subject /ˌduː ə ˈsʌbdʒɪkt/
do/take an exam /ˌduː/teɪk ən ɪgˈzæm/
drop a subject /'drɒp ə ˌsʌbdʒɪkt/
educate /'edjʊkeɪt/
education /ˌedjʊˈkeɪʃən/
elementary school /ˌeləˈmentəri skuːl/
fail an exam /ˌfeɪl ən ɪgˈzæm/
field trip /'fiːld trɪp/
grade/mark /greɪd/mɑːk/
learn by heart/memorise /ˌlɜːn baɪ ˈhɑːt/ˈmeməraɪz/
leave school /ˌliːv ˈskuːl/
literate /'lɪtərət/
miss/skip lessons /mɪs/skɪp ˈlesənz/
pass an exam /ˌpɑːs ən ɪgˈzæm/
playground /'pleɪgraʊnd/
primary school /'praɪməri skuːl/
revise /rɪˈvaɪz/
revision /rɪˈvɪʒən/
schedule /'ʃedjuːl/
school gate /ˌskuːl ˈgeɪt/
school uniform /ˌskuːl ˈjuːnəfɔːm/
schoolwork /'skuːlwɜːk/
secondary school /'sekəndəri skuːl/
single-sex school /ˌsɪŋgəl seks ˈskuːl/
subject /'sʌbdʒɪkt/
take a break /ˌteɪk ə ˈbreɪk/
timetable /'taɪmˌteɪbəl/

University

academic /ˌækəˈdemɪk/
academy /əˈkædəmi/
apply for (a place) /əˌplaɪ fər (ə ˈpleɪs)/
diploma /dəˈpləʊmə/
do a course /ˌduː ə ˈkɔːs/
entrance exam /'entrəns ɪgˌzæm/
gap year /'gæp jɪə/
tuition fee /tjuˈɪʃən fiː/

Phrases with get

get a good job /ˌget ə ˌgʊd ˈdʒɒb/
get a lot out of sth /ˌget ə ˈlɒt aʊt əv ˌsʌmθɪŋ/
get a place at university /get ə ˌpleɪs ət ˌjuːnəˈvɜːsəti/
get a reply /ˌget ə rɪˈplaɪ/
get a tattoo /ˌget ə təˈtuː/
get better /ˌget ˈbetə/
get cold /ˌget ˈkəʊld/
get dark /ˌget ˈdɑːk/
get exhausted /ˌget ɪgˈzɔːstəd/

get good marks /ˌget gʊd ˈmɑːks/
get home /ˌget ˈhəʊm/
get ill /ˌget ˈɪl/
get into trouble /ˌget ˌɪntə ˈtrʌbəl/
get into university /ˌget ˌɪntə ˌjuːnəˈvɜːsəti/
get late /ˌget ˈleɪt/
get nervous /ˌget ˈnɜːvəs/
get on with /ˌget ˈɒn wɪð/
get out of /ˌget ˈaʊt əv/
get ready /ˌget ˈredi/
get rid of sth /ˌget ˈrɪd əv ˌsʌmθɪŋ/
get stressed about sth /ˌget ˈstrest əˌbaʊt ˌsʌmθɪŋ/
get there /'get ðeə/
get tired /ˌget ˈtaɪəd/
get to school /ˌget tə ˈskuːl/
get to the station /ˌget tə ðə ˈsteɪʃən/
get to work /ˌget tə ˈwɜːk/
get up /ˌget ˈʌp/

Other

background /'bækgraʊnd/
be friendly with /ˌbi ˈfrendli wɪð/
beanbag /'biːnbæg/
blinds /blaɪndz/
carry on /ˌkæri ˈɒn/
chill out /ˌtʃɪl ˈaʊt/
collect /kəˈlekt/
collection /kəˈlekʃən/
community /kəˈmjuːnəti/
compete against /kəmˈpiːt əˌgenst/
conditions /kənˈdɪʃənz/
decide /dɪˈsaɪd/
decision /dɪˈsɪʒən/
donate /dəʊˈneɪt/
donation /dəʊˈneɪʃən/
exhaust /ɪgˈzɔːst/
exhaustion /ɪgˈzɔːstʃən/
explain /ɪkˈspleɪn/
explanation /ˌekspləˈneɪʃən/
flexible /'fleksəbəl/
follow your interests /ˌfɒləʊ jɔːr ˈɪntrəsts/
fundraising /'fʌndˌreɪzɪŋ/
have a good time /ˌhæv ə ˌgʊd ˈtaɪm/
invest /ɪnˈvest/
isolate /'aɪsəleɪt/
isolation /ˌaɪsəˈleɪʃən/
keep a promise /ˌkiːp ə ˈprɒməs/
meet up with /ˌmiːt ˈʌp wɪð/
on your own /ˌɒn jɔːr ˈəʊn/
provide /prəˈvaɪd/
provision /prəˈvɪʒən/
put on /ˌpʊt ˈɒn/
reach /riːtʃ/
relax /rɪˈlæks/
relevant /'reləvənt/
remote /rɪˈməʊt/
rigid /'rɪdʒəd/
scrape /skreɪp/
stumble into /'stʌmbəl ˌɪntu/
summit /'sʌmət/
swipe card /'swaɪp kɑːd/
take it easy /ˌteɪk ɪt ˈiːzi/
take off /ˌteɪk ˈɒf/
uncluttered /ˌʌnˈklʌtəd/
waste of time /ˌweɪst əv ˈtaɪm/

Jobs

accountant /əˈkaʊntənt/
actor /ˈæktə/
airline pilot /ˈeəlaɪn ˌpaɪlət/
babysitter/childminder /ˈbeɪbiˌsɪtə/ˈtʃaɪldˌmaɪndə/
banker /ˈbæŋkə/
beautician /bjuːˈtɪʃən/
builder /ˈbɪldə/
bus driver /ˈbʌs ˌdraɪvə/
businessman /ˈbɪznəsmən/
camp supervisor /ˈkæmp ˌsuːpəvaɪzə/
carer /ˈkeərə/
carpenter /ˈkɑːpəntə/
computer programmer /kəmˈpjuːtə ˌprəʊɡræmə/
design consultant /dɪˈzaɪn kənˌsʌltənt/
DJ /ˈdiː ˌdʒeɪ/
doctor /ˈdɒktə/
driving instructor /ˈdraɪvɪŋ ɪnˌstrʌktə/
electrician /ɪˌlekˈtrɪʃən/
engineer /ˌendʒəˈnɪə/
estate agent /ɪˈsteɪt ˌeɪdʒənt/
flight attendant /ˈflaɪt əˌtendənt/
hairdresser /ˈheəˌdresə/
interpreter /ɪnˈtɜːprətə/
journalist /ˈdʒɜːnələst/
lifeguard /ˈlaɪfɡɑːd/
mechanic /mɪˈkænɪk/
model /ˈmɒdl/
musician /mjuːˈzɪʃən/
nurse /nɜːs/
office assistant /ˈɒfəs əˌsɪstənt/
photographer /fəˈtɒɡrəfə/
plumber /ˈplʌmə/
police officer /pəˈliːs ˌɒfəsə/
politician /ˌpɒləˈtɪʃən/
receptionist /rɪˈsepʃənəst/
scientist /ˈsaɪəntəst/
secondary school teacher /ˈsekəndəri skuːl ˌtiːtʃə/
secretary /ˈsekrətəri/
shop assistant /ˈʃɒp əˌsɪstənt/
skiing instructor /ˈskiːɪŋ ɪnˌstrʌktə/
specialist /ˈspeʃələst/
taxi driver /ˈtæksi ˌdraɪvə/
tourist guide /ˈtʊərəst ɡaɪd/
travel agent /ˈtrævəl ˌeɪdʒənt/

Employment

apply for a job /əˌplaɪ fər ə ˈdʒɒb/
banking /ˈbæŋkɪŋ/
boss /bɒs/
candidate /ˈkændədət/
career /kəˈrɪə/
communication skills /kəˌmjuːnəˈkeɪʃən skɪlz/
conference call /ˈkɒnfərəns kɔːl/
contact details /ˈkɒntækt ˌdiːteɪlz/
CV /ˌsiː ˈviː/
employee /ɪmˈplɔɪ-iː/
employer /ɪmˈplɔɪə/
finish work /ˌfɪnɪʃ ˈwɜːk/
have a job /ˌhæv ə ˈdʒɒb/
holiday job /ˈhɒlədi ˌdʒɒb/
interview /ˈɪntəvjuː/
job advert/advertisement /ˈdʒɒb ˌædvɜːt/ədˌvɜːtɪsmənt/
look for a job /ˌlʊk fər ə ˈdʒɒb/
male-dominated job /ˌmeɪl ˌdɒmɪneɪtɪd ˈdʒɒb/
manual job /ˌmænjuəl ˈdʒɒb/
marketing /ˈmɑːkɪtɪŋ/
office /ˈɒfəs/
oil industry /ˈɔɪl ˌɪndəstri/
part-time job /ˌpɑːt taɪm ˈdʒɒb/
personal skills /ˌpɜːsənəl ˈskɪlz/
position /pəˈzɪʃən/
profession /prəˈfeʃən/
promotion /prəˈməʊʃən/
retail /ˈriːteɪl/
retire /rɪˈtaɪə/
self-confidence /ˌself ˈkɒn fɪdəns/
start work /ˌstɑːt ˈwɜːk/
training /ˈtreɪnɪŋ/

university degree /ˌjuːnəˈvɜːsəti dɪˌɡriː/
work experience /ˈwɜːk ɪkˌspɪəriəns/
work full-time /ˌwɜːk fʊl ˈtaɪm/

Collocations – terms and conditions

be badly paid /bi ˌbædli ˈpeɪd/
be/work in (IT) /ˌbi/ˌwɜːk ɪn (ˌaɪˈtiː)/
be on your feet all day /ˌbi ɒn jɔː ˈfiːt ɔːl deɪ/
be self employed /ˌbi ˌself ɪmˈplɔɪd/
be well-paid /ˌbi ˌwel ˈpeɪd/
do physical work /ˌduː ˈfɪzɪkəl ˌwɜːk/
do/work flexible hours /ˌduː/ˌwɜːk ˌfleksəbəl ˈaʊəz/
do/work long hours /ˌduː/ˌwɜːk lɒŋ ˈaʊəz/
do/work overtime /ˌduː/ˌwɜːk ˈəʊvətaɪm/
do/work regular office hours /ˌduː/ˌwɜːk ˌreɡjələr ˈɒfəs ˌaʊəz/
do/work shifts /ˌduː/ˌwɜːk ʃɪfts/
get a bonus /ˌget ə ˈbəʊnəs/
get/earn a high/an average salary /ˌget/ˌɜːn ə ˌhaɪ/ən ˌævərɪdʒ ˈsæləri/
get/earn low wages /ˌget/ˌɜːn ˌləʊ ˈweɪdʒɪz/
get/have a pay rise /ˌget/ˌhæv ə ˈpeɪ raɪz/
get/have/take a day off /ˌget/ˌhæv/ˌteɪk ə deɪ ˈɒf/
get/have/take five weeks' paid holiday /ˌget/ˌhæv/ˌteɪk faɪv wiːks ˌpeɪd ˈhɒlədi/
get/have/take time off /ˌget/ˌhæv/ˌteɪk taɪm ˈɒf/
work for/at (Citibank) /ˌwɜːk fə/ət (ˈsɪtibæŋk)/
work for (a construction company) /ˌwɜːk fər (ə kənˈstrʌkʃən ˌkʌmpəni)/
work from home /ˌwɜːk frəm ˈhəʊm/
work in (a hospital/advertising) /ˌwɜːk ɪn (ə ˈhɒspɪtəl/ˈædvətaɪzɪŋ)/
work in/as part of a team /ˌwɜːk ɪn/əz ˌpɑːt əv ə ˈtiːm/
work outside /ˌwɜːk aʊtˈsaɪd/
work with your hands /ˌwɜːk wɪð jɔː ˈhændz/

Other

be a fast learner /bi ə ˌfɑːst ˈlɜːnə/
be dependent on /ˌbi dɪˈpendənt ɒn/
benefit /ˈbenəfɪt/
deal with sth /ˈdɪəl wɪð ˌsʌmθɪŋ/
driving licence /ˈdraɪvɪŋ ˌlaɪsəns/
enclose /ɪnˈkləʊz/
find out /ˌfaɪnd ˈaʊt/
foreign /ˈfɒrən/
give up /ˌɡɪv ˈʌp/
grow /ɡrəʊ/
have a shave /ˌhæv ə ˈʃeɪv/
native /ˈneɪtɪv/
set up /ˌset ˈʌp/
shelter /ˈʃeltə/
sum up /ˌsʌm ˈʌp/
throw out /ˌθrəʊ ˈaʊt/
waste /weɪst/
work sth out /ˌwɜːk ˌsʌmθɪŋ ˈaʊt/

Types of shops

baker's /'beɪkəz/
bookstore /'bʊkstɔː/
butcher's /'bʊtʃəz/
charity shop /'tʃærəti ʃɒp/
clothes shop /'kləʊðz ʃɒp/
designer shop /dɪ'zaɪnə ʃɒp/
greengrocer's /'griːngrəʊsəz/
jeweller's /'dʒuːələz/
newsagent's /'njuːz,eɪdʒənts/
pet shop /'pet ʃɒp/
shoe shop /'ʃuː ʃɒp/
shopping centre/mall /'ʃɒpɪŋ ,sentə/mɔːl/
store /stɔː/
supermarket /'suːpə,mɑːkət/
toy shop /'tɔɪ ʃɒp/

Places in town, services

aquarium /ə'kweəriəm/
cinema /'sɪnəmə/
manicure /'mænəkjʊə/
museum /mjuː'ziːəm/
post office /'pəʊst ,ɒfəs/
theatre /'θɪətə/
theme park /'θiːm pɑːk/
the dentist /ðə 'dentəst/
the doctor /ðə 'dɒktə/
wedding chapel /'wedɪŋ ,tʃæpəl/

Goods

beauty products /'bjuːti ,prɒdʌkts/
boots /buːts/
carpet /'kɑːpət/
electrical goods /ɪ'lektrɪkəl gʊdz/
face cream /'feɪs kriːm/
friendship bracelet /'frendʃɪp ,breɪslət/
game console /'geɪm kən,səʊl/
headphones /'hedfəʊnz/
leisurewear /'leʒəweə/
light bulb /'laɪt bʌlb/
plant /plɑːnt/
purse /pɜːs/
sandals /'sændəlz/
swimwear /'swɪmweə/
toiletries /'tɔɪlətriz/
trainers /'treɪnəz/
vacuum cleaner /'vækjuəm ,kliːnə/

Shopping

advertising /'ædvətaɪzɪŋ/
branding /'brændɪŋ/
broken /'brəʊkən/
buy on impulse /,baɪ ɒn 'ɪmpʌls/
changing room /'tʃeɪndʒɪŋ ruːm/
complain /kəm'pleɪn/
complaint /kəm'pleɪnt/
consumer /kən'sjuːmə/
damaged /'dæmɪdʒd/
delivery /dɪ'lɪvəri/
economical /,ekə'nɒmɪkəl/
fashionable /'fæʃənəbəl/
faulty /'fɔːlti/
fit /fɪt/
out of stock /,aʊt əv 'stɒk/
package /'pækɪdʒ/
packaging /'pækɪdʒɪŋ/
product /'prɒdʌkt/
quality /'kwɒləti/
reduced /rɪ'djuːst/
replacement /rɪ'pleɪsmənt/
sell-by date /'sel baɪ deɪt/
sell out /,sel 'aʊt/
service /'sɜːvəs/
size /saɪz/
suit /suːt/
try on /,traɪ 'ɒn/
value /'væljuː/

Shopping and services – collocations and useful phrases

attract attention /ə,trækt ə'tenʃən/
close an account /,kləʊz ən ə'kaʊnt/
do some research /,duː səm rɪ'sɜːtʃ/
do the shopping /,duː ðə 'ʃɒpɪŋ/
exchange sth for sth /ɪks'tʃeɪndʒ ,sʌmθɪŋ fə ,sʌmθɪŋ/
get a refund /,get ə 'riːfʌnd/
go shopping /,gəʊ 'ʃɒpɪŋ/
go window shopping /,gəʊ ,wɪndəʊ 'ʃɒpɪŋ/
have a sale /,hæv ə 'seɪl/
I can't afford it /aɪ ,kɑːnt ə'fɔːd ɪt/
keep the receipt /,kiːp ðə rɪ'siːt/
on (special) offer /ɒn (,speʃəl) 'ɒfə/
pay attention to /,peɪ ə'tenʃən tə/
pick up a bargain /,pɪk ʌp ə 'bɑːgən/
shop online /,ʃɒp ɒn'laɪn/
some parts are missing /səm ,pɑːts ə 'mɪsɪŋ/
trust sb with sth /'trʌst ,sʌmbədi wɪð ,sʌmθɪŋ/

Partitives

a bottle of perfume /ə ,bɒtl əv 'pɜːfjuːm/
a bottle of shampoo/mineral water /ə ,bɒtl əv ʃæm'puː/ ,mɪnərəl 'wɔːtə/
a bunch of flowers /ə ,bʌntʃ əv 'flaʊəz/
a bunch of grapes/bananas /ə ,bʌntʃ əv 'greɪps/bə'nɑːnəz/
a can of beans/cola/tomatoes /ə ,kæn əv 'biːnz/'kəʊlə/ 'tə'mɑːtəʊz/
a jar of jam/instant coffee/mayonnaise /ə ,dʒɑːr əv 'dʒæm/ ,ɪnstant 'kɒfi/,meɪə'neɪz/
a packet of biscuits/tea/crisps /ə ,pækət əv 'bɪskɪts/'tiː/'krɪsps/
a pair of jeans/skis/scissors /ə ,peər əv 'dʒiːnz/'skiːz/'sɪzəz/

Personality and emotions

anger /'æŋgə/
angry /'æŋgri/
creation /kri'eɪʃən/
creative /kri'eɪtɪv/
elegance /'elɪgəns/
elegant /'eləgənt/
excitement /ɪk'saɪtmənt/
greed /griːd/
greedy /'griːdi/
honest /'ɒnəst/
honesty /'ɒnəsti/
jealous /'dʒeləs/
jealousy /'dʒeləsi/
loyal /'lɔɪəl/
loyalty /'lɔɪəlti/
mysterious /mɪ'stɪəriəs/
mystery /'mɪstəri/
passion /'pæʃən/
passionate /'pæʃənət/

Other

competitive /kəm'petətɪv/
focus on /'fəʊkəs ɒn/
make a living /,meɪk ə 'lɪvɪŋ/
market /'mɑːkət/
old-fashioned /,əʊld 'fæʃənd/
protect the environment /prə,tekt ði ɪn'vaɪrənmənt/
reduce poverty /rɪ,djuːs 'pɒvəti/
secure /sɪ'kʊə/
security /sɪ'kjʊərəti/
trade /treɪd/
wealthy /'welθi/
wealth /'welθ/

Society and politics

African American /ˌæfrɪkən əˈmerɪkən /
black community /ˌblæk kəˈmjuːnəti/
Board of Education /ˌbɔːd əv ˌedjʊˈkeɪʃən/
capital city /ˌkæpətl ˈsɪti/
citizen /ˈsɪtəzən/
Civil Rights Movement /ˌsɪvəl ˈraɪts ˌmuːvmənt/
constitutional monarchy /ˌkɒnstəˌtjuːʃənəl ˈmɒnəki/
corruption /kəˈrʌpʃən/
declare /dɪˈkleə/
democracy /dɪˈmɒkrəsi/
discriminate /dɪˈskrɪməneɪt/
discrimination /dɪˌskrɪməˈneɪʃən/
equal /ˈiːkwəl/
fight for /ˈfaɪt fə/
freedom /ˈfriːdəm/
general elections /ˌdʒenərəl ɪˈlekʃənz/
head of government /ˌhed əv ˈgʌvəmənt/
head of state /ˌhed əv ˈsteɪt/
human race /ˌhjuːmən ˈreɪs/
humiliate /hjuːˈmɪlieɪt/
humiliation /hjuːˌmɪliˈeɪʃən/
make a speech /ˌmeɪk ə ˈspiːtʃ/
Nobel Peace Prize /nəʊˌbel ˈpiːs praɪz/
political system /pəˌlɪtɪkəl ˈsɪstəm/
Prime Minister /ˌpraɪm ˈmɪnəstə/
racial discrimination /ˌreɪʃəl dɪˌskrɪməˈneɪʃən/
racial segregation /ˌreɪʃəl ˌsegrɪˈgeɪʃən/
racism /ˈreɪsɪzəm/
run a campaign /ˌrʌn ə kæmˈpeɪn/
segregate /ˈsegrɪgeɪt/
segregation /ˌsegrɪˈgeɪʃən/
separate /ˈsepəreɪt/
separation /ˌsepəˈreɪʃən/
sexism /ˈseksɪzəm/
slave /sleɪv/
slave trade /ˈsleɪv treɪd/
slavery /ˈsleɪvəri/
statistics /stəˈtɪstɪks/
the Supreme Court /ðə suˌpriːm ˈkɔːt/
tax /tæks/
terrorism /ˈterərɪzəm/
unemployment /ˌʌnɪmˈplɔɪmənt/
vote /vəʊt/

Crime

arson /ˈɑːsən/
assassinate /əˈsæsəneɪt/
assassination /əˌsæsəˈneɪʃən/
break into /ˈbreɪk ˌɪntə/
break the law /breɪk ðə ˈlɔː/
burglary /ˈbɜːgləri/
burgle /ˈbɜːgəl/
car crime /ˈkɑː kraɪm/
commit a crime /kəˌmɪt ə ˈkraɪm/
crime scene /ˈkraɪm siːn/
cyberbullying /ˈsaɪbəˌbʊliɪŋ/
damage public property /ˌdæmɪdʒ ˌpʌblɪk ˈprɒpəti/
deal drugs /ˌdiːl ˈdrʌgz/
drug dealing /ˈdrʌg ˌdiːlɪŋ/
gang /gæŋ/
graffiti /græˈfiːti/
hacking /ˈhækɪŋ/
illegal /ɪˈliːgəl/
mug /mʌg/
mugging /ˈmʌgɪŋ/
murder /ˈmɜːdə/
murder rates /ˈmɜːdə reɪts/
mystery /ˈmɪstəri/
online piracy /ˌɒnlaɪn ˈpaɪərəsi/
pirate /ˈpaɪərət/
rob /rɒb/
robbery /ˈrɒbəri/
set fire to /ˌset ˈfaɪə tə/
shoplift /ˈʃɒpˌlɪft/

shoplifting /ˈʃɒpˌlɪftɪŋ/
steal /stiːl/
theft /θeft/
vandalise /ˈvændəlaɪz/
vandalism /ˈvændəlɪzəm/
victim /ˈvɪktəm/

Criminals

arsonist /ˈɑːsənəst/
burglar /ˈbɜːglə/
drug dealer /ˈdrʌg ˌdiːlə/
mugger /ˈmʌgə/
murderer /ˈmɜːdərə/
pickpocket /ˈpɪkˌpɒkɪt/
pirate /ˈpaɪərət/
robber /ˈrɒbə/
shoplifter /ˈʃɒpˌlɪftə/
thief /θiːf/
vandal /ˈvændl/

Justice

appear in court /əˌpɪə ɪn ˈkɔːt/
arrest /əˈrest/
case /keɪs/
catch /kætʃ/
collect evidence /kəˌlekt ˈevədəns/
community service /kəˈmjuːnəti ˌsɜːvəs/
court /kɔːt/
guilty /ˈgɪlti/
identity /aɪˈdentəti/
innocent /ˈɪnəsənt/
interview victims/witnesses /ˌɪntəvju ˈvɪktɪmz/ˈwɪtnəsɪz /
judge /dʒʌdʒ/
police officer /pəˈliːs ˌɒfəsə/
prison /ˈprɪzən/
punish /ˈpʌnɪʃ/
report a crime /rɪˌpɔːt ə ˈkraɪm/
search /sɜːtʃ/
sentence /ˈsentəns/
suspect /ˈsʌspekt/
witness /ˈwɪtnəs/

Body language

bite your nails /ˌbaɪt jɔː ˈneɪəlz/
blink your eyes /ˌblɪŋk jɔːr ˈaɪz/
cross your arms /ˌkrɒs jɔːr ˈɑːmz/
fiddle with your hair /ˌfɪdl wɪð jɔː ˈheə/
liar /ˈlaɪə/
lie /laɪ/
raise your eyebrows /ˌreɪz jɔːr ˈaɪbraʊz/
stare at /ˈsteər ət/
tell a lie /ˌtel ə ˈlaɪ/
tell the truth /ˌtel ðə ˈtruːθ/

Other

boring /ˈbɔːrɪŋ/
convincing /kənˈvɪnsɪŋ/
effective /ɪˈfektɪv/
fake /feɪk/
false /fɔːls/
fascinating /ˈfæsəneɪtɪŋ/
genuine /ˈdʒenjuən/
life savings /ˌlaɪf ˈseɪvɪŋz/
shocking /ˈʃɒkɪŋ/
true /truː/

Pearson Education Limited,
Edinburgh Gate, Harlow
Essex, CM20 2JE, England
and Associated Companies throughout the world

www.pearsonelt.com/focus

© Pearson Education Limited 2016

The right of Sue Kay, Vaughan Jones, Daniel Brayshaw, Bartosz Michałowski and Lynda Edwards to be identified as authors of this work has been asserted by them in accordance with the Copyright, Designs and Patents Act, 1988.

First published 2016
Eleventh impression 2020
ISBN: 9781447997887

Set in Avenir
Printed in Slovakia by Neografia

Sue Kay and Vaughan Jones's acknowledgements

We would like to thank all the students and teachers we have met and observed during the development of Focus. We are also especially grateful to our wonderful editorial team for their expertise, encouragement and dedication. Finally a big thank you to our families without whose support and understanding none of this would have been possible.

Acknowledgements

The publishers and authors would like to thank the following people for their feedback and comments during the development of the material:
Humberto Santos Duran, Anna Maria Grochowska, Inga Lande, Magdalena Loska, Rosa Maria Maldonado, Juliana Queiroz Pereira, Tomasz Siuta, Renata Tomaka-Pasternak

We are grateful to the following for permission to reproduce copyright material:

Text

Extract on page 26 from *David Copperfield Penguin Readers series, Level 3. ISBN 978-1405862400*, Pearson Education Ltd. (Dickens C); Extract and book cover on page 26 from *"Dracula": Level 3 (Penguin Readers (Graded Readers)) ISBN 9781405855440*, Pearson Education Ltd. (Bram Stoker); Quote on page 77 from *The Moneyless Man*, Oneworld Publications (Boyle M); Quote and Book Cover from The Moneyless Man, Oneworld Publications (Boyle M); General Displayed Text on page 86 after http://www.fairtrade.org.uk, Granted subject to approval of final proof; Article on pages 88–89 adapted from Tutorials: How the colour of a brand affects our perception, www.macuser.co.uk (Caplin S)

Logos

Logo on page 24 from http://www.youtube.com/; Logo on page 25 adapted from http://www.classmates.com/; Logo on page 50 from http://www. couchsurfing.org/; Logo on page 86 from http://www.fairtrade.org.uk.

In some instances we have been unable to trace the owners of copyright material, and we would appreciate any information that would enable us to do so.

Photo acknowledgements

The publisher would like to thank the following for their kind permission to reproduce their photographs:
(Key: b-bottom; c-centre; l-left; r-right; t-top)

123RF.com: Tamas Panczel - Eross 75 (handshake), Wong Yu Liang 75 (clock); **Alamy Images:** Ammentorp Photography 10b, Arterra Picture Library 23cl (bottom), Rafael Ben-Ari 103l, Big Cheese Photo LLC 81, Clark Brennan 100cr, Jack Carey 103tr, colinspics 67cr, Tony Cordoza 87 (E), Design Pics Inc 93, Ersoy Emin 77bl, Martin Harvey 59c, Jim Holden 88-89, Ian Dagnall Commercial Collection 84l, Interfoto 25tr, Janine Wiedel Photolibrary 75tl, Niall McOnegal 104, MIKA - Images 80, Motoring Picture Library 30tc, Murad RM 75 (money), Ivan Nesterov 46, Andrew Paterson 97 (B), PCN Photography 75 (weightlifter), David Pearson 23tr, Niels Poulsen 23bl, PSL Images 68-69, PYMCA 97 (E), Simon Rawles 86cl, Realimage 57, Stuart Rimmer 23cl (top), Robert Harding World Imagery 23cr, Gavin Rodgers 23br, Tetra Images 62br, Washington Imaging 97 (D), Jan Wlodarczyk 53tl; **Mark Boyle:** James Barke 77tr; **The BRIT School:** 38l; **Copernicus Science Centre / Centrum Nauki Kopernik:** 32; **Corbis:** Alloy / Aurora Open / Kennan Harvey 31, Bettmann 28, 29t, 29bc, Bohemian Nomad Picturemakers 60b, C.J. Burton 9cr, CNP / Ron Sachs 29br, Epa / Kimmo Brandt 60t, Juice Images / Ian Lishman 71t, Ronnie Kaufman 51tc, Jutta Klee 68, James Lauritz 63t, Ocean 8l, PhotoAlto / Odilon Dimier 4tr, Oliver Rossi 23tl, Rubberball / Jessica Peterson 97 (A), Flip Schulke 100bl, Science Photo Library / Victor Habbick Visions 9tr; **DK Images:** Nikid Design Ltd 87 (H), Paul Wilkinson Collection 25tl; **Fotolia.com:** air 45, Helder Almeida 73br, anidimi 77 (background), antonel 36-37 (background), Yuri Arcurs 20, auremar 75cr, bds 13bl, Mario Beauregard 30tr, CandyBox Images 66bl, Innovated Captures 83t, Richard Carey 27 (E), cbckchristine 95, Close Encounters 7, Christian Delbert 30bc, Oleksandr Dibrova 76, DioGen 37bc, Elenathewise 30tl, eurobanks 40/5, Dmitrijs Gerciks 87 (B), Warren Goldswain 15c, Scott Griessel 92, Jörg Hackemann 19l, 102, Heartland 55br, HuHu Lin 103br, Brian Jackson 86cr, Jenner 72r, Hayati Kayhan 27 (F), Kurhan 73bl, Yahia Loukkal 88l, magcom 50tl, 62tl, 79t, 96, Maxim Malevich 87 (F), Monkey Business 44b, mr.markin 10l, nyul 78t, 78c, Tyler Olson 72l, Ioannis Pantzi 50bl, Paulista 77tl (book), Pressmaster 4tl, René 65t, Rido 15l, Sabphoto 74, Gina Sanders 97 (F), Gino Santa Maria 27 (A), Gordana Sermek 87 (A), Smileus 27 (C), squidmediaro 51r (girl); **Getty Images:** AFP 101bl, AFP / Anne-Christine Poujoulat 43c, AFP / Karen Bleier 85b, Airbus 9br, airportrait 47t, The Asahi Shimbun 9tl, Steve Debenport 75tr, Design Pics / Ben Welsh 56, Jonathan Elderfield 43t, Rebecca Emery 4cl, Don Farrall 98br, Matt Henry Gunther 59tr, Hulton Archive 101tr, Hulton Archive / Consolidated News Pictures 29cl, The Image Bank 9cl, Ryan Lane 30br, Jason Merritt 38r, Michael Ochs Archives 100cl, Karen Moskowitz 54, Redferns 43b, Carolyn Schaefer 85t, Science & Society Picture Library 29bl, Joseph Carl Stieler 36tr, SW Productions 105, UK Press via Getty Images 55bc, AFP / Vanderlei Almeida 39t; **Imagestate:** Michael Duerinckx 55bl; © **JR :** 39c, 39b; **Courtesy of the London Dungeon:** 55cr; **Mall of America®:** Courtesy Mall of America 84r; **Pearson Education Ltd:** 26tc, 26cr, 52, 67tl, 79b, Gareth Boden 40/1, 50r, Trevor Clifford 11 (A), 11 (B), 11 (C), 11 (D), Lord and Leverett 98t, Studio 8 40/2, 40/3, 50tc; **Press Association Images:** AP 36bl, AP / Morry Gash 100br, PA Archive / Ian West 5; **Reuters:** Ho New / Handout 65b, Oleg Popov 64; **Rex Features:** Steve Bell 14l, Daily Mail / Michael Fresco 15r, Paul Grover 36br, Image Source 63bl, Isopix 79c, Tony Kyriacou 47b, Nara Archives 36tl, OJO Images 44t, Sipa USA 14r, View Pictures 66c, 67br, View Pictures / Dennis Gilbert 66cr, View Pictures / Hufton + Crow 66cl; **Science Photo Library Ltd:** Christian Darkin 9bl; **Shutterstock.com:** Antonio Abrignani 100tl, Andresr 63br, Andrey_Popov 83b, Sergey Andrianov 87 (G), art&design 51l, ArtmannWitte 67tr, auremar 73tl, Barbara Barbour 53br, Nancy Bauer 87 (D), cloki 98bl, crydo 27 (D), Dropu 53bl, East 40/4, Endless Traveller 53tr, Angelo Ferraris 55cl, Fritzphoto 13br, Goodluz 71b, Paul Michael Hughes 75 (computer), ILeysen 55tr, JMiks 24bl, Anastasiia Kucherenko 107t, JinYoung Lee 61, Lightspring 24-25 (background), Maridav 35, MilaLiu 24tr, Neamov 87 (C), Odua Images 78b, Pres Panayotov 55tl, riekephotos 27 (B), ronstik 75 (graduation), sianc 13t, rui vale sousa 62tr, StockLite 73tr, Togataki 51r (background), Tsyhun 64-65 (background), zetwe 107b; **Simon Dale:** 48, 49tl, 49cl, 49bl; **SuperStock:** Image Source 16-17, 19r, Juice Images 4br, Library of Congress / Science Faction 100tr, Photononstop 97 (C), Stock Connection 4bl, Underwood Photo Archives 101cr; **The Kobal Collection:** 20th Century Fox / Morton, Merrick 42, Everest Entertainment 40cr, Hammer Film Productions 41b, Mark Johnson Productions 41t, See-Saw Films 41c, Silver Pictures 40tr, Touchstone Pictures 40br, Universal / Working Title 6; **Toms Shoes:** 90l, 90r; **Webb Chappell Photography:** Media Lab 26cl

Illustrations

(Key: b-bottom; c-centre; l-left; r-right; t-top)
Nicolas Gremaud (GREMS) p. 8t, 18, 35, 59, 91, 95, 99; Virus Group pp. 4–7, 8b, 9–11
All other images © Pearson Education

Every effort has been made to trace the copyright holders and we apologise in advance for any unintentional omissions. We would be pleased to insert the appropriate acknowledgement in any subsequent edition of this publication.